100 YEARS
SIMON & SCHUSTER

ALSO BY NANCY PELOSI

Know Your Power: A Message to America's Daughters

THE ART OF POWER

MY STORY AS AMERICA'S FIRST
WOMAN SPEAKER OF THE HOUSE

NANCY PELOSI

Simon & Schuster

NEW YORK   LONDON   TORONTO
SYDNEY   NEW DELHI

1230 Avenue of the Americas
New York, NY 10020

All Bible passages quoted herein are taken from the Revised
Standard Version, Catholic Edition, 2006, National Council
of the Churches of Christ in the USA.

"Prayer for St. Francis of Assisi" can be found at
http://www.shrinesf.org/franciscan-prayer.html.

First Simon & Schuster hardcover edition August 2024

SIMON & SCHUSTER and colophon are registered trademarks
of Simon & Schuster, LLC

Simon & Schuster: Celebrating 100 Years of Publishing in 2024

For information about special discounts for bulk purchases,
please contact Simon & Schuster Special Sales at 1-866-506-1949
or business@simonandschuster.com.

The Simon & Schuster Speakers Bureau can bring authors to your
live event. For more information or to book an event, contact
the Simon & Schuster Speakers Bureau at 1-866-248-3049
or visit our website at www.simonspeakers.com.

Book text design by Paul Dippolito

Manufactured in the United States of America

1   3   5   7   9   10   8   6   4   2

Library of Congress Cataloging-in-Publication Data is available.

ISBN 978-1-6680-4804-7
ISBN 978-1-6680-4806-1 (ebook)

To Paul, aka Daddy, aka Pop
A wonderful husband, father, and grandfather

Contents

THE ART OF POWER

Preface: Know Your Why

In November 2006, after the Democrats won the majority in the House of Representatives, I was nominated by my colleagues to be Speaker. As I approached the podium to accept the honor, our new caucus chair, Rahm Emanuel, whispered in my ear, "Your parents would be so proud."

I was taken aback by the comment. Why would my parents be proud? They did not raise me to be Speaker. They raised me to be holy. After having six sons, my mother wanted me to be a nun. Now you're talking proud!

People have asked me what role my faith has played in my political life. While I believe, of course, in the separation of church and state, I do believe that the values of my faith have informed my priorities. For example, my commitment to human rights springs from my belief that, as John Lewis always used to say, there's a spark of divinity in every person that needs to be respected.

When I was young and people would ask, "What is your favorite word?," I would always say the Word. It's a term used for Christ: "And the Word became flesh and dwelt among us" (John 1:14). Christ participating in our humanity enabled us to participate in His divinity—hence the spark. A Hebrew scholar in the third century said that because of the spark of divinity that we all have, hundreds of angels precede us when we walk. My deep commitment to honoring the spark of divinity in every person is why I turned to public service.

That's also why it's hard for me to imagine how people could ignore this spark and perpetrate heinous atrocities, especially the Holocaust. And in our own time, the tragedy of hundreds of thousands of people I saw in refugee camps in Darfur, the brutality of the Taliban in Afghanistan, the genocide of the Uyghurs and other repression in China, hunger in Sudan, suffering in Gaza, and massive poverty worldwide, to name just a few. How could we ignore that?

One of the most striking contradictions between values and action that I have witnessed was in 2019 when I joined a delegation of the Congressional Black Caucus to visit the nation of Ghana. We came to mark the passage of four hundred years since the arrival of the first slave ships on American shores. We visited the place where kidnapped Africans, soon to be sold into slavery, were imprisoned: a dark dungeon with low ceilings, and where they were abused and tortured under the most brutal and inhumane conditions imaginable. Those who did not die in the dungeon were forced to crawl through the Door of No Return to board the death ships bound for the Americas and the Caribbean—a journey that many would not survive. What made it even more appalling was the structure located directly above the dungeon. In a sickening display of hypocrisy, on top of the dungeon was the church where their oppressors had prayed. How could these men have prayed as they callously disregarded the spark of divinity below them? In our own country, we saw the same hypocrisy displayed in the act of slavery and in the repression of indigenous peoples, repellent practices that were often perpetrated by people who claimed to be of devout faith.

My "Why"

If the spark of divinity has been my inspiration, my core values are shaped by another passage in the Catholic Bible, from the Gospel of Matthew 25: "For I was hungry and you gave me food, I was thirsty and you gave me drink, I was a stranger and you welcomed me, I was naked and you clothed me, I was sick and you visited me, I was in prison and you came to me." This beautiful statement is the foundation of my "why." When people ask me, "What are the three most important issues facing Congress?," I always answer: our children, our children, our children.

The children have always been my "why" in public service and in my running for office. As a mother of five, my "why" is the one in five children in America who go to sleep hungry each night. How could it be that in America, the greatest country in the history of the world, one in five children lives in poverty? Children's health, their education, the economic security of their families, a safe environment in which they can thrive, including protection from gun violence, and a world at peace in which they can reach their fulfillment—these are my priorities. That is also why when I was sworn in as Speaker, I called up the children and grandchildren of my colleagues on both sides of the aisle and called the House to order . . . For the Children.

The security and strength that I draw from these values are also the "why" that allows me to withstand the many slings and arrows that have been directed at me for as long as I have been in public life.

When I speak to women or others who are considering running for office, I tell them that it is not a decision for the faint of heart. So, when you decide to run, you must know your "why." Why are you running? What is your vision, knowledge, and judgment? How do you hope to succeed? When you run, you become a target. Being certain of your "why" makes it worth it.

But to achieve your why, you will need three other pieces of advice. The best advice I received when I initially ran for Congress was "be yourself." Be true to yourself, your values, and who you are. And "be ready." You never know when the opportunity will come knocking, so be prepared to answer and say yes.

But the final piece of advice is the first piece of advice I received years before I ran. It was "know your power."

I never intended to run for elected office. Instead, I spent my political time volunteering for the California Democratic Party. I enjoyed the behind-the-scenes work of advancing our candidates and our agenda and mobilizing the VIPs—our volunteers in politics—to get the job done. In 1981, I became the state's Democratic Party chair. Nineteen eighty-four was a presidential election year, and in preparation, I assumed two additional roles: I became chair of the Democratic National Convention's Compliance Review Committee, which oversaw the convention's delegate selection, and I was named chair of the San Francisco Host Committee, placing me in charge of San Francisco's bid to host the Democratic National Convention—which we won.

While speaking with the legendary Louisiana congresswoman Lindy Boggs, I mentioned that I thought I had too many titles—three—and should probably give one up. In her lovely drawl, Lindy replied, "Darlin', no man would ever make that statement."

"Know thy power," she said, "and use it." I never forgot that vital lesson.

In 1987, when Sala Burton, our exceptional and kind congresswoman in San Francisco, decided not to seek reelection for health reasons, she asked me to run for her seat. She told me that she believed "you are ready to reach your heights." Her untimely death forced a special election, and very quickly, the race was on. When I won after a hard-fought campaign in the trenches where I was myself, I realized I was indeed ready, and I knew my power. Lindy Boggs, who was still serving in the House of Representatives, was there to be a mentor to me and to so many congressional women. She was a model of grace and legislative acumen, and today her name adorns the Women's Reading Room in the Capitol.

Congresswoman Sala Burton had told me I was ready. Lindy Boggs told me to know my power. And my message to women today is: the world needs you to be in the arena for peace, justice, and liberty. But know your individual power. There's no one in the history of the world like you. Your individuality is needed. Be yourself. Be ready. Know your power.

A Seat at the Table, Finally

When I arrived in Congress in 1987, women representatives were not just a minority, we were a rarity. There were only twelve of us among the Democrats (including my fellow Californian Barbara Boxer) and eleven among the Republicans. I'm forever grateful to Barbara for the guidance she gave me when I was a new member and for her personal friendship. I was determined to increase our numbers. After the election of 1992—dubbed the Year of the Woman—we added sixteen to the House Democratic roster, thanks in large measure to the help of Ellen Malcolm's pioneering political action committee, EMILYs List. And over the years, a main priority for House Democrats was to recruit, fund, and elect Democratic women to Congress. In 2024, we have ninety-four Democratic women, of which I am very proud.

But as late as 2001, no woman had ever served in the top leadership of either party in the House. This fact hit me when I arrived at the White House for my first meeting with President George W. Bush as part of the Democratic leadership. Walking into the West Wing, I was not apprehensive. I had frequently attended White House meetings on intelligence and appropriations issues as part of my committee work. But as I entered the meeting room, I realized that this meeting was unlike any other I had ever attended at the White House—it was, in fact, unlike any meeting that any woman had attended in the White House. It was a true first. While other women, who had been appointed as cabinet secretaries, had also been seated at the table as full participants, I was at the White House under different circumstances. I was there because I had been selected by my colleagues to represent the House Democratic Caucus and reflect their views—I was serving at the will of the House Democrats, not at the pleasure of the president.

When he opened the meeting, President Bush was very gracious in his welcome. He noted my historic role, and added that as the first woman to participate, I might have some different things to say. As he spoke, my chair started to feel crowded, and I had the sensation of being surrounded. It was as if I were being joined by the great women's rights activists and leaders Susan B. Anthony, Elizabeth Cady Stanton, Lucretia Mott, Sojourner Truth, and Alice Paul. I was not alone in my chair; all of them were sitting with me saying, **At last, we have a seat at the table.** My next thought was, "We want more." More women. More diversity. More seats at the table. Because this moment was not just the fulfillment of the courageous leadership of generations of women, as far back as the Seneca Falls Convention in 1848, which launched the women's rights movement and women's suffrage in the US, it was a manifestation of our responsibility to them, to women today and into the future. We stood on their shoulders, and today, newer generations stand on ours.

To recruit more women candidates, it was important for women members—especially those with small children—to share their stories, to share what their life experiences had given them, including confidence in their vision, their knowledge and judgment, and their strategic thinking. Their experiences gave them the courage to show the voters what is in their hearts, to empathize with and care about people.

Again, running for office is not for the faint of heart. I have often quoted Teddy Roosevelt's famous Man in the Arena speech to the candidates. I add my own update by saying to women: when you're in the arena, you have to be able to take a punch, and sometimes you have to be able to throw a punch . . . **For the Children**.

Over the years, opponents who feared the larger number of women on our side of the aisle have run a predictable campaign against them. Knowing that women have generally been shown to be highly ethical, critics cynically misuse this positive trait and make false claims against them. I mention this tactic because it is so cruel. It brings tears to the eyes of the candidates' children to see on TV or hear from someone in school phony charges against their mother's reputation. Opponents have often claimed that women candidates are "big spenders," especially on poor immigrant children and families. In some places, sadly, that rhetoric has had an appeal.

We must eliminate those tactics from our political system if we are to attract underrepresented candidates to public service. The number of women we elect is not just about the quantity of women members but the quality of their leadership. It is about having a diversity of opinion in the room, about truly representing America.

When I won the speakership of the House, I was overwhelmed

by the messages I received from women: young women said, "Thank you for opening a door for me," and older women said, "I never thought I would see the day." It was also a joy to hear from so many fathers of daughters. They thanked me for the opportunities that seeing a woman in my role provided for their daughters and for the confidence that it gave them. One father even wrote to me on stationery imprinted with poignant words often loosely attributed to Eleanor Roosevelt: "The future belongs to those who believe in the beauty of their dreams."

The dreams of the early suffragists—for women to have a seat at the table—is finally being realized. Now, however, more than ever, we still need to secure the beauty of their dreams, and the future for all Americans. Nearly two hundred fifty years after our country was born, the fight for democracy in America is, sadly, ongoing and challenging. It will take all of us, working together, to prove through the night that our flag is still there and to do so "with liberty and justice for all."

For me, that work begins in the hallowed halls of our nation's Capitol.

This book is a rendering of the most consequential challenges of my time in the leadership of the US House of Representatives: my decision to oppose the Iraq War and why; my nearly four decades of fighting for human rights in China; the epic struggle to respond to the 2008 financial crisis; the all-consuming fight to pass the Affordable Care Act (ACA); the January 6 attack on the Capitol; and the traumatizing assault on my dear husband inside our own home. I will take you inside the leadership room, but also inside the transformation of America's political landscape. To those who ask, How did she do it?, my answer is that the more important question is why.

What is her touchstone? What is her why?

Leadership's Price

Knock, Knock, Knock

Knock. Knock. Knock. Pound. Pound. Pound. Louder and louder. Then I heard a second noise, the doorbell, ringing over and over. And again, the knocking, someone was knocking, knocking hard—pounding and banging—on the door of my Washington apartment in the complete darkness of the early morning of October 28, 2022.

I looked at the clock. I could make out the number 5—still dark on the East Coast and the middle of the night in California. Clearly, I thought, someone had the wrong apartment. I heard more loud banging. Anxiously, I got out of bed and ran to the door. Outside I heard the voices of my Capitol Police security detail. I opened the door. The officers' expressions were grim. "Madam Speaker, we need to come in to speak to you," the detail leader said. I was beyond panicked.

"What are you doing here at this hour?" I asked in fear and desperation. "Does it have anything to do with my children or grandchildren?" Immediately I began thinking of who might be out or possibly hurt late at night.

"No," they said, "it's Mr. Pelosi. He's been attacked in your home."

Attacked? In our home? We had been together in our home just twenty-four hours before.

"Is he okay?" I asked.

"We don't know."

Horrified, I asked, "Is he alive?"

"We don't know."

"Where is he?"

"He has been taken to the hospital."

"Which hospital?"

"We haven't been informed yet."

I would soon learn that Paul was alive, thank God, and that he had been taken by ambulance to Zuckerberg San Francisco General Hospital and Trauma Center, the leading trauma center in Northern California. There are many great hospitals in San Francisco, including three that are just blocks from our home. But SF General, as it is known, is a preeminent Level 1 trauma center.

That was the moment when it sank in just how much danger Paul was in.

The Attack

Paul has never discussed the attack with me or with our children. It is "too traumatic," he says. It would also be inconsistent with his somber and stoic attitude. Most importantly, Paul's doctors did not want him to relive the events of that night—they just wanted him to focus on healing. He did talk to the police and investigators, and he had to tell his story on the witness stand during a federal criminal trial in November 2023 and again for a state trial in 2024. But in our home and family life, we have done everything possible to wall off this moment, which was truly a centimeter away from a disaster.

Invariably, I am asked, "How could this have happened?" Like most tragedies, it was the result of multiple things going profoundly wrong, starting with the bargain that most of us in high-profile elected office make. We know we are targets, and we recognize what that risk entails. But my thinking—and I am hardly alone in this—has been, Why would anyone want to harm our families? Until that awful early morning of October 28, despite the threats, including death threats, that I personally received, and all the horrible things that have been said about me, I didn't think that my family would be a target—especially in our own home.

On October 27, I left San Francisco for Washington, DC. I had congressional responsibilities and high-level security briefings scheduled for the morning of the twenty-eighth, and my security detail was with me. As the Speaker of the US House of Representatives, I was second in line to the presidency after the vice president. Consequently, I had twenty-four-hour security provided by the Capitol Police. But that robust security detail followed only me, not my family.

A few minutes after 2:00 a.m. West Coast time, a six-foot-four, two-hundred-sixty-pound man used a hammer to fiercely break the double-paned glass on the back-door windows of our San Francisco home and enter the house. Security cameras positioned around our house captured it all, but no one observed it happening in real time.

The attacker made his way to our bedroom, where Paul was asleep. The attacker then awakened Paul by asking, "Where's Nancy? Where's Nancy?"—the same question asked by the insurrectionists who overran the Capitol on January 6, 2021. The attacker was still carrying the hammer, and he also had zip ties, which are frequently used as makeshift handcuffs, and which were also carried by some of the January 6 insurrectionists.

As Paul testified during the federal criminal trial, "It was a tremendous sense of shock to recognize that somebody had broken into the house and looking at him and looking at the hammer and the ties, I recognized that I was in serious danger, so I tried to stay as calm as possible." As Paul recounted, he told the attacker that I was in Washington and would not be home for several days. The attacker said that I was the "leader of the pack" against Donald Trump and that the attacker was going to have "to tie" Paul up and "wait" for me. Hearing that, Paul tried to escape into the hallway.

In our hallway, we have a small elevator that we use for grocery bags and luggage so that we do not have to lug heavy bags up and down the steep stairs in our home. Paul testified that he thought if he could reach the elevator, he could press the emergency button and stop it between the floors and also use the emergency phone inside to call for help. But as the attacker testified in the federal trial, when Paul got into the elevator, the attacker followed, and, wedging himself in partway, he loomed over Paul, preventing him from seeking help. The attacker then testified that he said to Paul, "Do you really want to do this?" To which Paul looked up at him and said, "You're a big guy, no."

Paul then went back into the bedroom and had the presence of mind to go into the bathroom, which is the opposite direction from the bedroom door. This time, the attacker didn't try to stop Paul. Paul picked up his cell phone, which was charging on the counter, and dialed 911. To this day, I have not been able to listen to the 911 call and hear Paul's voice. I cannot watch any of the security footage or police body camera footage. I have avoided them all.

When you are a public figure—especially when an event involves a physical attack—it is not that the images are played once or twice. Instead, they dominate the news cycle, and the footage, in bits and pieces or in its entirety, is played around-the-clock. Being in the vicinity of a TV or a digital news stream means reliving these awful moments over and over. Paul did not want us to watch it—not our children, our grandchildren, or me. The attack on Paul caused our family its own deep trauma and my own survivor's guilt.

But I do know that Paul saved his own life with that 911 phone call. He kept his cool and gave just enough information while under tremendous physical threat—the attacker was standing behind him, holding the hammer and the zip ties. The attacker was close enough to Paul to be heard on the phone as he lied and claimed to be "a friend" of Paul's.

Paul kept the conversation going with the 911 operator and conveyed enough information that she dispatched the police. Paul testified that he knew his best chance was to get the attacker to go downstairs with him and hope the police would come to the front door.

When the officers did arrive and the door was opened, the police body cam footage showed the attacker holding the hammer. The police instructed him to drop the hammer. Instead the attacker used the hammer to assault Paul three times, striking him on the head. The next thing Paul knew, he was waking up on the ground, surrounded by a pool of his own blood.

Not long after, my security detail was banging on my door in Washington.

I could think only of two things: finding out everything and anything I could about Paul's condition, and that I had to call our children. Paul and I have five precious children and, at that time, had nine precious grandchildren (now ten), who are spread across the country in every time zone. I did not want them to hear about what had happened to our Pop from anyone other than me. But as I thought about telling the children and grandchildren, I also wanted to be able to awaken everyone with some hope as well as with the terrible news.

It would turn out that the media news cycle was moving so quickly that I could not reach each child first; only two would hear about what had happened to their father directly from me.

My first calls were to our San Francisco–based children. I called our son, Paul Jr., who lives nearby. He was shocked when I tried to explain what I knew. He immediately rushed to track down our Pop.

My next call was to our daughter Christine. Teen, as our family calls her, didn't answer, so I left a message, which she saved:

> Teen . . . it's Mom. Somebody broke into our house. They hurt Dad. . . . We just don't know what Dad's condition is, but they took him to Zuckerberg, which is a trauma thing. . . . They caught the guy. I mean, he was fighting with Dad when the police got there, and there was danger. And the guy had a hammer, that's what I'm worried about. . . . Okay, okay, that's what I know now. I'm sorry that this happened . . .

Christine had heard the phone but thought I was up early in Washington and had called her by mistake—a butt dial. Then she saw the voicemail notice pop up on her phone. Immediately, she called back. She rushed to get dressed, told her husband, Peter, what had happened, and raced to the hospital. On her way, she called Paul Jr. He had gone outside to discover that his car had a flat tire, so the two of them decided that he would walk to our house and she would continue straight to the hospital.

Our home, the house that our Pop loved and had carefully renovated over the years, was now a crime scene. Paul Jr. was needed to make sure the media didn't try to go inside—to protect the scene from everyone except law enforcement.

When Christine arrived at the hospital, she was not able to see Pop, because he had already been taken from the Emergency Department into a sterile pre-op area to be readied for surgery. His skull had been fractured. The doctors gave her a brief update on his condition—mostly focused on the critical blows to his head and their work to save his life. They told her Pop would have to be in surgery and post-op recovery for several hours. Meanwhile, Paul Jr. had to wait outside in the pre-dawn darkness for the police and then the crime scene investigation unit to sweep our entire house. Law enforcement feared that other weapons or even a bomb could be inside.

Not long after Christine arrived at the hospital, a TV anchor whom she knew called to offer his deep concern. In a matter of minutes after the attack, the media had already tracked down all kinds of reports both about the assault and about Pop being at the hospital. Some members of the press had information before we did and before we could reach everyone in the family. That meant that the first person who told some of our family was not me but a reporter, even possibly a reporter hoping for a comment. Others heard about Paul from their friends, who had been alerted earlier in the morning to the "breaking news."

Whether the information that the press uncovered about Paul came from the hospital or law enforcement, I don't know, but it created a terrible and very difficult reaction for many in our family. The reporting was often incorrect and incomplete, and it would grow worse as the hours dragged on. I cannot even begin to describe how painful and devastating it was for them to learn of a vicious assault on their father or grandfather in this way. Let alone the fact that there was no time for us to even process in private what had happened or even any way to know what Pop's condition was. He was eighty-two years old and had been hit in the head three times with a hammer. We knew anything could happen. We could not be certain that our Pop would survive.

I didn't have to call our youngest daughter, Alexandra, on that terrible early morning. She called me from New York. A documentarian, Alexandra has many friends in the news media. They had already called to alert her about the assault on Pop and share what they knew. Zon (her family nickname) was distraught.

Zon first yelled at me and said she was "done with all of this," *this* meaning politics, Congress, the speakership, and everything about a public political life. In a range of emotions from anger to sadness to worry, she demanded: What went wrong with the security cameras? How could this happen? This isn't fair. Pop doesn't deserve this.

Quickly the news continued to spread through the media. Alexandra could track it moving through outlet after outlet as her phone filled up with hundreds of calls and texts. She was desperate to rush to the airport. She asked her husband, Michiel, to just drive toward LaGuardia or Kennedy Airport while she tried to get the earliest flight to DC or San Francisco. She ultimately took the first flight to Washington so she could fly west with me.

When Congresswoman Sala Burton wanted me to run for her seat in Congress, I asked Alexandra for permission before I gave my answer. She was sixteen years old, in high school, and our only child still living at home—her siblings were away at college. I told her that if I won, I would be gone three nights a week in Washington when Congress was in session. "Mother," she answered, "get a life!" What teenage girl doesn't want her mother out of the house three nights a week? But when we were sitting in the ICU with Pop after the attack, she told me, "If I had known what we were

KNOCK, KNOCK, KNOCK

signing up for, if I had known this was where it was going to go, I would never have given you my blessing thirty-five years ago."

Christine had started a group text with all her siblings as she was reaching the hospital, but even that was not fast enough to beat the instant news cycle. Our daughter Jacqueline, in Texas, had been up early, driving to the gym. Four blocks from her home, she stopped at a red light and saw that her phone had lit up with a text from Christine. Jacqueline told me that if she hadn't been lucky enough to be in her car and to see the text, she likely would have learned about the attack on her father from breaking news, which would have been traumatizing. "It was remarkable how quickly the news was covering this nightmare," she told me later. "It was heartbreaking to imagine that had I been home, I would have seen this on CNN or NBC before hearing from my own family."

From her car, Jacqueline immediately called Christine, who was remarkably calm as she navigated the situation at the hospital. Christine said that she would give an update as soon as she heard anything more. Jacqueline quickly turned around and drove the four blocks back to her home. Almost immediately, her phone also began blowing up with messages from friends. By 8:00 a.m.—still only 6:00 a.m. in San Francisco—many of them began showing up at her home to be a support as Jacqueline awaited calls and texts from her siblings and reports from the doctors.

When I reached our daughter Nancy Corinne, in Arizona, she told me that she had already heard immediately from Alexandra. As the five children called each other and sent texts back and forth, everyone was scared to death. While Pop was in surgery, they began booking flights for San Francisco, afraid that they might not arrive in time. For the children who were able to leave immediately for San Francisco, it was a difficult flight. On

19

their planes, many of the passengers were glued to their phones or iPads or laptops, watching the horrible news. Buckled into their seats, our daughters tried to avoid it, saying prayers while ignoring the breaking headlines. When each of them landed, they went straight to the hospital.

As complicated as it was to tell all five children, telling the grandchildren was even more agonizing.

With Christine at the hospital, her husband, Peter, went to awaken their daughter, Bella, and her older brother, Octavio, to tell them what had happened to Pop. But he was too late. Bella's middle school friends had already heard, and her phone was filled with their texts and comments. Rather than have her stay at home, waiting and worrying, Bella and her parents decided that she should go to school, but before she left, she prepared a get-well card for her Pop. Imagine sitting down to make a card for your beloved grandfather after hearing such horrendous news.

Alexandra's son, named Paul after his grandfather, was in high school, and he was angry when he learned the news but remained composed. His younger brother, Thomas, had already left for his high school. He had to be privately taken aside and updated by a school counselor that his grandfather had been attacked and was in the hospital, heading for surgery. After learning the news, Thomas and his friends were joined by Xavier High School's president, and together they went to the school's chapel to pray for Pop.

Jacqueline had to call her husband, Michael, and their three sons—Liam, Sean, and Ryan, two of whom were away at college—to tell them what had happened, hoping as she dialed that they had not seen the news reports first.

Alexandra spoke to her niece, Madeleine, Nancy Corinne's daughter, from LaGuardia Airport. Madeleine, who was in graduate school, was crying hysterically on the phone, something Alexandra had never heard her do before. How, she kept saying, could anyone do this to Pop? In those hours, it was almost impossible to comfort these children and young people, who were heartbroken that something this awful could have happened to their Pop. Meanwhile, Alexander, Nancy Corinne's young adult son, had rushed to my Washington apartment to be with me as we awaited Alexandra.

In tears, in prayer, in utter shock and disbelief, and in anger, every child and grandchild of ours was deeply affected by the unfairness of this attack. Everyone had questions: Who would do this to Pop? How did we fail to protect Pop from this man?

Rushing Back to San Francisco

President Biden called me as soon as he heard the news, early in the morning. He was so prayerful, kind, and thoughtful in his comments about Paul.

Just before Paul went into surgery, the medical personnel placed a call to me, and I was blessed to be able to hear my husband's voice, even though he sounded foggy. I told him that we all sent our love, that President Biden sent his warm wishes, and that I was on my way as quickly as possible to be with him. When I told Paul about President Biden's kindness, he said, "How did the president even know about this?" Paul didn't imagine that people would know about what had happened—let alone that there would be a national and indeed a worldwide outpouring of sympathy and prayers for him.

Alexandra's and my five-and-a-half-hour flight across the

country felt endless and agonizing. We were both numb, but I held on to the thought of my brief call with Paul. Hearing his voice, weak and dazed as it was, made all the difference.

Almost immediately that morning, Cynthia Birmingham, among our family's dearest friends, had joined Christine at the hospital—she had thoughtfully arrived with thick socks, a cozy sweater, and a soft blanket for Paul. Lovingly, she had also stopped by Christine's home to pick up Bella's get-well card so it would be waiting for Pop when he awakened. Christine and Cynthia were the first to see Pop when he came out of the recovery room after the surgery to repair his skull. When he emerged, he was his usual stoic and unselfish self. He had no idea of the news reports swirling or the public impact of his assault, and his first thoughts were to reassure our family.

But he gratefully accepted the blanket that Cynthia delivered—and he didn't let it go for at least a week. When Paul Jr. called to tell Pop that "Mommy is on her way," Pop's first comment was, "She'll be happy because the Ravens won last night." He knows that I have a soft spot for all Baltimore sports teams—it is the city I grew up in—second only to San Francisco teams.

Although Pop seemed lucid, Cynthia told me that later she could see that underneath he was very shaken and somber—and everyone was still uncertain as to how or how well he would recover. He was seriously injured, and no one knew what the next hours and days would hold.

In addition to his skull injuries, he needed twelve stitches to the back of his right arm, and his left hand had to be reconstructed by plastic surgeons because it was so badly damaged.

By the time I reached the hospital in the afternoon, Paul was settled in the intensive care unit. When Alexandra walked in and saw Pop, she was frightened and declared that he looked like Frankenstein's monster, with deep wounds and bandages covering his head, hands, and arms. He had been struck with the hammer three times in separate places on the top of his head; by some miracle, the blows had not pierced his brain. Surgeons had to remove part of his skull and reshape it because of the blows he had suffered, as well as watch for serious bleeding and brain swelling. Paul's hand and arm would require multiple surgeries in the days and months to come. It was not merely skin wounds; the tendons and other structures had been seriously damaged. He needed his hand to be reconstructed for functionality. In February 2024, I would still be changing bandages on his arm after another round of surgical repair.

As our family kept vigil in the ICU during those early anxious hours and days, what was calming to observe, and a blessing, was the care that SF General provides to its patients, including Paul. The physicians Michael Huang, Geoff Manley, and John Rose, who treated Paul that day, truly saved his life. We are grateful to them, and to the caring nurses, physical therapists, and support staff, as well as to the health care providers, EMTs, and first responders who cared for him.

So much emotion descended on all of us that evening: tears, thoughts, and prayers from so many friends and family, love for Pop, friendship from the people in our lives and from so many others who cared.

The one person who left the hospital after seeing Pop was Paul Jr. Around 4:45 p.m.—after law enforcement had swept the house and garden for bombs and explosive devices and after a search warrant had been executed and evidence documented—Paul Jr. went inside to begin cleaning up. The horrible task of cleaning up a crime scene and the mess fell to him that afternoon. He vacuumed a million tiny shards of glass from the broken windows. He picked up his father's pajamas, which had soaked for hours in a pool of his father's blood. I cannot even begin to imagine what those moments were like. "Devastating" seems to hardly convey what Paul Jr. went through in our family home. Cynthia also went to our home to help restore order, bringing a shop vac with her assistant, who would later say with concern, "I hope Paul Jr. is feeling better. He was so distraught—it's going to take some time to heal from the trauma of it all."

Because our house still had a heavy police presence and remained a crime scene, it was clear that our family could not return to our home to sleep that night. Nor did we want to. That evening, Cynthia and her husband, Rob, invited us to have dinner and stay with them so we did not have to face the trauma of going home and seeing the broken windows and bloodstains, which would be a tragic reminder of the horror that had happened less than twenty-four hours before.

By the next night, the broken windowpanes had been boarded up; Paul Jr. had removed all the glass and cleaned up as much of the blood as he could. We could go home, but it was strange to be getting into bed in the room that had been invaded thirty-six hours earlier by a violent attacker calling out, "Where's Nancy? Where's Nancy?"

But this was our home, and the one, God willing, that Paul would return to after he was released from the hospital. Aware of our responsibility to make our home truly be home for Pop, we swallowed our doubts and fears and embraced the house despite everything that had happened inside those walls and the pain from that night, which we will carry for a long time.

After Surgery

Paul never wanted to talk about what happened that night. "I've made the best effort I possibly can to not relive this," he has said. We would not know the full extent of the danger he was in until more than a year later, when one of his doctors testified during the federal trial that when the attacker fractured Paul's skull, he came within a centimeter of hitting the superior sagittal sinus vein, which connects to the brain and, via the internal jugular vein, also to the heart. We learned that this could have been a life-threatening blow. The assault was so violent that the attacker thought he had killed Paul. In the federal trial, the attacker testified that he was surprised that Paul had survived.

In the days that followed, we recognized that it would be a long recovery—but thank God, a recovery. For many months, Paul wore a hat to cover the grotesque wounds on his head and a glove to protect and cover his badly injured hand. The blows to his head had also left Paul with post-concussion syndrome. He tired easily and had dizzy spells. His doctors were adamant that he needed to avoid bright light, noise, and especially electronic screens.

Paul, our Pop, came home from the hospital on November 3. But rather than returning to an atmosphere of peace and quiet at our home, he was met by a media barrage outside: reporters, cameras, even a helicopter noisily circling overhead. It was a bombardment of light and sound, bright and loud—exactly what his doctors had directed him to avoid. This media onslaught outside our home continued for days.

———

The story of Paul's attack would not go away. And from the moment news of the attack was reported, it was like a second assault was being waged on Paul and our family. Piled on to our deep shock and grief, we now had to confront lies and misrepresentations.

A true horror was the dehumanizing jokes. It was beyond offensive to hear high-profile Republicans make cruel jokes and misrepresentations about the attempt on Paul's life—from the former president and his children to governors, party leaders, and other high-ranking Republicans and Republican candidates looking to score cheap points, as they "joked" about sending me back to San Francisco. Donald Trump Jr. was among the worst. On Twitter (now X), he shared a meme of a hammer with the tagline, "Got my Paul Pelosi Halloween costume ready." It was equally horrible to hear crowds laugh, cheer, and applaud or "like" these cruel remarks, egging on this type of despicable violence. More than twenty-two thousand people "liked" Trump Jr.'s post; others denounced it as "vile." Sitting vigil at his bedside, we found their mockery of Paul and our family deeply painful, even as we worked very hard to keep this cruelty from him.

Again and again, it made me profoundly sad for our country that some individuals with high visibility would repeat these lies and stray so far to separate themselves from the facts and the truth. But our family tended to Paul's immediate needs, and we were comforted by a tremendous outpouring of love and support.

Hours after the assault, the attacker voluntarily told law enforcement that he had "a target list" and that "Speaker Pelosi" was on his list. He said that he planned to interrogate me, and that if "Nancy" told him the "truth," he would let her go, and if she "lied," he would "break her kneecaps." After he had broken my kneecaps, he added, Nancy would have to be wheeled into Congress, which would show other members of Congress that there were consequences to their actions. Hatred of me was his rationale to violently attack my husband.

Paul was not the intended target that night, but he is the one who paid and is still paying the price physically. And our entire family is paying the price emotionally and traumatically.

Recovery

For years, we've had guests come to our house, look at the steep stairs, and say, as San Francisco newspaper columnist Herb Caen observed, "Your house is made for mountain goats, because only mountain goats would want to go up and down those stairs." Many of them also wondered if we had an elevator. After the surgery, Paul's head, left hand, and right arm were heavily bandaged. When he came home from the hospital, it would have been much easier for him to use the elevator to go up and down. Instead, he chose to very slowly and carefully make his way up and down the stairs. He didn't want to set foot near the elevator, where he had tried to escape and had his way blocked.

Another spot that Paul avoided for months was one of his favorites, his happy place in the house, the garden room. He had renovated it out of the old laundry room and basement area. It was where he would watch the 49ers, the Giants, and the Warriors games, and occasionally smoke his cigars (which he was only allowed to do with the doors to the garden open). But that was the room where the attacker had broken the glass and entered.

So our daily life now centered on the living room on the second floor, where we worked, hung out, and watched sports on the iPad. That room was still a safe haven when other parts had bad memories.

I still struggle with passing through the entry hall, where the attack occurred.

I'll never understand how Paul could ever sleep in our bedroom again after being confronted by the attacker there. But my children told me that for a long time, he would only sleep in the bedroom when I was home—when I was in Washington and he was alone, he slept in another bedroom.

For months I was very aware of how Paul carefully avoided the key scenes of the crime. Until one day he simply said, "Let's watch the game downstairs." Those five words were such a big deal, such a hopeful sign that Paul was truly healing and trying to move beyond that horrible night.

We all have been so deeply proud of Paul's strength, courage, discipline, and resilience. He's not one to complain: he's faithful to his daily physical therapy program, designed to strengthen the damaged muscles and tendons and to help him regain function in his hand and arm. And he follows the doctors' orders. He always encourages all of us to be confident in his recovery. But more than one year later, Paul still needs to do exercises every day to strengthen his balance. He still suffers from headaches and dizzy spells, although they have become less frequent. When we go to an event, we rarely stay very long. We get our glasses of water and sit down to preserve Paul's stamina and make sure he doesn't get dizzy. And we are confident that he will continue to improve.

Our family has been blessed not only with the gradual healing of our Pop but with the thousands of prayers and the love and messages and warm wishes extended to Paul from so many during this difficult time. It all makes such a big difference in his, and our, recovery.

What seems especially unfair is that Paul is such a lovely and gentle person. When we were married sixty years ago, he never signed up for how political our lives would become. He was a wonderful father as we raised our five children—whom we had in the span of six years and one week. Years later, when I was asked to run for Congress without my ever having given it a thought before or having it be any part of our life plan together, he willingly signed on, without question or complaint. He wanted me to be able to pursue my passion for public service. He has been my biggest champion.

From housewife to House member to House Speaker, I certainly would never have broken the marble ceiling without Paul's support, encouragement, and love.

And I would never have done it if I thought it would one day cause him to risk his own life.

One chapter of our ordeal ended in May 2024 when the attacker was sentenced in federal court to thirty years in prison. But the scars from that night will never truly heal. As I wrote to the court before the sentencing, "Even now, eighteen months after the home invasion and assault, the signs of blood and break-in are impossible to avoid. Our home remains a heartbreaking crime scene."

But Paul's letter to the court was even more painful for me to read. As Paul described it, the attacker "kept me hostage in my own home," adding that the attacker "repeatedly said that he could 'take me out.'" Paul's letter described that his left hand was "de-gloved," exposing raw nerves and blood vessels. He wrote: "Surgeries and treatments mostly healed the skin, but underneath

I still feel pinched nerves in my left hand. This makes basic tasks like using buttons, cutlery, and simple tools more difficult."

Paul's headaches and dizziness continue to this day. I have seen him faint and fall twice from vertigo. He must take care before going to social events, avoiding extended exposure to bright lights and loud noises, and spending most of his time seated.

I do not know that we will ever feel safe. Paul noted in his letter that I remain under twenty-four-hour security. He wrote, "We do not answer our landline or our front door due to ongoing threats. We cannot fully remove the stain on the floor in the front entryway where I bled." It is almost an understatement to say, as Paul did, that his life has "irrevocably changed." This assault has truly had a devastating effect on three generations of our family.

We Must Have an End to Political Violence

The assault on Paul was violent and frightening for the future, not just of the Pelosi family but of the United States. Our family, of course, was privately consumed with Paul's recovery. It is so unfair because Paul's a perfect gentleman. He is someone who never wants to engage in political combat. Imagine how it was for him, watching as I was turned into one of the longtime villains of the Republican Party—starting in 2010, when the party spent millions of dollars to demonize me, running countless ads that featured my picture engulfed in hellish flames. Year after year, these personal and demonizing attacks that made me a target continued. The then-Republican Minority Leader Kevin McCarthy had even "joked" in 2021 about hitting me with the Speaker's gavel. By the 2022 election, the Republicans spent tens of millions on ads personally attacking me. It was common for me to see an image of myself defaced with devil's horns or worse.

That the same taunting chants and jeers of "Where's Nancy? Where's Nancy?" that echoed through the hallowed halls of the Capitol on January 6 would less than two years later echo through our family home must teach all of us a lesson about the politics of personal destruction. It was the Republicans who engaged in this dangerous tactic with me—it's unworthy of what we once called the Grand Old Party, the GOP, and it is also disrespectful of our democracy.

The current climate of threats and attacks must stop.

We must be able to have disagreements on policies and issues without those disagreements immediately escalating into nasty personal attacks and angry threats of violence. This change in tactics began in the 1990s, when then-Republican House Speaker Newt Gingrich began targeting President Bill and First Lady Hillary Clinton. But it has grown far worse, especially since the 2016 election and the tactics of Donald Trump and his surrogates.

When I first arrived in Washington, there was limited security at the Capitol and almost none for individual members and senators, including in the leadership. That changed after 9/11, when the top leadership in the House and Senate joined the Speaker in receiving a protective detail. Individual House members or senators who are the targets of specific threats can also receive temporary protection. Frequently, the Capitol Police will need to work with local police departments in a member's district. During the health care legislation debate, for example, as many as one-third to one-half of Democratic members received threats, and some needed local police protection when they held health care town halls back home.

There is no one uniform standard for personal protection across the three branches of the federal government. In Congress, we don't even know the full extent of the protections offered to people serving in the executive or judicial branches and their families. But it is fair to say that Congress has historically had the least personal protection, even though the Capitol Police's threat assessment teams examine thousands of cases of "credible threats" against lawmakers each year.

My San Francisco house had long been a magnet for all kinds of protests, starting with anti–Iraq War protesters back in 2007— even though I led the opposition to the war for the House Democrats. But the tone and substance of the protests has grown far more aggressive and angry in recent years. No longer is it just noisy sit-ins on the block. During the night of January 1, 2021, our garage was spray-painted with graffiti, "We want everything" and "Cancel rent," apparently referring to Covid financial assistance legislation. In case that didn't make the point, someone left a severed pig's head and a small river of red paint, looking like blood, in front of the garage door. In the 2023 federal trial for Paul's attacker, an FBI agent testified that the "pig's head" was a top Pelosi-searched image on the attacker's computer.

Five days after the severed pig's head was left outside my home, the whole nation would witness the brazen and destructive events of January 6 on Capitol Hill. With the January 6 attack, Capitol Police and Congress realized that members' homes could become possible targets. Following a discussion and assessment of the most pressing needs, in August 2022, the House Sergeant at Arms William J. Walker began a program to provide each House member with up to $10,000 to cover security system equipment for their residence, including motion sensors, video recorders, indoor and outdoor cameras, and door locks, as well as professional security surveys. But the truth is, protection for some high-profile members costs far more. Increasingly, members are spending their own money or are using allowable campaign funds to pay for personal security for themselves and their families. The political rhetoric has gotten that personal and that violent. The fact that the exterior of my house was a constant target made everyone focus on the outside—not the possibility that someone would violently break in and enter, with an agenda to harm me or my family.

In just four years, between 2017 and 2021, the number of threats and concerning statements against all members of Congress doubled—to nearly ten thousand. In the year following January 6, the Capitol Police reported that threats against lawmakers increased by 107 percent. My house is still a target. Protesters routinely splash red paint on the garage and otherwise deface it, they defecate in front of the house, they pound on the door, and they yell in the street. And it's not just my house; similar behavior is on the rise outside the homes of elected and appointed officials around the country. I'm all for people expressing their views, but I have to ask how they think these violent actions are making a persuasive argument on the merits of an issue or furthering their cause.

Amid this poisonous rhetoric, I also do not hear serious, sustained calls by the other side saying that threats of political violence and personal demonization are unacceptable. This is not the way our country should be—if you engage in public service, you should not be a target, and your family should not be a target. When I speak to dynamic young people about running for office, especially to young women, too often I hear their reluctance to put their families in harm's way. What they most often mention now as their greatest fear is the attack on Paul—and that something like that could happen in their own homes.

We cannot ask people to serve in public life if the cost is risking the safety of their families and those they love. I believe we as Americans want better and are better. I pray that another family will never know the fear and pain that ours did that morning when I awakened to that desperate knock, knock, knock at my door.

Leadership in Congress

"We Have Made History, and Now We Must Make Progress"

One of my early first overseas trips as Speaker of the House was to Kuwait, Iraq, Pakistan, Afghanistan, and Germany in late January 2007. American troops were embroiled in deadly conflict in Iraq and against a growing Taliban-backed insurgency in Afghanistan. Joining me was a delegation of key House foreign and defense policy committee and subcommittee chairs and a Republican ranking member. We wanted to see with our own eyes what was happening on the ground, talk to leaders, and especially talk to and support our American troops. In Kuwait, the country's leaders had called me "Your Excellency"—as they called their Speaker.

But now I was huddled inside a massive, cold military transport plane, circling the high, jagged, snow-capped mountain peaks separating Pakistan and Afghanistan. Looking out the window, it seemed as if our plane was flying over the top of the world.

Rep. Nita Lowey, the chair of the House Committee on Appropriations, and I were in the cockpit, and I could hear the pilot speaking with air traffic controllers, informing them that we were planning to approach Kabul, the Afghan capital. I interjected and said, "No. We are supposed to be landing in Bagram. I want to see the troops first." Not only was a visit to this massive US military

37

base the main reason for our trip, but I knew from previous visits that anything could happen. Sometimes, one touchdown and takeoff inside Afghanistan was all that weather and other troubles would allow a visiting delegation.

The military pilot responded, "Our instructions from the embassy in Pakistan were to take you to Kabul." I stood firm: We were going to Bagram. That had been our plan and our schedule, that was what we had decided when we organized the trip. For our delegation, the troops came first. The pilot got back on the radio. "The embassy told us to go to Kabul first; Payload is insisting that we go to Bagram." Apparently "Payload" was my ID in the air. In a short span of time, I had gone from "Your Excellency" to "Payload."

And in case you are wondering, "Payload" landed at Bagram first.

"Who Said She Could Run?"

The path to the speakership involved the toughest political race I ever ran. It had only 215 voters and took place on October 10, less than one month after the attacks of 9/11. It was a special election: then-whip David Bonior was stepping down to run for governor of Michigan, and my opponent was Steny Hoyer, a longtime friend. Some of the most powerful men in Congress not only wanted me to lose this race—they also never wanted me to run. When I announced my candidacy for House Democratic whip, the number two position then available on the Democratic leadership team, one of my gentleman colleagues bluntly asked: "Who said she could run?" The men explained to me that the House had a pecking order, that other male representatives had been dutifully waiting in line for an upper-level leadership spot to open, that I was cutting in and overturning the established order of things. When the women members spoke out in favor of having a woman in the Democratic leadership, the same gentlemen said: "Why don't you just make a list of what you want to do, and we will do it for you?"

My reply was no, thank you. I told them that women had been waiting for more than two hundred years, which made our timeline a heck of a lot longer than theirs. But I also said to my fellow members that I didn't want anyone to vote for me because I was a woman or vote against me because I was a woman. For years, in fact, members had been asking me to run for a leadership position, which I initially had no interest in doing. I loved my legislative work on the Appropriations and Intelligence Committees and even spending a record seven years on the House Ethics Committee. What triggered my change of heart was four straight election-year losses from 1994 to 2000. I believed Democrats needed to start winning elections for our country and our country's children. The House of Representatives, as run by Republican Speaker Newt Gingrich, was not a healthy place for children and other living things. So I presented to my fellow Democratic Caucus members my vision and policy priorities and explained how I believed both could lead us to achieve political success.

Looking back on the day of that crucial vote, it is important to recognize that one of the hardest "asks" of a member is to choose among or between colleagues. Therefore, I started my campaign with the confidence that I would win. I did not want to subject members to a difficult choice if there was not a likely prospect of success. Well before the day of the vote, I knew that I had the votes. Members who make a public commitment to support you will hold true to their word. But when the conversation occurs in private, some members will make more than one commitment. Therefore, I built a 20 percent "fudge factor" into my count—confident that those who might say one thing and do another would not matter. And I largely knew which members might be inclined to do that. I've always known how to count and trust votes.

Nevertheless, the day before the whip vote in the caucus, one member who was advocating for the opposition began telling other members that the race wasn't over. And this member was speaking those words within earshot of me. He claimed that there was a one-vote difference in the whip race. It was certainly a tactic—but I knew it wasn't a fact. With confidence, not arrogance, I showed up to the beautiful Caucus Room in the Cannon House Building, with its ornate ceiling and walls, on the morning of the vote. The feeling of making history hung in the air. My team was prepared—and we won.

My victory was quite remarkable, not only because I was a woman but also because no House Democratic leader had ever previously invited me to any leadership meetings or offered me any role, which kept the men's pecking order inside the caucus intact. Indeed, until I was elected Speaker, I had never set foot in or even been invited to a Democratic Speaker's office. My own election was the first time.

After the whip voting ended, California representative Anna Eshoo, one of my longtime friends, opened the heavy wooden doors and called out to the waiting staff and gaggle of reporters, "It's Pelosi." Some of the men grumbled that "gender and geography" had won—because California has such a large state delegation of representatives, and all but one were supporting me. My answer was simply, "We have made history, and now we must make progress."

A year later, on November 14, 2002, I was elected by our caucus as the House Democratic leader after Dick Gephardt stepped down to prepare for a presidential run. That leadership vote, 177–29, was not even close. A central part of my message was about the deep value of our House Democratic Caucus: I saw our caucus as a source of strength, intellectually, legislatively, and politically. We were motivated by ideas, we understood the legislative process needed to be able to execute our ideas, and we had the political acumen to market our ideas to the American public. I wanted to tap into those abilities to regain the House of Representatives for the Democrats.

As fate would have it, I served as either the Democratic leader or House Speaker for the next twenty years, through multiple wars and international standoffs, dire economic crises, a global pandemic, the historic remake of American health care, an attack on the United States Capitol, and an unprecedented attack in my own home. Over more than two decades, I served alongside four presidents. One hundred five major cabinet secretaries, including defense secretaries, attorneys general, and secretaries of state, and twelve White House chiefs of staff came and went during my tenure.

The founders designed the House speakership to be the most important elected legislative position in our national government; it is the only congressional leadership position mentioned in the Constitution. The Senate majority and minority leaders are not in the line of presidential succession (that role falls to the person who holds the ceremonial post of Senate president pro tempore). But the Speaker is in the line of succession, directly following the vice president.

I assumed the speakership on January 4, 2007, when, after twelve years in the minority, the Democrats recaptured control of the House. We won thirty-one seats, more than double what we needed to regain the majority, and our party's largest seat gain since 1974, in the aftermath of Watergate. We ran on a positive agenda: "Six for '06," emphasizing an increase in the minimum wage, health care for all and lower prescription drug costs, redeployment of US troops out of Iraq, protecting Social Security, college access, and energy independence. We knew the public was deeply upset by the direction of the Iraq War, but other grave challenges, including a global economic meltdown, would await us.

Becoming Speaker

When I was sworn in as Speaker, I was surrounded by my grandchildren—and the children and grandchildren of my colleagues from both sides of the aisle. I also looked out to the Speaker's box to see Paul and my gray-haired champions: my brother Tommy—the former mayor of Baltimore, who had first shown me the Capitol when I was six—and my friends Tony Bennett and Richard Gere as they watched me take on this historic role.

In my remarks, I thanked my colleagues for electing me—for bringing us closer to the ideal of equality that is America's heritage and hope. I wanted my words to be healing and unifying. I told everyone assembled, "I accept this gavel in the spirit of partnership, not partisanship," adding, "In this House, we may be different parties, but we serve one country. . . . This openness requires respect for every voice in the Congress. As Thomas Jefferson said, 'Every difference of opinion is not a difference of principle.' . . . Let us all stand together to move our country forward, seeking common ground for the common good."

When I became Speaker of the House, I announced that we would strive to govern with bipartisanship, transparency, and accountability. That same philosophy had guided me from the moment I became Democratic leader: "Where we can find our common ground on the economy and other domestic issues, we shall seek it." But I noted, "Where we cannot find that common ground, we must stand our ground."

While the speakership is daunting, I embraced it confidently because of my experience with the domestic and global issues facing our country and my awareness of the possibilities to make improvements. Quite simply, there is no substitute for preparation and doing your homework. Globally, I was the first House member in recent history to assume a leadership position having already had national security experience, dating from my earliest years in Congress. I was the top Democrat on what was then, in the 1990s, called the Appropriations Subcommittee on Foreign Operations, which funded foreign assistance (I prefer to call it foreign cooperation) and some military assistance where appropriate; it also dealt with issues that relate to the global environment, health, and human rights. Next, I became the top Democrat on the House Permanent Select Committee on Intelligence, which I joined in 1993 to protect civil liberties and to stop the proliferation of nuclear weapons. In the course of my service in Congress, I have traveled to eighty-seven countries: some once, others many times, particularly to visit our troops deployed to war zones. I have met with leaders overseas and also hosted some as guests of Congress to address a joint session of the House and Senate.

I've always been grateful to my constituents for the latitude they gave me to engage in global affairs while at the same time remaining deeply involved in our domestic kitchen table issues as a rank-and-file member, whip, leader, and then Speaker.

As the first woman Speaker, it was necessary for me to assert myself in a very strong way on a core value: diversity. In my first meeting with all House committee chairs, whom I respected, I presented the case for diversity—that our caucus should reflect the diversity of America and honor that value. That diversity is what Americans should see when they look at our members and our staff. I put that value into practice by appointing women chairs to the three committees where I had the power of appointment: Louise Slaughter to the House Rules Committee, Juanita Millender-McDonald to the House Administration Committee, and Stephanie Tubbs Jones to the House Ethics Committee. Nydia Velázquez became chair of the Small Business Committee by right of her seniority. We had more than one hundred leadership gavel positions at the subcommittee level for women, people of color, and LGBTQ+ and other representatives. Later, working with our colleagues, I spearheaded the creation of the Office of Diversity and Inclusion. In fifteen years, our caucus has grown to be 70 percent women, people of color, and LGBTQ+ individuals—far removed from when I arrived in Congress in 1987 as one of twelve Democratic women.

Not only was I proud of our caucus coming together to pass legislation, but another source of pride for me as Speaker and Democratic leader was the expansion of our leadership team. By changing the composition of our team, expanding our team, and ensuring that its selection is more "democratic," we have made House Democratic leadership more representative and inclusive. When I became Speaker in 2007, there were just eight members of the Democratic leadership (I had served in three of those positions: Speaker, leader, and whip). In addition, we had a chair and vice chair of the House Democratic Caucus, two co-chairs of the Steering and Policy Committee, and a chair for the Democratic Congressional Campaign Committee.

When we lost control of the House in 2010, in order to avoid a race for whip between Steny Hoyer and Jim Clyburn, I established the position of assistant Democratic leader (later to become assistant Speaker when we regained the majority). I expanded our Steering and Policy Committee chairs to three, appointing Barbara Lee, who became the first Black woman to serve in the Democratic leadership. Then, our newer members suggested that we create a position for those who had served five terms or less, so that more junior members would have a crucial voice in leadership discussions and decisions. I also broadened our selection process: rather than appointments by the Speaker, many of our positions are now directly elected by our members. And to expand the reach of our caucus and its messages, in 2015, I created the Democratic Policy and Communications Committee, which now has four co-chairs. Additionally, I added a parliamentarian, whose knowledge of the rules of the House is designed to help members resolve differences.

By the end of my term as Speaker in January 2023, we had grown from eight to eighteen members on our leadership team—and I'm sure that number will continue to expand.

In addition to the leadership changes, I launched another initiative, which I named "Crescendo," to indicate that I wanted it to increase the impact of our House Democratic policies. This group, comprised of eight elected chairs (of the Black Caucus, the Hispanic Caucus, the Asian Pacific American Caucus, the Equality Caucus, and the Progressive Caucus, as well as the three coalitions, the Freshmen Class, the New Democrats, and the Blue Dogs), meets weekly with the Speaker to exchange views. And by popular demand, we established the Select Committee on the Modernization of Congress, suggested by Congressmen Joe Kennedy and Derek Kilmer, where members could share their views about a Congress of the future. I believe in open doors and open communication in the Speaker's office.

Being Speaker of the House is probably the most challenging position in government. You have to address the same vast array of issues as the president (but lack the advantage of making appointments across the executive branch and proposing judicial nominees). The Speaker has a much smaller staff, and does not have the benefit of the bully pulpit. As opposed to leading just your political party, you are also responsible for leading the entire House of Representatives, 435 voting members and 6 non-voting delegates. Being Speaker is obviously also very different from being a member of Congress. As members of Congress, we most often act deductively: we subject ideas to hearings, town hall meetings with constituents, and other forms of public comment. Members have time to decide on and refine or amend a proposal as it passes through the committee process and reaches the House floor.

The speakership is different. It is both a uniquely powerful and an executive position that requires a combination of a policy background, strategic knowhow, and, above all, intuition. A successful Speaker can't ever be surprised by anything. You must know what all the possibilities are, all of the time. Those possibilities include how each member of your caucus will vote, what you are willing to concede in negotiations with the Senate or the White House and what you are not, and what resonates with the American people and why. Every challenge you face requires a decision, and you're not always given much time to make that decision. Anticipation is the order of the day. You must immediately be able to articulate your answers to the questions why, what, and how. You must demonstrate a plan, and you must act without hesitation. The minute you hesitate, your options are diminished. The longer you wait, the more your options are diminished. Everyone with an agenda will chip away at your delayed decision.

While a Speaker's actions must be both intuitive and quick to succeed, that alone is not enough. The thinking that informs and supports a Speaker's intuition must be strategic and respected. That is why I believe it is absolutely vital to maintain a constant level of member contact—you need to know what members are thinking. This contact benefits everyone in two ways: not only are you learning from your members, but when members see your investment in them, it gives them confidence in your knowledge and judgment, which is essential. The advice to trust your gut only works if your gut is informed from both the head and the heart.

For twenty years, the word that dominated my approach to and my work with my colleagues is "respect." Our job title and our job description are one and the same: "representative." On the Democratic side, we have deeply shared values and highly respected diversity, in terms of ethnicity, geography, generation, gender, gender identity, and sometimes even philosophy, and thus sometimes we differ. As I always say to the members, "Our diversity is our strength, our unity is our power."

I'm often asked, "How did you keep your caucus together?" I always reply, "With respect." Power does not come from the top down; it comes from the bottom up. To achieve that, I always demonstrated my respect for all our Democratic members. I listened to their views; I wanted them to know that we were a community, and that their time was valuable. If we came to serve, our objective was to get things done. I also wouldn't ask members to vote with me on an issue unless I thought I could win.

Recognizing the differences among our caucus members, I considered myself a weaver at the loom. Every member is an essential thread in the tapestry our caucus is weaving. The beauty is in the mix. Therefore, it is necessary to build consensus respectfully. Our vision on a particular issue might not always lead to unanimity. However, as a responsible leader of our caucus, it was my role to ask those who disagreed or needed to represent a different point of view for their constituents to please respect the larger consensus. For example, our caucus has always overwhelmingly supported a woman's right to choose, but it wasn't until the 2018 election that we built enough support for that position to hold a majority in the full House of Representatives. When it comes to some highly contentious issues on our own side or when we deal with Republican members, I apply the same test of respect: I truly believe that it is possible to have eternal friendships with those with whom you agree or disagree. I do believe that we can avoid eternal animosities with those with whom we disagree.

This leads from my vision of the loom to another key metaphor in my approach: the kaleidoscope. I've always professed that in Congress, we know that after a vote is over, tomorrow is another day. As with a kaleidoscope, the coalition that works in one design is not necessarily replicated in another combination. A crucial kaleidoscope design appeared when the House took on the historic repeal of the "don't ask, don't tell" policy, which banned openly LGBTQ+ service members in the military. The policy was enacted in 1993, but only when we held the majority in 2010 did we finally have the votes to overturn the provision. However, there was a catch: the repeal of "don't ask, don't tell" was attached as an amendment to the annual defense authorization bill. The vast majority of Democrats were jubilant when the amendment to repeal "don't ask, don't tell" was passed and included in the defense bill. I told our progressive caucus members: "You are making history today!"

Yes, they replied, we finally repealed "don't ask, don't tell."

"Yes," I said, and then I added, "and you are also making history because some of you will be voting for a defense bill for the first time."

"Oh no," they said, "don't ask us to do that!" Many of our progressives had never voted for a defense authorization bill—and they told me they couldn't cast their vote in favor of the bill that day. I replied that without the passage of the defense bill, our amendment to repeal "don't ask, don't tell" was dead. "Oh no," they countered, "the Republicans always vote for the defense bill. They will pass it."

"No," I replied, "not today. Today we will need your votes." Many of the members openly scoffed at me, asking, "How do you know?"

I reminded them, "I'm Speaker. I can see it in the Republicans' eyes . . . and I can read lips. The Republicans are not going to vote for this bill. So, before you vote, at least wait and see if your vote will be needed to pass the bill and thus the amendment." Thankfully, these members honored my request. They stood back and held their votes. The clock ticked and the vote count climbed—but it was overwhelmingly against the bill. The progressive members watched as only 9 Republicans voted yes—while 160 voted no.

I'll never forget the sight of John Lewis, Barney Frank, Barbara Lee, Anna Eshoo, Dennis Kucinich, and the full array of Democrats who, up until that day, had a 100 percent record of voting against any defense authorization bills. But many of them joined to help us reach the final vote count: 220 Democrats in favor. The bill passed, but our progressive members weren't jubilant when I congratulated them on having made history twice that day. That, however, was a true kaleidoscope. On any given day, as we turn the dial, we bring in new elements and new alliances. We can never assume that support for one issue automatically leads to support for another. Inside our caucus, those of us in leadership must always be in discussion with each other, with committee chairs, and with members. We don't want to weaken or dismiss anyone for one position they may hold—because they may be vital to the overall design of another issue and another important vote—and soon.

Congress has multiple responsibilities, outlined in the Constitution, including raising and appropriating funds, declaring war, legislating, and exercising oversight. But because we are a legislature—the legislative branch, Article I of the Constitution— often an important expression of our role is negotiating legislation and then voting on it. Many steps must be taken before a Speaker calls a vote. Successful initiatives begin with respecting the experience and values of your colleagues and working together to put people over politics.

The vast majority of legislation originates in committees, where each bill is scrutinized and refined. Once a bill is voted out of committee, it may be eligible to be brought to the House floor for a vote by the entire House. However, before a vote occurs, a successful Speaker wants to ensure that members know what provisions are contained in the bill. That means having the relevant committee chairs and the House leadership brief members before they vote. Then, members must decide how to cast their votes based on what I refer to as the four Cs: to honor the Constitution, to represent their constituents, to obey their conscience . . . and sometimes it takes courage.

Some of the most consequential moments of my time in the House have been votes requiring the Constitution, constituents, conscience, and courage. The Affordable Care Act is one such example. So were the decisions on the Iraq War and the 2008 financial crisis. Other times, it is not simply one final vote tally that matters, but many votes and efforts over many years, such as on the issue of human rights in China. More recently, support for democracy in Ukraine and the battle to save the planet have unified or divided members of Congress.

The legislative process requires broad debate, not only within the Democratic Caucus but across the aisle, with the Senate, and then with the White House. Sometimes we find common ground. Sometimes we don't, and we look to the public to weigh in. We don't agonize; we organize—mobilizing for success, as we did by turning out grassroots support for the Affordable Care Act.

A House Speaker should and must lead in each of these arenas. How that is accomplished often determines the success or failure of a legislative agenda—indeed, of their speakership. But winning in the House is only the first step. A Speaker also faces two other formidable institutions: the Senate and the White House.

The House v. the Senate v. the White House

There's an old adage among House Democrats that was frequently voiced by the late John Dingell, chairman of the Committee on Energy and Commerce and the longest-serving member of Congress in history: "The Republicans are our opposition, but the Senate is our enemy." It's old and often repeated because it reflects House frustrations with the Senate.

The House and Senate have very different approaches to legislation. In the House, a majority rules. Build a coalition of one party, of both parties, of an overwhelming majority, or simply by one vote, and your legislation passes. But in the Senate, having the support of ninety-nine senators is not enough. Due to Senate rules requiring unanimous consent (meaning the agreement of all senators) before a motion is made on the Senate floor, a single senator can hold up a piece of legislation or an appointment. And that senator's colleagues, some suspect, are loath to change the rules because they each know they may want to be the one holding up their ninety-nine colleagues the next time. At one point, I vowed to send the Senate one hundred powdered wigs because the glacial pace of that so-called deliberative body seemed far more at home in the eighteenth century than the twenty-first.

Another striking difference is engagement with constituents. Representatives face the voters every two years, but senators only every six years. House members return to their districts, host town hall meetings, and can't fear taking strongly worded feedback from voters. Our House experience has been that senators tend to be less face-to-face with their constituents. Nevertheless, it has been my experience—and challenge—that White House administrations tend to play to the Senate. Sometimes this is because our presidents served as senators and have a natural affinity for that branch: they are "Senate-centric," and their White House staffs may have many former Senate staffers. But if a president wants to put forth any idea that requires funding, that legislation must start in the House.

Time and again, I have watched different White Houses side with the Senate version of a bill or praise senators and ignore the House committee chairs who made sure that a vital piece of legislation passed—sometimes on a tough vote.

At one point or another, all presidents (some far more than others) just want to get their way. They arrive in the Oval Office convinced they know more than Congress and fail to appreciate Congress's important role. In Congress, we joke that there must be something in the air ducts inside the White House. It's as if they have all breathed in the same intoxicating air.

During the 2008 financial crisis, President George W. Bush thought that the vote to pass the Troubled Asset Relief Program (TARP) legislation would be easier than it was. Ultimately, working directly with Congress was necessary for a successful outcome. And with the greatest respect for President Barack Obama's indispensable leadership, having Congress write the Affordable Care Act is a major reason why the health care reform effort succeeded in 2009–10. Congress, as a representative body, has a different approach that is inclusive and from the ground up.

Members of Congress also often have invaluable expertise. Administration officials measure their tenure in months—twelve, twenty-four, thirty-six. The average presidential chief of staff lasts about two years in that role, which is the equivalent of one term in Congress (Trump went through four chiefs of staff in four years). Administration turnover can make the executive branch insensitive to the unique challenges of being a House member. Congress held some difficult votes in 2009 to pass the American Recovery and Reinvestment Act to continue to respond to the 2008 financial crisis and its impact on our economy. House Democrats were absolutely mystified when a top Obama administration political strategist told us that he hadn't expected that our members would receive such a pummeling for their support of the bill from "the cables," meaning cable news, primarily Fox News. I thought to myself, Do you not have televisions in your offices?

Of course, one of the House Speaker's most important roles is working with presidents. I have worked with four presidents as House Speaker and three more as a House member. Each brought different approaches and leadership styles to the table, and there is much to be learned—some good and one bad—from how they approached problems, as well as a better understanding of how our government process works. It is also important to recognize that sometimes a Speaker and a president will be from different political parties.

Since 1969, the same party has controlled both houses of Congress and the presidency for only eight congressional sessions (sixteen years). Divided government is more the norm, and that means each side has to learn to work with the other. It also matters whom you are working with—and when there is divided government, particularly in times of crisis, your relationship and your ability to trust in the opposition are essential.

Both George W. Bush and I came from political families, and I had a particularly warm relationship with his parents. Even though President George H. W. Bush and I disagreed on China policy, I always had tremendous respect for him and Barbara Bush. For my twenty-fifth anniversary in Congress, while I was Speaker, they invited me to give a presentation at the Bush Presidential Library in College Station, Texas, over Presidents' Day weekend. Barbara Bush warmly greeted me at the library's front door. It was a very welcoming gesture, and with her trademark humor, she told me that she was "disappointed," adding, "I thought you'd have far more protesters," referring to the crowd waving signs out front. I had a lovely visit with them in their apartment inside the presidential library. I believe there were about eleven hundred people gathered for the event—and I think about one thousand of them were Republicans. But it was a great occasion and a lovely dinner with their family and foundation.

Perhaps my sweetest memory of President Bush 41 was seeing him at the White House's congressional Holiday Party after

I became Speaker, when his son was president. We spent some minutes chatting about Christmas and our families. Then, at the end of our conversation, with a twinkle in his eye, he said, "Hey, Madam Speaker, can you give my kid a break?" As a mom of five, I knew exactly where that impulse came from. It's a good reminder that although today we may live in a very divided and too often uncivil time, it has not always been that way.

While we had many political differences, working with the George W. Bush administration was made easier because whomever the president tasked to negotiate on behalf of the administration, that person spoke for him. They had the president's confidence and would not be wasting your time. Whenever I had a suggestion for President Bush related to the economy, the president would tell me: "Convince Paulson"—because he had such great confidence in his Treasury secretary, Hank Paulson. Indeed, one of my most successful instances of working across the aisle happened early in my speakership with President Bush.

In 2007, the Democratic majority tried to persuade President Bush to support a stimulus package. We were pushing for an infrastructure bill, which would be job-creating and promote growth in our economy. President Bush was not interested in a stimulus package, especially with the infrastructure approach. But one day, he called me to say that he would support a stimulus package based on the tax code. He then tasked the Treasury secretary to be our contact for negotiations. As we compared the merits of our proposals, the president was clear—again, he wanted the legislation to address the tax code. In response, we suggested that we would yield on certain infrastructure priorities if the administration in turn would yield on doing more to help America's working families.

Hank and I conducted our negotiations in a room whose

location was unknown to the press to keep our deliberations inside a cone of silence and avoid leaks. In doing so, we earned each other's trust. I reminded Hank that as we moved forward, I needed to show our progress to my Democratic leadership; it would have to be a plan they could approve. As Speaker, I had to be sure that I had the votes for what would be perceived as a Bush tax proposal, and I needed to listen to the House Democratic leadership. In turn, I wanted to know how far the Bush administration would go to reach a compromise, and we both wanted House Minority Leader John Boehner to sign off as well.

Initially, the administration's proposals for tax code reforms would only benefit workers making $27,000 or more per year. Democrats, however, wanted "refundability"—or rebates—which would be available to those who made less money per year. The concept of refundability means that, if you have a lower income level, rather than simply giving you a "credit" on your income tax and thus lowering your final income tax payment, the government will return money to your pocket—you will receive money, even if you don't make enough to receive a tax refund. In my discussions with Hank Paulson, a main area of interest was providing rebates for families with children. Our tax code already provides a tax credit for each child, based on income levels. But this proposal would return money to families. The key question was: How far down the income scale was the administration willing to go to provide a rebate for lower-income, working-class Americans? Rosa DeLauro, the Democratic representative from Connecticut, was the leader who had made this a vital issue in our caucus; she was the one who had first pushed for an expanded child tax credit. Hank ultimately came back with a final number: the annual income requirement was $3,000 in the first year for refundability, meaning many more people of very low income would be eligible for these funds. And because of economic need, many people who received this money would be putting it right back into the economy: rebates helped pay for groceries and school clothes and supplies. The tax cut/stimulus package was ultimately a very successful negotiation. For every infrastructure area where the Bush administration turned me down, I was able to find another area where we got something that would support low-income families in return.

When I presented the final proposal to the Democratic leadership, with the $3,000 refundability number for the first year, Rosa DeLauro jumped for joy. In early 2008, when the bill passed, Barney Frank said it was "the most progressive piece of tax policy in American history" because of the billions it steered to lower-income Americans. Hank Paulson negotiated for the White House with integrity, which is a must for successful governance and government, divided or not.

The Trump Deviation

My legislative career has had many facets, but I'm still amazed by how many people I meet who ask about only one topic: Donald Trump.

My first interaction with Donald Trump came in 2016, after he had won the election, but not, I would remind everyone, the popular vote. Following Hillary Clinton's concession, I called Trump to congratulate him. The phone rang, and when a voice said hello, I responded, "This is Nancy Pelosi. I'm trying to reach President-elect Trump." Immediately, I heard, "This is Donald Trump." Then, without stopping, he launched into a short monologue on how I had gotten his cell number. The message of his monologue was that he thought he had given me his phone number a decade or so before, and he asked me if I had saved it all these years. Finally, I was able to reply, "No, I've never had your phone number. My staff got this number from your staff."

I tried to swing the conversation to put the campaign behind us and to do what I have done with every new president: seek areas of common ground. I thought that, given his background as a developer, infrastructure would be a natural discussion point. I then referenced human infrastructure, such as affordable childcare. He broke in to say, "Oh yeah, Ivanka is into that," and the next thing I knew, he had put Ivanka on the phone. She was indeed "into that," and Ivanka and I had a very positive conversation about children's issues. I was cautiously optimistic that perhaps the Trump White House and House Democrats could work together on some issues. Almost every day of the next four years, Donald Trump would prove me wrong.

Always wanting a president of the United States to succeed, I tried to remain hopeful going into our first meeting at the White House after Trump's inauguration. The first meeting between a new or reelected president and the congressional leadership is an event of unique significance: the new president presents his vision to us. Many of us in the House and the Senate had already been appalled by Trump's grotesque inaugural address, where he talked about "American carnage" and "tombstones," but we hoped for a more mature presentation at this iconic meeting. I wanted to think that he would rise to the occasion and recognize the honor of the office of the presidency. In the weeks before, many of us had already congratulated him and wished him success, offering our cooperation on health care, infrastructure, global security, and other matters. And I spoke to President Trump just as I had spoken to Presidents Bush and Obama, understanding that each president has his own agenda and political needs and offering to help with issues where we could find common ground, such as making improvements to the Affordable Care Act.

Perhaps I should have lowered my expectations. The location of our initial meeting was already a major departure from other prior presidential new term meetings. It was held not in the West Wing, in the Cabinet or Roosevelt Rooms, as had been the case with Presidents Bush and Obama, but in the East Wing, a space used primarily for social functions, and not generally a substantive working location. The new president had also opted to serve everyone in attendance pigs in a blanket (small hot dogs wrapped in pastry), which he would assure Senate Democratic leader Chuck Schumer were "kosher." My disappointment wasn't about the venue but about Trump.

As we were standing around waiting for the meeting to begin, Jared Kushner, Trump's son-in-law, who had already been named a senior advisor to the president, came up to me and made a rather unusual statement to the leader of the opposition party in the House: "Hi, aren't you so excited about everything that is happening? Is everybody excited about what's happening now?"— meaning Donald Trump becoming president. I said that everyone I knew was "excited about the Women's March"—a global demonstration on behalf of women's rights, directly in response to some of Trump's statements about women, which took place the day after the inauguration. Jared Kushner seemed oddly oblivious to his remarks and to mine. I wondered what was next.

In January 2005, 2009, and 2013, when I had previously participated in these occasions, Presidents Bush and Obama sought to inspire and acknowledge the tremendous honor and opportunity they had been given to hold this office and preside in the White House. How would Trump begin the meeting—quoting from the Bible, telling a personal story about America, or referencing an important moment in history, as other presidents before him had? We solemnly awaited Donald Trump's inspirational words to open this meeting.

Once we were seated, Donald Trump leaned forward with his elbows on a table and began by saying, "You know I won the popular vote." He then used examples of non-citizens whom he claimed had voted illegally. Trump even named a supposed witness—who, it had been proven, was not there. Even from him, it was deeply disappointing.

There is a certain protocol for speaking at these meetings. Looking around the room, I realized that Chuck Schumer, House Speaker Paul Ryan, and others had never attended before, and that no one on the president's team had any knowledge of or allegiance to protocol. Only Mitch McConnell and I had attended these meetings before. So I spoke up and said: "Mr. President, that is not true. You did not win the popular vote." He returned with: "And I wasn't even counting California."

Persisting, I said: "If we are going to work together, we must adhere to the facts. My colleagues here can tell you that when we begin a discussion, we stipulate a fact—budget numbers, for example—before we proceed. If we are going to work together, for instance, on infrastructure, we must start with a number."

He then chimed in and said: "Oh yes, infrastructure. I have it right here." It wasn't clear if he was holding a napkin or a hankie, but he waved his supposed infrastructure proposal in the air, saying, "Here it is, one trillion dollars, which can pass right away." Then he looked over at Senate Republican Leader Mitch McConnell and added, "Right, Mitch?" Leader McConnell responded in a deadpan voice, "Not unless it is paid for, Mr. President." And that ended that discussion.

I had to leave the meeting before it officially concluded because votes on legislation had been called in the House. (Paul Ryan was able to stay because House Speakers don't have to vote on individual bills.) When a Republican senator left, he told the waiting press corps that the president said he had won the popular vote. Perhaps he thought this news would sound better coming from a Republican than being characterized by the Democrats. However, when Chuck Schumer walked out, the press asked him if Trump had indeed said that he had won the popular vote. Chuck said, "Yes, and Nancy Pelosi told him it wasn't true."

By then, I was back at the Capitol, and the press asked me for a comment. I said I prayed for Trump—and more importantly, I prayed for the United States of America.

Donald Trump himself set the tone for his term at that first meeting. While I wanted to believe that he would value the dignity of the office and move beyond his name-calling—"Crazy Nancy," "Crooked Hillary"—it quickly became clear that the man in the Oval Office was even worse than the one we had seen on the campaign trail. So many things with Trump were for theatrics. He invariably tried to make the moment about him or his insults. No topic was too small. One December, Trump looked at me and said, "You liberals aren't really religious. Nancy, you don't say, 'Merry Christmas,' you say, 'Happy Holidays.'" I looked right back at him and said, "Well, Mr. President, I just received my invitation to your congressional 'Holiday Party' at the White House. Your invitation was to a Holiday Party, not a Christmas Party." In reply, he began sputtering about "White House staff."

But we could have gotten past that childishness if Trump had remotely been a president of his word. He wasn't.

Whatever differences occur in the legislative debate, it is always important to respect others' points of view—but it is necessary to trust that the people you are working with speak the truth.

"Truth" is a word that Donald Trump exploits but never engages in. I saw this even more clearly when the Democrats retook control of the House in 2018 and I returned to the speakership.

Before I was even sworn in as Speaker, Trump had proudly sent the federal government into a partial shutdown over his demands regarding payment for his border wall. The shutdown lasted for thirty-five days, the longest in US history. Flights were canceled due to the lack of air traffic controllers; federal employees went for weeks without a paycheck. The president finally capitulated in late January, and the federal government reopened. After that, the congressional leadership optimistically began working with the White House on an infrastructure bill to address roads, bridges, water systems, and broadband internet. At the same time, the House was conducting multiple investigations of Trump, including into his personal finances for improper foreign influence. No fewer than three committees had issued subpoenas for his tax and financial records. And Trump had been fighting all of them.

Against this backdrop, however, we had a productive meeting at the White House on April 30 for a $2 trillion infrastructure bill. The House, the Senate, and the White House had spent months preparing and finalizing the details. We had one last hurdle: how to pay for the bill, through offsets (finding money already in the federal budget) and/or new revenue (taxes). In late May, the congressional leadership and our committee chairs returned to the White House for what we hoped would be the final meeting to conclude the agreement. After we had assembled, Trump came into the room and angrily said that I had offended him publicly. He referenced my statement that he needed to comply with congressional subpoenas; I had added that the House Democrats "believe that the president of the United States is engaged in a cover-up." Trump announced that because of what I had said, he wasn't going to participate in our infrastructure meeting. And he didn't. He stormed out after less than three minutes. I had to wonder if he even wanted an infrastructure bill to pass. It was clear that he didn't want to pay for one.

That moment made me think back to a memorial service I had attended a few weeks before for Dr. David Hamburg, a distinguished psychiatrist who, among his many accomplishments, had served as the president of the Carnegie Corporation, where he had been a great voice for international peace. At the service, doctors and other mental health professionals came up to me, unsolicited, to tell me that they were deeply concerned that there was something seriously wrong with the president and that his mental and psychological health was in decline. I'm not a doctor, but I did find his behaviors difficult to understand.

Unlike in previous administrations, where presidents were either willing to participate directly themselves or gave authority to their staff to speak on their behalf, Trump would do neither—instead, my staff and I came to suspect that he was secretly following the discussions. Chief of Staff Mark Meadows and his minions would keep an open phone line to the White House while they sat in the room meeting with us, either furiously texting what we said back to the West Wing and not responding until they had received a reply, or even literally dialing into the West Wing and having every word of our private meetings surreptitiously listened to by the White House. (This behavior was not unique to our meetings. Apparently Trump had House Minority Leader Kevin McCarthy do much the same during meetings of the House Republican Conference. According to then-chair Liz Cheney, McCarthy seemed to have Trump listening in on an open cell phone line.) This gamesmanship by Trump's "representatives" became so bad that when top White House staff came to my Capitol Hill office for discussions, we had to ban all cell phones from the meeting rooms. In the Speaker's office, we simply couldn't trust the people from the White House.

It said something to me that John Kelly, Trump's longest-serving chief of staff, who lasted less than eighteen months, pointedly told me that he had taken an oath of office to the Constitution and not to any one man.

Yet we did manage to pass some legislation, including an appropriations package. But it often took a lot of pounding on tables and slamming of doors by the administration to get there—unless the administration wanted something, which happened, too. In the fall of 2020, we had just completed an appropriations bill. One of Trump's main stipulations was that the bill would contain no additional foreign assistance. The bill was complete and the vote was pending when Steve Mnuchin, the Treasury secretary, called me. His message was direct: he needed $700 million added to the bill for "Sudan" in exchange for the Sudanese leader's signature on the Abraham Accords, agreements for normalizing relations between Israel and several Islamic countries, including the United Arab Emirates and Bahrain. In return for Sudan's signature, the Trump administration pledged to remove Sudan from its list of state sponsors of terrorism and provide a $1.2 billion loan. The $700 million was part of that payment.

This money was news to me. Mnuchin pressed on that he had already "promised" the money to Sudan. I didn't want to torpedo the accords, but I reminded Mnuchin that our understanding was no new money for foreign purposes. I had given that same message to Bono, Elton John, Bill Gates, and other global health leaders. I told Mnuchin that if we reopened our legislative agreement to include foreign assistance, I needed to add $4 billion for global health focused on Gavi, the international alliance that provides access to vaccines for children in the world's poorest countries. We both got to yes.

Not all of our encounters had to do with legislation, however. Donald Trump also seemed to like phone calls. On April 6, 2017, I was in Boston when the calls started coming, first from Vice President Mike Pence, saying that the White House was going to launch a retaliatory missile strike into Syria after a chemical attack by the Bashar al-Assad regime, then from the secretary of Homeland Security, saying that the Tomahawk cruise missiles had been launched, and finally, at midnight, from President Trump. I was in my hotel room when my security detail informed me that the president was on the phone.

Usually, calling at midnight signals something serious. This time, the president was telling me he had ordered fifty-nine missiles to be fired at a Syrian air base. I was concerned, because Russian military personnel were operating at that base, and I did not want this strike to allow them to gain more of a foothold inside Syria. I said that I did know of the missile strike, but that I was concerned that it would ultimately benefit the Russians. (Indeed, less than two and a half years later, the Russians would take control of an air base that US troops had abandoned.) Trump began blaming this outcome, and the need for a US strike, on President Obama, because he had refused to initiate hostilities against Syria after the government of Assad was reported to have used chemical weapons in 2013. After listening to these statements, I interjected and said, "Mr. President, you and I both opposed the war in Iraq. On this we agree. You know that there was no public appetite to go to war in Syria. You know the difference." I added, "It's midnight. I think you should go to sleep."

One of his more contentious phone calls occurred at 8:16 a.m. on September 24, 2019. Trump started by saying that he was "up here at the UN," and then added, "We are making progress on guns. Next week is a whole big deal. We are making good progress . . . some on my side, some on your side." I replied, "I hope the House Democratic position is represented," adding, "I have not heard our members have been present at your meetings."

"Good movement on behalf of a lot of people," said Trump. That bipartisanship, of course, was not real—nor was it the real reason for his call. Trump's real purpose for this call to me was to try to explain away another, far more serious phone call, one that he'd had with Ukraine's newly elected president, Volodymyr Zelenskyy. That morning, I was going to announce that the House would open an impeachment inquiry into Trump's efforts to pressure Zelenskyy into granting him political favors and his withholding of congressionally appropriated funds until that happened. In fact, I was scheduled to call Trump, but he called first.

Again and again during our more than twenty-minute call, Trump repeated, "It was a perfect call. . . . The call was so perfect. You'd be impressed with my lack of pressure." I then tried to explain the whistleblower act—a whistleblower had alerted us to the call's existence—and automatic congressional requirements for an investigation. I also explained my intelligence credentials, as well as House rules and the federal laws for evaluating the allegations—while Trump played defense. "The call is actually the whole thing. . . . I didn't threaten anyone," he told me. "There's no reason to impeach me." This back-and-forth continued, with the president becoming increasingly whiny by the end. "I've done a great job as president," he said, and he kept repeating, "It's very, very unfair."

Trump also fell back on the timing and complained about how this announcement was happening today, the day when he was speaking to the UN General Assembly. I was thinking, Well, good for you. That's what you are doing today. I'm telling you what I am doing today, and I ended the call by saying that "the truth will come out." I've had a lot of conversations with this man, and at the end of nearly all of them, I think, Either you are stupid, or you think that the rest of us are.

By mid-December, the House had voted to approve articles of impeachment. The trial began in the Senate on January 16, but Republican senators outrageously refused to allow witnesses to be called or subpoenas to be issued for documents. On February 4, 2020, Donald Trump gave his State of the Union address to both Houses of Congress. His impeachment trial had just concluded. The next day, on a party-line vote, the Senate Republicans would vote to acquit him of abuse of power and obstruction of Congress. The only exception was Sen. Mitt Romney, who voted to convict on the abuse of power charge.

That night, the atmosphere was already tense in the House chamber. When he arrived, the president refused to shake my outstretched hand. As I listened to the speech, what I heard was a manifesto of lies, including claiming nearly three times the number of jobs as had actually been created by a trade agreement with Mexico and Canada; claiming an end to "catch and release" along the border, when in fact Trump had released thousands of migrants; taking credit for oil and gas production that started under President Obama; and claiming nonexistent manufacturing growth. But the lies did not stop there. The man who promised to repeal the Affordable Care Act even pledged to protect people with preexisting conditions—although his repeal bills did not. I had intended to mark each page of the speech that contained a lie with a little tear in the paper so I could go back and easily find the pages. But as Trump continued speaking, it was not just one, two, three, or four pages with lies. It was pages and pages of them. At the close of the speech, disgusted with what I heard, I ripped the pages from end to end. To me, that speech was certainly not worth the parchment it was printed on. I told the press it was a manifesto of lies, and when reporters asked me why I had called it that, I answered, "Because I was being polite."

But the worst was yet to come. While I tore up his speech on February 4, by March 12 I was tearing up the phone in reaction to Trump's early Covid actions. Indeed, Trump's extremism and his delay and denial of the deadly Covid pandemic would soon cost lives and livelihoods.

On March 12, I was sitting with the taoiseach of Ireland, Leo Varadkar, at the Ireland Funds dinner when our phones started to explode with major news. The administration had announced that the United States would no longer allow travelers from certain European countries to enter the US because of transmission of the Covid virus.

A call ensued with Dr. Anthony Fauci, one of the leaders at the National Institutes of Health. I had worked for years with Dr. Fauci on HIV/AIDS issues. President George H. W. Bush had called Dr. Fauci a hero in regard to HIV/AIDS—I agreed and was especially grateful for his leadership. During our call, I told Dr. Fauci not to stand with Trump while he put forth his unscientific junk. "Don't legitimize his quackery," I warned—knowing that when NIH leaders stood beside Trump in the White House briefing room, even as they rolled their eyes at his ill-advised comments, the public could still get a false impression.

Trump's leadership during Covid was a sharp contrast with another Republican president with whom I had served. In February 2023 we marked the twentieth anniversary of the President's Emergency Plan for AIDS Relief, better known as PEPFAR, which

has dramatically reduced the scourge of HIV/AIDS in Africa—
and is a bipartisan success story of how to respond to a health
crisis. Dr. Fauci had been a great force for PEPFAR as well. In my
thank-you remarks for the recognition I received for the important role House Democrats played in passing PEPFAR, I praised
Dr. Fauci as we paid tribute to President and Mrs. Bush for their
visionary and scientific leadership. I take great pride in my two
decades of work with President Bush to establish and support
PEPFAR's lifesaving mission—and we worked together again to
save it in 2024 government funding legislation.

Two different presidents, two different results.

Twenty-six million lives saved by President Bush and PEPFAR.
Untold death and destruction from President Trump's delay-and-
deny role in Covid.

The theme of the Trump years might well have been: I gave
him every chance to work together, and he gave me no choice but
to impeach him.

But more than the personal insults, which I can certainly take,
or the theatrics or the duplicity that accompanied the Trump
presidency, what I find so appalling is Donald Trump's repeated
examples of complete disrespect for America and Americans. I
cannot imagine any president or any political leader saying to his
supporters, as Donald Trump did in February 2024, "Russia, what
did they do? They defeated Hitler." No, the US and Great Britain were central to defeating Hitler. The Soviet Union was Hitler's
ally until the Nazis attacked them in June 1941. Only then did
the USSR fight against Hitler, and at the end of the war, they took
Eastern Europe as their spoils and forced millions to live behind
the repressive Iron Curtain.

The America that Donald Trump was born into was saved

by young men like my uncle Johnny D'Alesandro, whom I never knew and who died in the fighting on the way to the Battle of the Bulge. He is buried in the Lorraine American Cemetery in France, the final resting place for the largest number of US military dead in Europe. Johnny was my father's younger brother, and my father mourned his loss for the rest of his life. What an insult to every family who lost a precious child, sibling, spouse, or parent on the beaches of Normandy, in the forests of France, in North Africa, Italy, or in the Pacific. The Soviet Union was not responsible for the defeat of Hitler. Trump may think that Americans who died in the war are "suckers" and "losers," as he told his then-chief of staff John Kelly. Trump made the remark after having refused to visit an American cemetery near Paris. But the only loser is him.

In some ways, however, Trump is a manifestation of a larger problem in our political life, one that has been slowly metastasizing: greed. Trump has a greed for power, but from my early days in Congress, I saw how greed for markets, at the expense of human rights and the inhumanity of prison labor, drove our China policy. In the 2008 economic crisis, it was the greed of too many financial institutions whose pursuit of profits put average Americans and their livelihoods and homes at risk. For the Affordable Care Act, greed on the part of insurance companies and Big Pharma had created both a health care and an economic crisis for millions of Americans. Finally, there is Trump's selfish greed or sense of entitlement that we saw on display after the 2020 election and when rioters attacked the Capitol on January 6.

Time and again, many of us have felt compelled to stand for the goodness I see and know in so many parts of America and against this type of greed. That's what has animated me to spend much of my life on airplanes, as well as packing and unpacking my suitcase, and changing time zones often several times a week.

I can't afford to get up from the table and storm out every time someone says something unkind about me. I don't even pay attention, because I know it says far more about them than about me. My focus is on what matters: putting people—especially our children—over politics.

Leadership to Meet Global Challenges

"The Intelligence Does Not Support the Threat"

Wednesday, March 19, 2003, was slated to be a routine day. Congress had been in session for just over two months; I had been elected by our Democratic members as leader. House Democrats had gathered for dinner so we could plan for the upcoming congressional session and the future. On the Catholic calendar, March 19 was also a hopeful day, the celebration of the feast of Saint Joseph. But that Wednesday became the day that the US went to war.

Our member dinner had just started when one of my aides approached with the message that Condoleezza Rice, the national security advisor to President Bush, was on the phone. Rice told me that she was calling at the direction of the president. She stated that the purpose of her call was to inform me that in two hours, at 9:00 p.m. Eastern Standard Time, the US military and its coalition partners would initiate hostilities in Iraq.

Misrepresenting the Case for War with Iraq

How did the United States end up initiating war with Iraq? The short answer is that the American people are traditionally trusting and patriotic. The Bush administration told the public a very self-serving story. In August 2002, Vice President Cheney told the

Veterans of Foreign Wars, "Simply stated, there is no doubt that Saddam Hussein now has weapons of mass destruction. There is no doubt he is amassing them to use against our friends, against our allies, and against us." The next step, the administration argued, was acquiring fully operational nuclear weapons. Indeed, the administration misled many people into thinking that Iraq possessed—or was on the verge of possessing—a nuclear weapon. On September 8, 2002, during an interview with CNN, Condoleezza Rice said, "We don't want the smoking gun to be a mushroom cloud," suggesting that our first proof of Iraq's successful nuclear program could occur when it detonated a nuclear device. Additionally, multiple members of the administration suggested that US troops would be seen by the Iraqi people as liberators. The number two official at the Pentagon, Paul Wolfowitz, publicly summed up much of the administration's position when he testified before Congress in February 2003 that US soldiers "are going to be welcomed" by the majority of Iraqis as "liberators," adding, "we will have millions of people witnessing on our behalf." Wolfowitz also told the public that the war's aftermath would be paid for by Iraqi oil revenue, explaining, "We are dealing with a country that can really finance its own reconstruction." None of these assertions would prove to be true, as the world would later learn. In the years to come, our troops' paths were strewn not with flowers but with deadly improvised explosive devices. And the costs would be monumental to incalculable, in lives lost and soldiers injured and maimed.

As the case for war built throughout the summer and early fall of 2002, our House Democratic Caucus had strong discussions about the looming Iraq War resolution. It was coauthored by Richard Gephardt, who had asked George Tenet, the director of the CIA, if Saddam Hussein had "weapons of mass destruction

[WMDs], especially components of nuclear weapons," and had also asked Tenet if it was a "worry that some components could wind up in the hands of terrorists." Tenet and other high-ranking intelligence officials replied yes, and, according to Dick Gephardt's recollections, "They said the other world intelligence services agreed that he [Saddam] did." This was not necessarily completely true.

By the time of the Iraq War, I had ten years of experience studying and reviewing intelligence. Due to my committee and leadership roles, I also had access to the highest levels of reports and briefings from the complete intelligence community that were offered to members of Congress. Based on everything my experienced intelligence staff and I had seen, read, and been told, I did not believe that the president and his administration were being fully transparent with the American people when it came to Iraq. My position was simply this: "The intelligence does not support the threat." And I stated that position repeatedly throughout September and early October 2002 in meetings, in interviews, and to members on the floor of the House of Representatives during the Iraq War authorization debate.

When it was my turn to speak before the vote, I broke with our very respected Democratic leader Gephardt, even though I was the Democratic whip and ranked second in the House Democratic leadership. I told my fellow Democrats that I could not vote and would not vote for the resolution.

Leading members of my own caucus (but not Dick Gephardt) told me that if I voted against the war, I would have no future in the Democratic Party. Their warning had no effect on me, because I was never going to vote for this war in Iraq. Because while every congressional vote is a vote of conscience, a vote to authorize war is in its own category. I would never ask a member to vote either for or against a war, but I was obliged to tell members why I opposed the war. Anyone voting to authorize war in Iraq should have been troubled by a central fact: the lack of an NIE (National Intelligence Estimate). One of the most important documents we have in the intelligence world is an NIE. An NIE is the intelligence community's most authoritative document on a particular threat. The most thorough NIEs are written based on a compilation of information from sixteen separate intelligence agencies. But during a closed hearing on September 5, 2002, when the Senate Intelligence Committee, led by Democrat Bob Graham of Florida, asked CIA Director George Tenet for the NIE analyzing the case for invading Iraq, and to examine possible military and post-invasion occupation scenarios, the committee members were told that there was no NIE. The White House had not requested one, and the intelligence community had not taken it upon itself to prepare one.

The absence of an NIE was a complete shock. Director Tenet said he couldn't provide a full one, but that he would provide a narrow one focused on Iraq's WMD program. Soon after, the CIA provided a limited, classified, roughly ninety-page NIE to Congress, but when those of us in the intelligence leadership saw it, it was clear to us that the document was not conclusive about the threat posed by Iraq. We asked the administration to declassify the NIE while protecting the sources and methods it contained.

The administration's response then was much quicker than it had been to our original request for the NIE; we received the new, twenty-five-page document within a few days. But what the administration gave us wasn't a declassification of the original document. Instead, it was a completely different presentation of intelligence on the threat from Iraq—and it wasn't true!

This document was making a case for war, whereas the previous document had contained an analysis of Saddam Hussein's intent, which was far less definitive.

Needless to say, Chairman Graham in the Senate and I in the House were deeply concerned by the disparity. Sen. Carl Levin, chairman of the Senate Committee on Armed Services, was also growing concerned about the administration's disregard for the underlying intelligence. If the American people had seen the original NIE, they would have seen the difference between what the administration was touting as a call to war and the scarcity of the facts to support it.

What none of us in Congress knew as our back-and-forth with the CIA continued was that on September 9, four days after Director Tenet had appeared before the Senate, Defense Secretary Donald Rumsfeld had sent an eight-page briefing to US Air Force General Richard Myers, chair of the Joint Chiefs of Staff, the highest-ranking military advisor. The briefing's subject was: "Status of Iraqi Weapons of Mass Destruction (WMD) Programs." To accompany the briefing, Rumsfeld had attached his own note to General Myers: "Please take a look at this material as to what we don't know about WMD. It is big." The Air Force major general responsible for the report had written, "A couple of weeks ago SECDEF asked me what we don't know (in a percentage) about the Iraqi WMD program. We've struggled to estimate the unknowns . . . We range from 0 percent to about 75 percent knowledge on various aspects of their program." One of the report's main conclusions was: "Our assessments rely heavily on analytic assumptions and judgment rather than hard evidence. The evidentiary base is particularly sparse for Iraqi nuclear programs." It went on to state: "Our knowledge of the Iraqi nuclear weapons program is based largely—perhaps 90 percent—on analysis of imprecise intelligence." This report never made it into the NIE, either in classified or unclassified form. Instead, the administration used different models and sources to produce its intelligence conclusions.

Traditionally, in Congress, many members in both chambers take the administration at its word. That was unfortunate in this case. Before the vote, not many senators and House members went to the SCIF (sensitive compartmented information facility) to read the top secret intelligence.

In the Senate, Bob Graham encouraged all of his colleagues to read these classified intelligence reports, "which is much sharper than what is available in declassified form." He also asked, "And what is the most urgent threat to our peace and security? In my judgment, it is that shadowy group of international terrorists who have the capabilities, the materials, conventional and weapons of mass destruction, the trained core of zealots united by their hatred for the United States, and the placement of many of those bomb throwers so they are sleeping among us, waiting for the order to assault." And then, as he would later explain, "I lost my cool." On the Senate floor, he told his colleagues, "If you reject that [premise], and believe that the American people are not going to be at additional threat, then, frankly, my friends—to use the term—blood is going to be on your hands."

While we could not stop the march to war, I was proud that on October 10, House Democrats voted 60 percent to 40 percent against the resolution, 126 nays to 81 yeas. But Republicans voted overwhelmingly for the resolution, 215 yeas to 6 nays, ensuring its passage. Early Friday morning, October 11, the Senate voted 77 to 23 to approve the war resolution, with 29 Democrats voting in favor and 21 against.

After that, the momentum was unstoppable.

———

Having secured the vote to authorize war, the administration began pressing its case to the American public and the international community. In addition to George W. Bush, two respected national security leaders—Secretary of State Colin Powell and George Tenet—contributed to the misrepresentations around Iraq. As part of their efforts to solidify their case for war, three events stand out: the first is a late-December meeting in the Oval Office during which President Bush reviewed the presentation that would be made by Colin Powell before the United Nations. During that meeting, George Tenet is reported to have said that the case for Iraq's WMD program and war would be a "slam dunk." (After he left office, Tenet claimed that he had been misquoted—that he was only saying "that we can put a better case together for the public case," so his use of "slam dunk" was simply referring to strengthening the public presentation.)

The second event took place on January 28, 2003, when George Bush gave his State of the Union address to Congress. The president made the case for war by offering specific claims about Iraq's WMD program—that Saddam Hussein had sought "significant quantities of uranium from Africa," which could be used to produce a nuclear weapon. Bush was referring to a substance known as "yellowcake," a lightly enriched uranium that the administration was claiming Iraq was trying to procure from Niger, along with specialized aluminum tubes to be used for enriching it.

I knew how the State of the Union addresses were reviewed; the lines about uranium had to have been approved by the intelligence community. But what the president had said differed from some of the classified intelligence, even though the speech, again, had to have been reviewed by the CIA and others before the president ever delivered it. Indeed, seven days later, on February 4,

———

the State Department specifically told the International Atomic Energy Agency (IAEA) that it "cannot confirm" the African uranium reports, and that it had "questions regarding some specific claims." But at the time, those questions did not deter the broader momentum inside the administration toward armed conflict with Iraq.

The speech also directly contradicted what international weapons and nuclear inspectors were finding inside Iraq. For nearly four months, starting in the fall of 2002, United Nations weapons inspectors and experts from the IAEA had been examining more than five hundred sites around Iraq, searching for evidence of Saddam Hussein's nuclear weapons program. But, as the nonpartisan Arms Control Association noted, ultimately, after nine hundred inspections, the inspectors would find no evidence of an operational nuclear effort. As Robert E. Kelley, one of the IAEA inspection team members, would later write, "By early 2003 we knew at a very high level of confidence that there was no nuclear weapons effort of any kind in Iraq, and we were regularly passing this information back to the UN Security Council."

Thus, to me, probably the saddest moment, and one that I will never understand, was the third event: what Secretary of State Powell said in a presentation to the United Nations on February 5. Seventeen times, Powell used the phrase "weapons of mass destruction." He had served in Vietnam and had achieved the rank of four-star general. He had served as national security advisor in the Reagan administration and had been chairman of the Joint Chiefs under George H. W. Bush, overseeing the earlier Gulf War. As I listened, I thought Secretary Powell was ill-served by his security staff, who had to know that the proof was not there.

There were some truth tellers, however. On February 25, 2003, less than a month before the US initiated hostilities with Iraq, Army Chief of Staff Eric K. Shinseki courageously told the Senate Armed Services Committee that "several hundred thousand soldiers" would be needed in Iraq, especially for the occupation that would necessarily follow the hostilities. The Pentagon immediately said that his numbers were "wildly off the mark." But as we all would learn, Shinseki was correct. Irresponsibly, Defense Secretary Donald Rumsfeld had already rendered General Shinseki a lame duck inside the Pentagon by announcing the general's replacement in April 2002, fourteen months before his term as army chief of staff expired. I was concerned by this apparent premature undercutting of General Shinseki for many reasons, especially because of my respect for the general. Years before, in the 1990s, I had traveled with a congressional delegation to a theater of war in the Balkans, in part to see firsthand the challenges and the needs of our troops; we visited them at night, for instance, to observe night warfare to better understand the need for night vision technology. General Shinseki had met with our delegation and was very impressive. It was clear that the troops respected him for his patriotism and his courage—as did our congressional delegation.

In late February 2003, less than a month before the first US missiles and bombs exploded over Baghdad, I traveled to Kuwait with Rep. Jack Murtha, who was the top Democrat on the House Appropriations Subcommittee on Defense, and Congressman David Hobson, a Republican from Ohio, who also was a member of the Defense Appropriations Subcommittee. Jack Murtha was a respected marine veteran and a strong supporter of national security. He had always been there to support the troops, to see what they needed in terms of equipment, and to hear the state of their morale. Jack had also voted to authorize the war.

Kuwait shares a border with Iraq—and Iraq had already tried

to claim Kuwait's territory, resulting in the 1991 Gulf War. We went to Kuwait primarily to support our troops stationed there. Among our concerns, we had been told that the administration believed Iraq would use chemical agents against our troops, and we were particularly worried for their safety.

It was a remarkable visit. But what was most remarkable was the size of the American military base. It looked as though it took up 30 percent of Kuwait. From the moment we arrived, I thought to myself, How could this have been built starting in the less than five months since the October vote to authorize war? I asked some of our military leaders on the ground how this transformation was possible. Their answer was, We've been doing this and preparing for more than a year, since Bush became president. Although the substantial deployment of troops and weapons did occur after the October vote, preparing the infrastructure to receive them clearly began well before. The Bush administration had long ago decided it would get its way, and I soon had additional evidence of their determination to initiate the war in Iraq with 9/11 as a pretext.

Many of us in Congress were already concerned that the administration had turned its attention away from Afghanistan. Bob Graham had stated that General Tommy Franks, the commander for the region, had told Graham in February 2002 that US military and intelligence personnel were being "redeployed" to "prepare for action in Iraq." While President Bush had said that US and coalition forces had "routed" the Taliban, routing the Taliban was not the same as defeating them. Indeed, Taliban fighters merely concealed themselves across the country, only to reemerge and eventually return to power in 2021.

At the time, Bob Graham and I and others in Congress had major questions: Why did the administration pull US forces out of Afghanistan? Why were they so eager to go into Iraq that they cut short their time and presence in Afghanistan? Those questions were now front and center in my mind when I saw just how large the US military presence was in Kuwait. The size of the US base also made it clear that the administration had planned to go to war in Iraq long before it sought Congress's approval or had made a sustained case.

Jack Murtha, Dave Hobson, and I had breakfast with General David Petraeus. He had just arrived at the Kuwaiti base to command the 101st Airborne Division. The base was swirling with rumors that the Iraqis planned to use chemical weapons and biological weapons on our troops. It was already very hot in the region, but the troops would have to wear heavy protective equipment in case of attack. We spent as much time as we could listening to the troops on the ground. I asked them: "How do you feel about this war?"

The troops told me that morale was very high. They said, "Ma'am, they hurt us, so now we're going to hurt them."

I asked, "Well, when did they hurt us?"

"On 9/11," they responded.

That's what the generals and other officers were telling the troops: "They hurt us on 9/11."

It broke my heart that our military leaders would exploit our troops in this way, with a message that was not supported by the facts. We did not have intelligence tying Iraq to September 11, yet here were young men and women being sent into harm's way, with 9/11 as their rallying cry.

While Jack and I were sitting with some National Guard members who had been called up for duty, I went around the table and asked each of the young men what he had been doing before he was deployed. A couple of them answered, "I was a firefighter."

Another said, "I was a police officer." The next young man answered, "I was in high school, ma'am."

For the administration, however, there was no turning back.

On the night of Wednesday, March 19, the start of hostilities, I could not hide my disappointment. I had many unanswered questions, but in our brief phone call, I was only able to ask Condoleezza Rice one: How can you initiate hostilities in Iraq when we have not finished the weapons inspections? She answered my question by saying, "If we go in now, we will save lives."

I replied, "Well, I know the president is probably very thoughtful about the loss of life, both Americans and Iraqis, but I'm just saying that I don't understand why you're going in now when we have not exhausted every remedy. War should be the last resort."

She answered, "Well, that's what it is." She added that she couldn't say any more on an open telephone line.

Later, congressional leadership heard that the administration believed it had found a reliable human intelligence source (HUMINT, as this kind of collection is known in the intelligence community). We suspected that this source had informed the administration that Saddam Hussein was hiding in a specific farm complex. Based on that apparent piece of HUMINT, the war planners claimed that if the US attacked now—most likely with bunker buster bombs capable of inflicting severe damage, as part of a larger military campaign that the administration was calling "shock and awe"—this initial strike would be enough to successfully decapitate Iraq's existing top leadership.

US and coalition forces did not, however, "decapitate Iraq" in that one strike. As we now know, Saddam was not killed at that farm. In fact, he would not be captured until December 2003, when he was discovered inside a hole in the ground on an entirely different farm near his hometown region of Tikrit. In between, thousands of lives were lost, with many more thousands of deaths and injuries to come as the conflict dragged on. Our troops would become locked in years of bitter insurgent warfare, fighting block by block in Iraqi city streets.

How Did We Get to This Place?

How did we get to this place?

A significant part of the rationale for the 2003 Iraq War can be traced to the incomprehensibly tragic morning of September 11, 2001.

On 9/11, Americans were shocked and devastated to find our country under attack. The Twin Towers were brought down by two hijacked commercial airliners. The Pentagon was rammed by a third hijacked plane, and a fourth jet crashed in a field in Pennsylvania after brave passengers fought back against the terrorist hijackers. Nearly three thousand Americans and citizens of other nations lost their lives that morning.

At 8:46 a.m., I was in the Capitol office of our longtime Democratic leader, Dick Gephardt, where the Appropriations Committee leadership was meeting to plan our legislative agenda. Dick was sitting at the head of the conference table. A television morning news show was playing in the background—the sound was off, but most of us could see the images on the screen. Suddenly, a few minutes before 9:00 a.m., we saw the images of flames and smoke billowing out of one of the towers of the World Trade Center. The reporting said a plane had crashed into the building.

The initial thought of those of us in the room was that, of course, we had just witnessed a tragic accident. We were very concerned, but did not suspect terrorism. We wondered how such a thing could have happened. Then, at 9:03, after Dick had reached out to his staff for more information, we saw another plane fly into the second tower. For a few seconds, we were in complete disbelief; we thought that we were watching a replay of the initial tragedy. But then we clearly saw smoke rising from the first tower. Stunned, we realized that our nation was under attack.

I doubt there is anyone alive who remembers September 11, 2001, and who does not know exactly where they were at the moment when they heard or saw the shocking news.

Somberly, we filed out of the meeting room and returned to our own congressional offices. Soon after, we saw gray smoke rising from across the Potomac River, in the direction of the Pentagon. The Capitol Police rushed to inform us that another hijacked plane was headed for Washington and ordered us to evacuate. My staff and I raced down the stairs and toward the exits, not even pausing to look behind. That hijacked plane ultimately crashed hundreds of miles away in Pennsylvania—after brave passengers fought back and rushed the cockpit. Because of the heroism of Flight 93's crew and passengers, there was no possible fourth attack on the Capitol or the White House.

That morning, our country would go to war.

Because of my leadership role on the House Permanent Select Committee on Intelligence, I was among the members of Congress immediately taken to a secure facility. We waited, anxious for any piece of news, but information was scarce; whatever we learned was largely also being shared publicly in real time. We didn't know much more than anyone with a television. President Bush was in Florida, visiting a school and sitting in a classroom with young children. After he made a brief statement, he was rushed to Air Force One, which reportedly took off for the safety of the middle of the country as the various intelligence agencies and the FBI struggled to piece together what had happened. As my colleagues and I watched the images of the devastation in New York City and Northern Virginia, it was simply shocking and unforgivable.

In Congress, we knew that our first job was to come together immediately on behalf of our nation. That evening, as the sun set just beyond the Washington Monument and the Lincoln Memorial, we stood together on the steps of the Capitol. After some brief remarks by the leaders and a moment of silence for the victims, everyone assembled, Democrats and Republicans, began to sing "God Bless America." Afterward, many of us embraced. It was a patriotic and unifying moment.

We knew our first task was, as Abraham Lincoln had once said, to bind up the nation's wounds. Privately, I found myself, as did many of my colleagues, feeling a strong combination of shocked, prayerful, thoughtful, and endless questioning: How could this have happened? Who are these enemies? How should we respond? But I knew one thing: we had to act in a unified way. Much of my time was spent reaching out to the representatives of the districts that had been most affected: those where the attacks had taken place and those with the greatest loss of life. They needed our immediate support to help the victims' families.

Three days later, on September 14, President Bush visited the site of the Twin Towers, by then known as Ground Zero. He spoke beautifully and sought to unify and reassure the nation. At one point, someone in the crowd said to the president, "We can't hear you"—to which he famously and resolutely responded, "I can hear *you*." Such an unprecedented attack as 9/11 would be a monumental challenge for any president. President Bush had been in office for less than nine months.

In early October, I was part of a somber congressional delegation that traveled to Ground Zero. I still remember approaching the site. There was total silence. The ground was treated with the reverence of a cemetery, but the smoking, dusty expanse, with its thick, indescribable odor of jet fuel, human remains, and incinerated building parts, looked, sounded, and smelled like something from a cinematographer's imagining of hell. We knew that the people who came to the site day after day to work were searching for human remains and the tiniest fragments of DNA. I often think of how the searchers found some two hundred Irish claddagh rings, with their trinity of a heart, two hands, and a crown, symbolizing love, friendship, and loyalty. In the violence of the collapse, the rings had become separated from the wearers; in some cases, they were all that remained.

September 11, 2001, was transformative. It forced our country to cross a threshold we never thought we would face. As public servants in Congress, our role was to bring people together to protect our country, to make sure that nothing like this terrible day could happen again, and to support the families of all those who were affected.

The immediate next step before us, however, was how we would address the assault on our country, and that meant declaring war.

War Powers Resolution

Many people in our caucus, I among them, believe that it is the responsibility and the duty of Congress to declare war. The importance of Congress's role is recognized in the War Powers Resolution, which was passed by Congress in 1973, in the wake of the Vietnam War. President Richard Nixon vetoed the bill, but Congress ultimately overrode his veto, and the resolution became law after the US had withdrawn its combat troops from Vietnam. The

War Powers Resolution very clearly defines the congressional role in declaring war, based on the language found in Article I, Section 8 of the Constitution. Specifically, the law directly restricts the power of the president to declare war without congressional action. However, the War Powers Resolution also states that if our country is attacked—"a national emergency created by attack upon the United States"—any and all immediate power goes to the president to respond.

So as we confronted the aftermath of 9/11 in Congress, we had a significant number of members who were very protective of, and firm believers in, the congressional prerogative to declare war. However, they also knew what the War Powers Resolution said: the president had the sole power to respond to an attack. The central question we in Congress had to confront was: How extensive was that power? In the past, wars had been fought against nation-states, like Germany and Japan, or insurgent armed forces like the Vietcong in Vietnam. Who we were fighting was clear. Now we were dealing with terrorists, who might have state sponsors. Were there any limits to where and how the president might pursue a "war" on terror? How could Congress clarify the scope of the president's role—in this case, responding to the 9/11 attack? That was the premise we started from and exactly how we proceeded: We focused our language and our response specifically on the president's role regarding the 9/11 attack on the US. And we did it in a bipartisan way, with bipartisan agreement.

The White House saw the situation differently and wanted a much broader—an open-ended—mandate from Congress. On September 12, the administration proposed the most sweeping interpretation of the War Powers Resolution possible in draft legislation submitted to Congress. The draft not only would have authorized the president to take military action "against those nations, organizations or persons he determines have planned, authorized, harbored, committed, or aided in the planning or commission of the attacks," but it would also grant the president the authority "to deter and pre-empt any future acts of terrorism or aggression against the United States." The combined effect of this draft language would have given this White House, and likely any future administration, a blank check to engage in new conflicts without authorization from or consultation with Congress, so long as the administration believed there was even a potential threat against the United States.

In Congress, on both sides, that sweeping language was not going to pass. Supporters of the War Powers Resolution believed that our role should be to give the president not simply more power, but responsible power to exercise on behalf of the nation. Speaking for the Democrats, Democratic Leader Dick Gephardt in the House and Majority Leader Tom Daschle in the Senate carefully presented a resolution that specifically addressed what had happened on 9/11 and what the military objectives should be. Senator Daschle and Sen. Trent Lott, the Republican minority leader, jointly sponsored the resolution. Its language made it clear that this authorization did not supersede or in any way replace the War Powers Resolution.

The post-9/11 resolution's final language shows how important a few words can be in crafting meaningful legislation: "That the President is authorized to use all necessary and appropriate force against those nations, organizations, or persons he determines planned, authorized, committed, or aided the terrorist attacks that occurred on September 11, 2001, or harbored such organizations or persons, *in order to prevent any future acts of international terrorism against the United States by such nations, organizations or persons.*" Congress ensured that the focus remained on 9/11 and "international" terrorism; the word "aggression" was removed, and we specified that the targets had to remain individuals, organizations, or nations that could be directly connected to September 11.

The measure passed unanimously in the Senate and in the House except for one vote: that of my colleague Barbara Lee, who did not want a vote to authorize war. Within weeks, US forces were at war with al-Qaeda and its Taliban hosts in Afghanistan. There was great unity in the country; most people believed that there should be no safe harbor for Osama bin Laden and al-Qaeda. A year later, the climate would drastically change.

The September 11 Inquiry

From the first hours after the 9/11 attacks, many Americans and many in Congress began asking questions—they wanted to know how the catastrophe of 9/11 could have happened. Sen. Bob Graham, who was the new chair of the Senate Select Committee on Intelligence, proposed a congressionally led investigation. He had served on the Senate Intelligence Committee for more than seven years, and he knew the territory. He advocated for a congressional Joint Inquiry, which would be overseen by the four leaders of the Senate and the House Intelligence Committees, two Democrats and two Republicans. From the Senate: Graham and Republican vice chair Richard Shelby. From the House: Republican chairman Porter Goss and myself (as the Democratic ranking member). Our committee roles were known as the Gang of Four, and our positions of leadership on these committees meant that we had access to our nation's most sophisticated intelligence.

I am proud of my many years in intelligence oversight. Like Bob Graham, I began my service on the House Permanent Select

Committee on Intelligence in 1993. When I was selected as the Democratic whip in the House, I became one of the rare members of the leadership who already had high-level security credentials. (In fact, my first vote as a member of Congress after my swearing in was a vote to bring the annual intelligence bill to the House floor.) By the time I stepped down as Speaker of the House, I had spent thirty years working in intelligence, first as a member of the committee and then as the committee's top Democratic member, and as the House Democratic leader and Speaker. Because of my leadership roles, I spent twenty-two of those years as a member of the Gang of Eight (the nickname given to the combination of the four top Democratic and Republican leaders in the House and Senate, along with the Intelligence Committee chairs and the ranking member or senator), receiving briefings and reports at the highest intelligence levels. I also traveled to eighty-seven countries, a few only once, but most more than once. I made a total of sixteen trips just to Afghanistan and Iraq.

I originally sought a seat on the Intelligence Committee for two reasons. One: to halt the proliferation of nuclear weapons. Two: in accordance with the law, I wanted to ensure that we protected the civil liberties of the American people so that they were not spied on in their own country.

In my early days on the Intelligence Committee, one of our primary areas of focus was force protection for our troops. We looked to the intelligence community to recognize emerging threats, so that we might be able to prevent conflict. But if preventing conflict was not possible, then we wanted our intelligence community to provide its best understanding of our enemy—so that we could know the strength of the other side in order to protect our troops and win.

As we got further and further from the end of the Cold War,

and a traditional, conventional war seemed far less likely, our committee's focus broadened to include issues related to money laundering and drug trafficking, which were the primary fundraising sources for terrorist movements. As the year 2000 approached, having experienced the bombing of the World Trade Center in 1993, the 1996 Khobar Towers bombing in Saudi Arabia (where some US and coalition forces were being housed after the first Gulf War), and the attacks on the US embassies in Kenya and Tanzania in 1998, our focus on counterintelligence intensified.

From the moment I joined the Intelligence Committee, when I was a relatively new legislator, I read everything available to committee members nearly every day. It became second nature to build an intelligence document review into my daily schedule. I would let the staff in the SCIF know that I was coming to read the daily threat assessment, the material that the combined intelligence services put out to their "customers." These "customers" are the select users of intelligence in the executive branch, the legislative branch, and parts of the intelligence community itself. If I or another member had questions or areas of specific interest, the staff in the SCIF could provide more information, up to our classification levels. We were allowed to take handwritten notes while we were inside the room, but nothing we read or wrote could leave the hermetically sealed secure space. Instead, the notes would be stored, along with any briefing materials, in each member's designated "safe place"—the equivalent of a locked, high-tech cubbyhole or file cabinet.

In the aftermath of the most devastating attack on the US since Pearl Harbor, the immediate bipartisan concern of the Intelligence Committees' Gang of Four was to understand what had led to 9/11. The Bush administration did not want us to conduct an inquiry; its official position was that we were taking critical staff time that should be devoted to the war on terrorism, as well as risking leaks and potentially compromising intelligence. But 9/11 was an unconventional terror attack, and Congress immediately wanted to know if there had been any intelligence failures or if key warning signs had been missed. So did the American public.

We established the Joint Inquiry, which was new, exceptional, and historic. It was only authorized to investigate intelligence, because it was convened by the Intelligence Committee; but the committee hired a completely separate staff: as the Congressional Research Service highlighted, it included twenty-four professionals with backgrounds in intelligence collection, analysis, management, law enforcement, investigations, and oversight. The Joint Inquiry then established five investigative teams. Three teams focused on the CIA, the FBI, and the National Security Agency. In addition, staff teams reviewed documents and conducted interviews at the Treasury, Defense, State, Justice, Transportation, and Energy Departments and with certain private-sector individuals and organizations.

By the time the Joint Inquiry began its public hearings, in September 2002, the staff, as Staff Director Eleanor Hill noted, had reviewed more than four hundred thousand pages of documents, identified more than sixty-six thousand pages of records, and conducted some four hundred interviews and technical discussions. It was a privilege to serve as one of the four congressional leaders co-chairing the Joint Inquiry. It was also heartbreaking to see how vulnerable to attack our country had been. And it is worth reviewing what we learned, because not only would this information be vital to protecting the US in the future, but, sadly, it also has direct bearing on the administration's misleading decision to go to war in Iraq and the majority vote in Congress to authorize the war.

Warning Signs

In the mid-1990s, an NIE highlighted a "new breed" of terrorist. According to this NIE, these terrorists lacked a specific state sponsor, were loosely organized, had, as the Joint Inquiry noted, a "penchant for violence" and sometimes for jihad, a so-called holy war. By 1996, the intelligence community was increasingly focused on a specific terrorist and a specific terror organization: Osama bin Laden and al-Qaeda, now operating out of Afghanistan, after previously operating out of Sudan. In August 1996, bin Laden issued a fatwa calling for holy war against the US. During the mid- and late 1990s, federal intelligence and law enforcement agencies created special units to track terrorists, work with foreign governments, and expand the FBI's presence overseas.

By the spring and summer of 2001, there were further warnings of possible (and more specific) attacks. Testifying before the Joint Inquiry, the committee's own excellent staff director, Eleanor Hill, shared a briefing that had been prepared in early July 2001 for senior US government officials: "Based on a review of all-source reporting over the last five months, we believe that UBL [bin Laden] will launch a significant terrorist attack against U.S. and/or Israeli interests in the coming weeks," it stated. "The attack will be spectacular and designed to inflict mass casualties against U.S. facilities or interests. Attack preparations have been made. Attack will occur with little or no warning." But the conventional thinking was still that the attack would take place overseas. In fact, and unfortunately, one of the findings of the Joint Inquiry was that no one in the intelligence community had prepared a comprehensive list of terrorist threats inside the United States. And there had been no serious effort to educate the American public about the dangers and possibility of a terror attack at home.

We, however, learned that individual FBI agents were very worried by the summer of 2001. The Joint Inquiry focused on a July 2001 communication from the FBI field office in Phoenix, Arizona, a message that became known as the Phoenix Memo. It had been forwarded to FBI headquarters in Washington. In it, an agent had warned the bureau about the presence of overseas "students" who had possible ties to foreign terrorist organizations and who were attending commercial aviation training schools in the US. The memo began by stating that its "purpose" was "to advise . . . of the possibility of a coordinated effort by Osama bin Laden to send students to the United States to attend civil aviation universities and colleges."

In August 2001, Minneapolis FBI agents detained Zacarias Moussaoui, a French national originally from Morocco who was seeking to learn basic commercial airliner flight operation in the US. An employee of the Minnesota aviation school where Moussaoui was enrolled had reported Moussaoui's "unusual" specific requests for flight training on a 747, particularly his interest in the protocols for how to communicate directly with flight towers. Moussaoui was also particularly interested in how the plane's autopilot and cabin doors worked and said he would "love" to do a simulated flight from Heathrow Airport in England to John F. Kennedy Airport in New York, performing all necessary navigation and communications. In FBI interviews, Moussaoui's roommate— a resident of Saudi Arabia—said that Moussaoui "is preparing himself to fight and has, in the past, expressed approval of 'martyrs.'"

Local FBI agents in Minnesota sought an emergency search warrant to investigate Moussaoui's notes and computer disks, but, as the US Department of Justice Office of the Inspector General would later conclude, FBI headquarters in Washington "did not believe sufficient grounds existed for a criminal warrant, and it also concluded that a FISA [Foreign Intelligence Surveillance Act] warrant could not be obtained because it believed Moussaoui could not be connected to a foreign power as required under FISA." Blocked by their superiors, the Minneapolis agents began the process to have Moussaoui deported to France, so French officials could search his belongings and report their findings to the US; but before Moussaoui could be deported, the calendar turned to September 11, 2001.

A third major missed opportunity was the realization that two hijackers of Flight 77, which crashed into the Pentagon, had been previously identified by the CIA as having attended an al-Qaeda meeting in Malaysia in 2000; but the two men were never placed on any watch lists maintained by the State Department, the Immigration and Naturalization Service, or the US Customs Service. The CIA only belatedly placed their names on a watch list, in August 2001, and by then it was too late. The men were already inside the United States and preparing for 9/11.

A major theme of the Joint Inquiry's findings was the inadequate communication between and among the various intelligence and law enforcement agencies.

But there was a second major theme that we were not initially allowed to present to the public: the Saudi Arabian connection, specifically a clear trail of funding and assistance to these 9/11 terrorists that was provided by Saudi citizens, and particularly by Saudi diplomats and royal family members. In retrospect, it was an almost obvious connection. Fifteen of the nineteen 9/11 hijackers were from Saudi Arabia, and Osama bin Laden was a member of one of the Saudi kingdom's wealthiest families. We found multiple links between the hijackers and Saudi citizens residing in the US. And even when we could not find direct links to Saudi support, there were many red flags and interwoven connections.

Omar al-Bayoumi, a Saudi national (who was also repeatedly alleged to possibly be a Saudi intelligence officer) living in San Diego, offered considerable assistance to two of the 9/11 hijackers, including signing their housing lease. And Bayoumi received money from a Saudi company with ties to the Saudi ministry of defense. His wife also attempted to deposit three checks written by Princess Haifa bint Faisal, the wife of Prince Bandar bin Sultan, the Saudi ambassador to the US. But because the three checks were made out to another Saudi national, the wife of a man named Osama Bassnan (Bassnan's wife regularly received money from Princess bint Faisal, and Bassnan himself had, our committee found, "close" ties to other individuals connected to the hijackers), the bank declined to accept them.

In Minnesota, FBI agents discovered that Moussaoui had deposited $32,000 in cash in a bank account upon arriving in the US and had paid for his flight lessons in cash; someone had to be funding him as well. Another senior al-Qaeda operative arrested in Pakistan was later found to have private telephone numbers closely connected to a leading Saudi diplomat and Saudi embassy personnel in Washington. But the intelligence community refused to declassify this section of our report. It took fourteen years, until 2016, before Congress was allowed to release some of our findings regarding possible Saudi Arabian involvement in 9/11.

Another troubling fact surfaced during our Joint Inquiry hearings. At one point during his testimony, the former FBI assistant special agent for San Diego, where two of the terrorists had lived, said that Saudi Arabia was "not a country identified by the State Department as a state sponsor of terrorism." Because of that, he explained, the FBI did not pursue Saudi leads.

While there were probably other allies to whose actions our intelligence and law enforcement agencies also turned a blind eye, here, in the case of Saudi Arabia, we had conspicuous evidence of deeply concerning behavior. But suspicious behaviors and financial transactions were essentially written off or excused as simply the actions of Saudi officials whose "primary objective was to monitor dissidents in the interest of protecting the royal family. So they were not viewed as an inimical threat to national security," as the former San Diego FBI special agent explained in his testimony. During a closed hearing on October 9, 2002, the FBI executive assistant director also testified that "the FBI did not treat the Saudis as a counterterrorism [redacted] threat prior to September 11, 2001."

And during that same hearing, under questioning by Ohio Republican senator Mike DeWine, then-FBI director Robert Mueller revealed that he had become aware of "some facts" only "as a result of the probing" of the Joint Inquiry staff. Mueller added that those facts "perhaps would not have come to light had the staff not probed." Director Mueller's words were a very bureaucratic way of saying that the FBI only became aware of the depth of the Saudi role in helping and sponsoring some of the 9/11 terrorists because of the work done by the Joint Inquiry.

Ultimately, the Joint Inquiry learned that the multiple intelligence and law enforcement communities had no common, formal system for placing suspected terrorists on watch lists. Furthermore, in the case of the FBI, that agency was set up primarily to gather evidence for criminal trials, rather than to focus on strategic analysis of threats. Thus while the FBI had uncovered different pieces of a terror plot, it had no organizational way to connect them. In addition, there was no designated government agency responsible for regularly assessing threats to the US homeland, because, again, the working assumption had been that a terror attack would take place abroad, even though the World Trade Center had been the target of a bombing by an explosive-laden van in 1993. As the Joint Inquiry staff director put it, "Law enforcement tools became the primary instrument of American counterterrorism strategy." Indeed, the US had indicted Osama bin Laden in November 1998. However, indicting bin Laden in no way deterred 9/11. It was clear to us that especially in the year leading up to 9/11, there had been multiple opportunities for better communication among law enforcement and the intelligence community, and that if information had been shared, it might have prevented 9/11.

The Joint Inquiry experienced repeated delays in receiving information from the administration, and even some stonewalling. Some delays were likely due to efforts to protect sources and methods. Overall, the administration would be very sparing in what they divulged. But given what they were planning for Iraq, the administration also may not have wanted the congressional investigation to get too close to the fuller picture that was emerging. We found strong evidence of multiple concerning links to Saudi Arabia, while they were trying very hard to link 9/11 to Iraq and Saddam Hussein.

The Joint Inquiry's report and main recommendations were completed in December 2002 and submitted to the intelligence community for declassification review. But by then Congress had already voted to authorize the use of military force against Iraq— the vote in the House, in October 2002, was 296 to 133, and it came one day after Director Mueller's closed-door testimony.

The 9/11 Commission

The misuse of the 9/11 attacks as a rationale for war in Iraq underlined the importance of another congressional initiative: the 9/11 Commission. Early on, both the House and the Senate, as well as much of the country, wanted a broader 9/11 Commission, tasked with a wider mandate than the Joint Inquiry (which, as we have seen, could only look at intelligence). I had authored legislation to establish a commission right away in the House Intelligence Committee. It passed in committee. But when we took the measure to the House floor, Republicans who had voted for it in the committee now said that we should not have an outside commission, because it would look as if we were investigating the president. That was not our objective. We just wanted to try to fully understand what had happened and why. But the measure failed.

But we did not give up on our efforts. By the summer of 2002, we were joined by the 9/11 families, who had turned their deep grief into strong action. They wanted an outside commission. For those of us supporting one, working with the 9/11 families was very much like walking on hallowed ground. Strengthened by their advocacy, we tried again. With their help and the leadership of Rep. Tim Roemer, a Democrat from Indiana and a member of the Intelligence Committee, we brought to the floor new legislation to create a National Commission on Terrorist Attacks Upon the United States. The Republicans were still skeptical or downright opposed. Finally, after multiple proposals and votes in the House and the Senate, on November 27, President Bush signed the legislation.

More than fourteen months after the attack, we finally had a 9/11 Commission.

The 9/11 Commission was bipartisan. Former Republican

governor Thomas Kean of New Jersey was the chair, and former Democratic congressman Lee Hamilton of Indiana, the past chair of the House Foreign Affairs Committee, was vice chair. Kean and Hamilton respected each other and worked well together. The findings that came out of their hearings would carry a great deal of weight.

The commission held its hearings against the backdrop of the Iraq War. Kean and Hamilton and the other distinguished members of the committee opened the first public hearing of the National Commission on Terrorism Attacks Upon the United States on March 31, 2003. After several months of work, the members noted that their work was being delayed, mainly because the Bush administration was slow in providing, or had refused to provide, the relevant and necessary material. In January 2004, the commission requested an extension of the deadline for delivering its final report. But, after slow-walking the intelligence material for months, Republicans in Congress and the administration initially said they opposed granting the commission extra time to complete its work.

I released the following statement in reply: "President Bush's opposition to extending the Commission is at odds with the enormity of the tragedy we suffered on September 11th, and with the necessity to do everything we can to make it less likely that we would experience another horrific attack." Our responsibility was to the families of 9/11, to the first responders, to the military, and to the future security of our country. The families deserved answers, and we needed to protect the American people. The majority of those in the best position to know, the Republicans and Democrats on the Commission, had said they needed more time, and we believed it was vital to grant their request. In early February, the administration reversed itself and supported a two-month extension of the deadline.

When the Commission published its final report, in July 2004, Chairman Kean and Vice Chair Hamilton came to my House Democratic leader's office and made their presentation to our Democratic leadership. It was a presidential election year, and the Democratic National Convention was being held in Boston. Immediately after the convention, I asked the Democratic members to return to Washington to push to authorize what the 9/11 Commission had recommended. These recommendations included changes to the organization of the US's homeland security, improvements to intelligence and to our global traveler screening efforts, visa modernization, more comprehensive monitoring for bioterrorism, and other important provisions to bring the government into the twenty-first century and better address the new threats facing us. Nearly all of the Democratic members came back to work. At that time, we had a significant number of veterans in our caucus, and they were very eager to pass these recommendations to protect the American people. Republicans were reluctant: so reluctant that it would not be until two and a half years later—January 2007, when the Democrats retook control of Congress—that the 9/11 Commission's final recommendations would be put to a vote. When the new term started in the House, our first bill was H.R.1, the Implementing Recommendations of the 9/11 Commission Act, which we passed on January 9. But the Senate didn't move its own version until July 9. After the differences between our bills were resolved, the 9/11 Commission recommendations finally became law, with President Bush's signature, on August 3, 2007—nearly six years after the attack on our country and nearly four and a half years after we had invaded Iraq.

When President Bush signed this legislation, the US was in the middle of a change in Iraq War policy, having undertaken what was dubbed "the surge," a plan that added more than thirty thousand troops to support the battlefield. The war that the administration had promised would be quick and almost costless, in a country where our troops would be welcomed as "liberators," had devolved into a grim contest of terror attacks against our soldiers and bloody urban combat.

Jack Murtha: "A Flawed Policy Wrapped in an Illusion"

Although President Bush had declared the end of major combat operations in Iraq under a banner that read "Mission Accomplished" on May 1, 2003, many Iraqis saw the conflict differently. They launched an insurgency, which began with bombings and escalated to roadside attacks on US troops and the ambushing and killing of US contractors. Saddam Hussein was finally captured in December 2003. The next month, January 2004, the Bush administration was told that inspectors had failed to find extensive stockpiles of chemical, biological, and especially nuclear weapons and components inside Iraq. David Kay, the former top US weapons inspector, testified before Congress on January 28: "We were almost all wrong." Despite declining public support for the war, President Bush still won reelection that year against Sen. John Kerry, a decorated Vietnam War veteran.

Although Iraq did hold elections in 2005, the violence continued. On November 17, 2005, a longtime champion of the troops in the House, Jack Murtha, addressed the Democratic Caucus and then the press. Murtha was a proud marine and a decorated war hero, with two Purple Hearts from his service in Vietnam. He had served as top Democrat on the Defense Appropriations Subcommittee, and he regularly visited the troops in the theater of war and in military hospitals in America and abroad. He had been a staunch supporter of the first Gulf War and had voted to authorize the Iraq War in October 2002.

With those credentials, in November 2005, Jack Murtha announced that he was introducing legislation to redeploy US troops out of Iraq. His words were blunt and strong: "The war is not going as advertised. It is a flawed policy wrapped in an illusion. . . . It is time for a change in direction. We cannot continue on the present course. The main reason for going to war has been discredited." Murtha spoke sadly and at length about the injured soldiers he had met, the impact on their families, and what he called "battle fatigue," or PTSD. He cited the abuse of Iraqi detainees at Abu Ghraib, the US-run prison, and said that attacks on our troops had doubled since the revelations of torture and abuse of prisoners. He said that, according to a British poll, 80 percent of Iraqis wanted us out of Iraq—and about 45 percent believed that the attacks on US troops were justified. And he said that the American public was way ahead of the members of Congress in its opposition to the war.

The public reaction to Murtha's comments and his plan was overwhelming. He could barely walk through an airport without being thanked and applauded. His presence was in demand across the country. Because of his national security credentials, he gave people confidence in a new path for our military and hope for peace.

Not long after Murtha's powerful speech, legendary *Star Wars* filmmaker George Lucas hosted a gala in San Francisco that was sponsored by the National Basketball Association. It was the first private-sector event to raise funds for the proposed Martin Luther King Jr. Memorial on the National Mall in Washington, DC. As the program began, the announcer said that he wanted to pay tribute to his hero, Jack Murtha—and the crowd roared in approval. Before Jack's statement on the war, hardly anyone in attendance would have known who he was. Now, although Jack wasn't even there, his importance was recognized.

I was very happy, because I loved Jack and his wife, Joyce—he had been my campaign chairman when I first ran for leadership in the House—but more importantly because of his courage.

Jack had led many congressional delegations to visit our troops, and we often visited our troops when they came home, particularly our severely injured troops. I remember one of our visits to Walter Reed, the US Army's military hospital. We were about to enter a patient's room when we were asked to wait a moment. This was not unusual—but on this occasion, the soldier wanted time to welcome Jack. When the door opened, Jack saw the young man, out of bed, standing and saluting him while wearing a Pittsburgh Steelers football team jersey. Jack represented western Pennsylvania, and the Steelers were his home team.

No one paid more visits to soldiers in hospitals than Jack, to comfort the patients and families, to witness their recuperation, and to understand their problems. Jack encouraged all of us to join him. During one visit, I was talking with a twenty-year-old soldier, and as he was describing his wounds, he said: "And ma'am, I don't have anything going on down below."

For him and so many other young men, another horrible price of war.

Opposing the War, Supporting the Troops

The year 2006 was a major midterm election year in Congress. As we looked toward the election, Harry Reid, the Democratic leader in the Senate, and I crafted a political strategy to win back

Congress. Democrats had not held the majority in both houses since 1994. But in 2005, President Bush had given us a gift when he said he would privatize Social Security. Our opposition to Bush's Social Security privatization plan and our "Drain the Swamp" ethical campaign led us to victory. In November, with President Bush's popularity falling, and by campaigning on our "New Direction for America"—and with Democrats united in supporting our "Six for '06" agenda—we won majorities in both the House and the Senate. We had made a decision to win—and we did.

But the Iraq War played a role as well. During the election and following our victory, there were thousands of people in the streets demanding an end to the war. Some of them were calling for the impeachment of President George W. Bush for his role in initiating it and his administration's misrepresentations surrounding the invasion.

While there were major disagreements over what I considered the largest destabilizing mistake in recent American history in terms of its consequences, I resisted the calls for impeachment. Sen. Bob Graham, in his book *Intelligence Matters*, had presented a case for impeachment on the basis of Iraq's nonexistent nuclear weapons and our leaving Afghanistan too early. Although I was strongly opposed to the war—and constantly pointing out the false statements by the administration—as long as American troops were in combat, I held that we had the responsibility to support them.

In December 2006, the bipartisan Iraq Study Group, chaired by former Republican secretary of state James Baker and former Democratic congressman Lee Hamilton (previously of the 9/11 Commission), began its report summary by saying: "The situation in Iraq is grave and deteriorating. There is no path that can

guarantee success, but the prospects can be improved." This statement, coming from a largely conservative study group, should
have been alarming to the administration, as it was to the American people. In an attempt to change the dynamic inside Iraq and
on the battlefield, some military and foreign policy experts began
recommending that the US send additional troops to Iraq. President Bush had been meeting with a range of advisors, and the
ultimate result was that he agreed with the plan to "surge" additional troops.

When I became Speaker of the House, almost four years after
we had invaded Iraq, George and Laura Bush invited Paul and me
to a private dinner in the upstairs residence dining room at the
White House. Before dinner, the president and I sat down for an
hour, just the two of us. He asked me what I thought about keeping a US presence in Iraq, similar to what we have had in South
Korea since the end of the Korean War in 1953. As much as I disagreed with President Bush on Iraq, I remained respectful, but I
was also very honest with him. I told him absolutely, positively
not—I was opposed to nation-building in Iraq. Respectfully, we
put our differences aside for dinner.

There were two immediate institutional challenges to this expanded US combat and occupation force inside Iraq: The US military had to increase its recruiting efforts to meet the troop goals
for the surge. And the Pentagon needed funding to pay for the
surge.

By the spring of 2007, the central debate in Congress surrounding the war was focused on funding legislation, including
accountability measures and timetables. The first bill that the
House Democrats brought to the floor had both funding for the
war and a deadline of August 2008 to remove US combat troops
from Iraq. The Senate had difficulty passing any legislation

that contained an exact date for the full removal of troops, but it could agree on a beginning point for the withdrawal. Instead, the senators presented a "goal" of ending the US combat troop involvement in Iraq by March 2008. The House then passed the diminished Senate bill—but even that was vetoed by President Bush.

We were back to the drawing board. And in terms of funding needs, we were confronting more than Iraq. Louisiana, Mississippi, and Alabama were still struggling to recover from the devastation of Hurricane Katrina in 2005. The House was called upon to pass a supplemental appropriations bill to fund the ongoing Katrina recovery, other domestic needs, and now also the ongoing war.

When all three issues were combined, all hell broke loose in our caucus.

Members were overwhelmingly opposed to funding the Iraq War effort—and they strenuously objected to voting for the war and Katrina in the same supplemental bill. It was necessary that any legislation that I proposed enable members to vote for Katrina aid and domestic priorities without having to vote for the Iraq funding. That formula meant that I needed to persuade Republicans to join us in voting to appropriate more money to fund the troops in Iraq, because so many Democrats were opposed to the war that I could not guarantee that the bill would pass solely on a party-line vote.

My personal sympathies were with the majority of the House Democratic Caucus, but I told my members that when we say that we support the troops, we must do so when it is difficult as well as when it is easy by enabling the House to work its will.

Supporting the troops financially meant I still needed to pass a defense supplemental. That is, it was necessary to divide the legislation into different bills to bring to the floor, which would then be joined and sent to the Senate. The chair of the Appropriations Committee—the smartest and most strategic of us all, Rep. Dave Obey of Wisconsin, who would be managing the bills—expressed concern that the Republicans would decide not to vote for the Iraq funding, intending to put Democrats on the spot and try to paint us as being unsupportive of the troops. But that didn't happen.

In May, we passed the very specifically named U.S. Troop Readiness, Veterans' Care, Katrina Recovery, and Iraq Accountability Appropriations Act of 2007 on the House floor. The bill was very clear in its support of our military service members and our veterans. Many provisions were directed toward their well-being and their care. Rep. Ike Skelton of Missouri, chair of the Armed Services Committee, proposed a 3.5 percent pay raise for troops and a $40 per month increase in survivors' benefits. (The administration said that this increase was unnecessary.) Rep. John Spratt of South Carolina, chairman of the Budget Committee, also brought a budget to the floor, with a $6.7 billion increase in funding to provide for our veterans. Rep. Chet Edwards of Texas, chairman of the Appropriations Subcommittee on Military Construction, Veterans Affairs, and Related Agencies, put forward the largest increase to the Veterans Affairs budget in the department's seventy-seven-year history.

So it was very clear that our debate was not about whether or not we supported our troops. We did, of course. It was about opposing the war.

In my speech on May 24, I said: "We think there should be a new direction . . . Many retired generals, including General William Odom, have stated that any strategy for success in Iraq must begin with the redeployment of troops out of Iraq . . . That is what we are proposing—a change of mission. A redeployment for a different purpose."

We passed both bills, combined them, and after the Senate approved the legislative package, President Bush signed the legislation into law. The troops had been funded—although I personally voted against the funding for the war in Iraq and Afghanistan. While the legislation did not contain a timetable for troop withdrawal, we were still hoping that the vast majority of US forces would be redeployed out of Iraq in the coming months.

In September 2007, General David Petraeus, now the commander of forces in Iraq, and Ryan Crocker, US ambassador to Iraq, issued a report that opposed a premature drawdown and endorsed continuing the surge of combat troop levels until summer 2008. The report hit us hard. Democrats were furious—in and outside of Congress. In the House, our "Out of Iraq" Caucus had been clear, determined, and forceful in its opposition to the war. And they were right. I'll never forget Congresswoman Lynn Woolsey of California, taking to the House floor nearly every day to speak truth about the falsehoods and failures of the war. Outside groups, particularly MoveOn, were relentless and persistent in their vocal opposition. Concurrent with the release of the Petraeus-Crocker report, MoveOn renamed Petraeus "General Betray Us."

After the report's release, the congressional leadership met with President Bush at the White House to discuss the surge. The president said that he wanted to hear our views about the policy. In reality, he wanted to ask us to hold our fire for six months.

My position was that the war had to end. I asked the president why he thought the surge would work when so many of his war initiatives had failed. He responded: "Because it has to." My parting message to him was that with no exit strategy, America's grandchildren would be serving in Iraq ten years later. We did not find common ground.

Iraq: The Consequences

By the time President Bush left office, a little over a year later, he had negotiated a status of forces agreement (SOFA), which, at the Iraqis' insistence, laid out the terms for US military forces to depart Iraq. With the SOFA, a departure date had been determined.

While there are some who claim the surge worked, I believe if you look at the facts, it only worked briefly, and then conditions inside the country fell apart again. The Iraqi government became unreliable, and new forms of terror began to emerge.

Beyond the tremendous loss of life and suffering inside Iraq, it was also clear that our initiation of hostilities had serious, lasting consequences for the region. For many years, Iraq and its next-door neighbor Iran were a check on each other. The two countries had fought a long war. They had remained focused on their extreme enmity toward each other.

Now, however, Iraq was greatly weakened, in the grip of strife between Sunni and Shia Muslims, and also had a very fragile government. That left Iran far more free to intensify its terrorist activities and its support generally for terrorists in the Middle East. And Iran also became an unchallenged force for developing a nuclear weapon. In its pursuit of weapons of mass destruction, Iran has sought components and scientists from China and has increasingly made itself a menace to the world. Iran has also been able to use its money to support Hezbollah in Lebanon, as well as Hamas in Gaza, and even to exert its influence inside Afghanistan.

Our shift in military focus and resources away from Afghanistan back in 2002—claiming that we had routed the Taliban—was clearly one of the biggest strategic mistakes historically in national security. Just "routing the Taliban" did not ensure that Afghanistan would not once again become a safe haven for al-Qaeda and other terrorist groups. Just "routing the Taliban" did not mean that they were defeated—they were simply lying in wait for the opportunity to return to power.

We never want our soldiers to think that their protection of our freedom is not respected or is in vain. But the loss of life—of Americans, Afghans, and Iraqis—was tragic. And conditions for women and children in both Afghanistan and Iraq remain a deep source of concern for Americans and many of us in Congress. The story of 9/11 and of the wars in Afghanistan and Iraq is, sadly, not finished. Nor are the consequences for us, for the region, and indeed for the entire world.

Lasting Lessons from 9/11 Through Iraq

As I have said, I believed then, and I believe now, that the Iraq War was the most destabilizing mistake in recent American history. There are crucial questions that have never been satisfactorily answered about the ultimate decision to go to war: Why would the administration engage in misrepresentations about the prospects of Iraq's nuclear capabilities? Why would they mislead the American people about the number of troops needed to occupy the country? Why would they wrongly tie Iraq to the attacks of 9/11? And why would we leave Afghanistan before the job was done?

I understand why different members of the House and senators voted how they did on Iraq. Many of the Republicans trusted their president and gave him the benefit of the doubt. But ultimately, a vote for war requires you to trust your own judgment.

I never asked anyone to vote with me; I simply explained why I was voting as I was.

Ultimately, it is my view that the failures that led to 9/11 were organizational and unintentional. But the intelligence failures that led to the Iraq invasion were bureaucratic and deliberate. For 9/11, we had many of the dots, but failed to connect them; our intelligence community was not structured to grasp the extent of this new threat and fully see the new patterns that were emerging. In the case of Iraq, there was a concerted effort to ignore (and even withhold) inconvenient analysis and to artificially inflate or elevate intelligence that supported invasion: to connect only some dots and dismiss others. As the Iraq Study Group noted in its report, "An extraordinary amount of sacrifice has been asked of our men and women in uniform, and of their families." But that level of sacrifice must always be matched by the same level of planning for the war and its aftermath. As an institution, Congress has a responsibility to honor the sacrifice of our troops as we work to protect our nation.

The world remains dangerous. Our responsibility matters every bit as much as it did on that bright, beautiful, and then tragic morning of September 11, 2001.

May 3, 2024: Receiving the Medal of Freedom, the nation's highest civilian honor, from President Joe Biden at the White House.

(*Left and Right*) The slogan of my first campaign for Congress in 1987 was "A Voice That Will Be Heard."

4

September 4, 1991:
Standing in Tiananmen
Square with Reps. Ben Jones
and John Miller to honor the
brave Chinese people who gave
their lives for freedom. Chinese
police chased us after we
unfurled our banner.

5

January 4, 2007:
After being sworn in as
the first woman Speaker,
I called the House to order
For the Children.

6

January 23, 2007:
The first woman to
preside at the presidential
State of the Union, greeting
George W. Bush.

(Top) Visiting US troops in Iraq in 2008. Although I opposed the war from the start, I have always supported our troops. *(Bottom)* In Afghanistan on Mother's Day 2012.

March 23, 2010: President Barack Obama signing the Affordable Care Act. Finally, health care is a right—not a privilege.

(Left) March 21, 2010: Walking to the House arm and arm with the great Rep. John Lewis to pass the landmark Affordable Care Act. *(Right)* Successfully rallying to save the ACA when it came under Republican assault.

12

(Left) October 17, 2007: President George W. Bush awarding the Congressional Gold Medal to His Holiness, the Dalai Lama. *(Right)* Meeting with Chinese President Xi Jinping in the Capitol in 2015. Dianne Feinstein and I challenged him on Tibet.

August 2, 2022: An inspiring welcome in Taiwan, even as the Chinese government rattled its sabers against our congressional trip.

With then–President Tsai Ing-wen in Taipei, honoring our commitments to Taiwan.

16

February 5, 2019: Returning to the Speakership and acknowledging President Trump at the State of the Union.

(Left) October 16, 2019: Confronting Trump in a congressional meeting at the White House's Cabinet Room. "With you, Mr. President, all roads lead to Putin." *(Right)* February 4, 2020: Tearing up Trump's manifesto of lies in the pages of his State of the Union.

(Left) January 6, 2021: With Sen. Chuck Schumer and Rep. Steny Hoyer at our secure location in Fort McNair. We were initially told it would take "several days" to secure the Capitol after the assault. *(Right)* Reconvening the House on the night of January 6th. We were determined to certify the election of Joe Biden and preserve democracy.

March 1, 2022: A celebratory State of the Union with Joe Biden and Kamala Harris, the first time two women have presided over the podium.

April 30, 2022: Leading a secret high-risk congressional trip to Ukraine to support President Volodymyr Zelenskyy and his nation shortly after Russia invaded.

December 21, 2022: Presenting Ukraine's President Volodymyr Zelenskyy with an American flag during his address to Congress. We must ensure our flag continues to symbolize freedom.

From Tiananmen to Taiwan

The tracking of our airplane began the moment it lifted off from the Malaysian capital of Kuala Lumpur, at a little before 4:00 p.m. local time on August 2, 2022. The US Air Force C-40C aircraft, code-named SPAR19, was carrying five other members of Congress and me. For the next seven hours, as we crossed southern Asia, carefully avoiding the South China Sea, about 2.92 million people around the world followed some portion of our flight. As our plane touched down in Taipei, the capital of Taiwan, more than 708,000 people were following SPAR19, making it the most tracked live flight at the time in Flightradar24's history.

Taiwan is the island to which opponents of Mao Zedong's hard-line Communism fled in 1949 when Mao took power. The Chinese government has threatened Taiwan's sovereignty from the beginning, and a hostile takeover is one of the leading international threats to global security.

Shortly before our courageous flight crew began the plane's descent, in an act of saber-rattling, the People's Republic of China had sent its fighter jets into the narrow Taiwan Strait, nosing the edge of Taiwan's airspace. The Chinese military also had announced it would soon conduct live-fire drills, firing ammunition in the vicinity of Taiwan.

Our delegation had received an invitation from Taiwan's government. We had originally planned to visit in April but had to delay after I tested positive for Covid. When I asked other members of the delegation if they wanted to proceed with the trip, they were eager and willing. Rep. Gregory Meeks, chair of the House Foreign Affairs Committee; Rep. Mark Takano, chair of the House Committee on Veterans' Affairs; Rep. Suzan DelBene, chair of the New Dems Coalition; Rep. Raja Krishnamoorthi, of the House Permanent Select Committee on Intelligence; and Rep. Andy Kim, of the House Armed Services Committee and the House Foreign Affairs Committee are to be commended for their steadfast commitment.

My view was and is simply this: despite Chinese President Xi Jinping's tantrum, we would not let Beijing isolate Taiwan. When our cars left the Taipei airport, we had no idea that at this late hour of the night thousands of people would be packing the streets of the capital, to cheer and celebrate our arrival. The city's tallest building was bathed in light, beaming messages of welcome. I could see the letters *U-S-A* glowing against the glass as we passed.

The Communist government of China immediately condemned our visit. But I believed we needed to affirm Taiwan's democracy, particularly in the face of increased repression inside China. As I wrote in the *Washington Post* on the morning of our visit, "The world faces a choice between autocracy and democracy. . . . It is essential that America and our allies make clear that we never give in to autocrats." For thirty-five years, I have tried to hold China's autocrats to account, particularly for their treatment of the country's own citizens—in Tibet; in the genocide of the Muslim minority population in China's northwest known as the Uyghurs; and in the crushing of democracy in Hong Kong.

In public life, there are issues that I consider issues of conscience that speak to us from the depths of our shared humanity. These are issues on which our conscience will not allow us to be passive or to be silent. They challenge us to act on behalf of those who cannot. Since I entered Congress, the lack of basic human rights in the People's Republic of China and Tibet has called out to my conscience. In pursuit of trade and profits, we have ignored the Chinese government's treatment of its own citizens, among them the people of Hong Kong and Tibet. And we know that the government of China continues to threaten Taiwan. The US has ignored the Chinese government's religious and ethnic persecution inside its borders and has not recognized how Beijing has destabilized other parts of the world. In the case of Iran, the Chinese government has sent its technology—including ring magnets to enrich uranium—its scientists, and its weapons delivery systems to the Iranian regime, increasing the risk of nuclear hostilities for the entire world.

Nor is this a new story; it is one that has been decades in the making. The Chinese rulers did not hide what they were doing. It was simply that too many of us have chosen to excuse or ignore, or to avert our eyes.

On June 4, 1989, the world saw how the Chinese government unleashed its People's Liberation Army to silence peaceful, defenseless citizens, many of them young students, who were asking for basic rights in Beijing's Tiananmen Square. The protesters occupied the square for nearly two months, starting in mid-April after the death of Hu Yaobang, who, as Chinese Communist Party general secretary, had called for democratic reforms and was forced to resign. By May, nearly one million people had been drawn to Tiananmen, and many others had gathered in over four hundred cities throughout China. In Tiananmen, the protesters built a Goddess of Democracy modeled after our Statue of Liberty and quoted the United States' founders. Students and their supporters sought freedom of expression, freedom of the press, transparency, accountability, and an end to rampant corruption. Instead, these brave souls who had stood up for freedom were met with a hail of bullets and a deeper era of repression. Hundreds, possibly thousands, of Chinese citizens died in the Tiananmen Square massacre. Many more were wounded, jailed, or forced to flee China.

As appalling as the events of June 4 were, even more appalling was the US response. In July, barely one month after the killings, after Chinese troops crushed young people under the treads of military tanks, and after publicly claiming that he was suspending high-level meetings with China, President George H. W. Bush allowed Brent Scowcroft, his national security advisor, and Deputy Secretary of State Lawrence Eagleburger to travel to China for a secret meeting, during which they pledged not to let anyone come between the two countries. Internal documents later made public show that Scowcroft and Eagleburger conceded to Chinese leaders that how they treated their own citizens was, "of course, an internal affair." The two men returned in December to toast Chinese leaders "as friends to resume our important dialogue," while enjoying a candlelit banquet.

Contrary to their statements, we in Congress wanted to hold the Chinese government accountable. We began in June by unanimously passing—with all Democrats and Republicans voting yes—a resolution to condemn the crackdown and the subsequent Chinese government executions of pro-democracy activists. A bipartisan congressional group also marched to the Chinese embassy in the rain to express our deep horror at what had taken place.

The next step was legislation to protect Chinese students in the US who had been involved in the pro-democracy protests. Just two weeks after the Tiananmen Square massacre, I introduced the

Emergency Chinese Adjustment of Status Facilitation Act of 1989, which would provide students additional time to apply for new visas or permanent residency status without fear of having to return to China. These students were being spied on by the Chinese government. Agents were filming them at US events and showing the footage to their families back home, to intimidate and suppress their voices. Working closely with the Chinese student community, including Zhao Haiqing and the Independent Federation of Chinese Students and Scholars, we mobilized outside advocacy and maneuvered inside Congress to pass the bill 403–0 in the House and by voice vote in the Senate a day later, thanks to the leadership of Majority Leader George Mitchell. But then in a shocking development, when the bill reached the president's desk, he vetoed it. The Senate had the votes to override the veto, but President Bush appealed to the senators, promising to extend the protections using an executive order. He even wrote personal notes to wavering senators and to some of their wives, again promising that an executive order would be issued to protect Chinese students. The Senate did not override his veto. We were told the executive order would be posted in the Federal Register.

For weeks, we carefully checked the Federal Register, searching for the executive order, but nothing appeared. Finally, when a group of us reached out to the White House, we were told that no order would be issued—we were getting nothing. Fortunately, I was able to get access to one of the president's personal notes that had been sent to a senator. We had the text published in the *Washington Post*. That proof forced the White House to reverse course and protect the Chinese students through an executive order. A final Chinese Student Protection Act was passed into law in 1992. It ultimately granted legal permanent resident status to more than fifty-four thousand Chinese nationals. Over the years, I have met many of the beneficiaries of the legislation and their families who have been able to avoid repression at the hands of China's government and have instead become scientists, engineers, and business leaders in our own country.

But more needed to be done.

As background, in 1974–75, George H. W. Bush spent fifteen months as the director of the US Liaison Office to the People's Republic of China, the precursor to our embassy. He had a personal affinity for China, and perhaps he thought that opening China up to trade would lead to a more open society inside the country. At the same time, many big money interests wanted to increase US-China trade ties. For them, the pro-democracy students were a hindrance to their long-term business interests. Along with a core bipartisan group of colleagues, I disagreed with these big money interests and their desire to subordinate freedom to finances.

For my entire time in Congress, I have held the exact same position: Yes, China is a very important country. The relationship between our two countries is very important economically, as well as in terms of security, climate change, culture, and in almost every way. But the size of the economy, the size of the country, and the size of the relationship doesn't mean that we should not speak out for the people of China who do not have a voice in their country. Because human rights in China is a very, very important issue. If we as Americans do not speak out about human rights in China because of commercial interests, then we lose all moral authority to speak out about human rights abuses in any other country in the world.

This position has put me at odds with every administration to occupy the White House, Republican and Democrat. It has put me at odds with members of my own party. It has at times aligned me with staunch Republicans; indeed, one of the strongest expressions of support for my bipartisan 2022 trip to Taiwan came from Senate Republican Leader Mitch McConnell and twenty-five other Senate Republicans, who immediately issued a statement strongly backing the visit when our plane landed in Taipei.

Following the Tiananmen Square massacre, our legislation on US-China policy received overwhelming support in Congress and in the country. It focused on three areas.

First, of course, the timing centered around the June 4 massacre of perhaps thousands of peaceful protesters in Tiananmen Square and the arrests of many more at demonstrations in the square and across China. Suppression in Tibet was already well known, so human rights were already a high concern. Second, the issue of trade—tying human rights to trade—greatly expanded the possibilities for our advocacy. The trade issue had several important economic components: market access for US manufacturers, Chinese use of prison labor, and pirating US intellectual property.

At that time, the Chinese government was depriving US products of market access to China. Small- and medium-sized manufacturers were told that if they wanted access to Chinese production and low-wage workers, they needed to submit their product designs. Once China's government had the designs, they told them: We don't need you. You can manufacture here, but you cannot have access to the Chinese market. Our businesses then had to compete in the world market with Chinese companies, which in many cases were using prison labor and our designs. Use of prison labor is both a human rights issue and an unfair trade practice. US unions were very aware of how that put our production at a serious disadvantage to Chinese production.

Another unfair trade practice was the pirating of our intellectual property. In the 1990s when Chinese leader Deng Xiaoping was promoting his policy of greater economic openness, which US businesses saluted, it was said that he spoke in a factory that was pirating US intellectual property. I would also learn from my daughter that the day after one of her movies opened in New York, it was for sale on the streets of China. Imagine being able to move that fast, but that was par for the course.

Third, in addition to human rights and trade violations, our coalition was also emboldened by security concerns—especially China's sale of missiles and technology to Pakistan and rogue states. When we challenged the executive branch to end that threat to our security, we were told that they punish the buyer of the goods and military equipment—not the seller. The US allowed these violations to happen because they were beholden to corporate America. Insurance companies and financial institutions ruled the day: largely because of them, our small- and medium-sized businesses suffered. And because of the revolving door in government and big business, we rode the dragon at the expense of our values—and today, we still pay the price.

The Fight Over Most-Favored-Nation Status

In July 1989, in the wake of the Tiananmen massacre, I supported a package of sanctions against the Chinese government. These sanctions restricted international loans and either banned or restricted arms sales, technology transfers, and crime control equipment, which the Chinese government was using to surveil its citizens. But there was one additional avenue that Congress had not used to impose a consequence on the Chinese leadership, a central feature of the US-China relationship: the trade imbalance.

For more than twenty years, starting in 1951, the two nations had a hostile relationship, until President Richard Nixon visited China in 1972. Diplomatic relations between the US and China resumed in 1979, and a trade agreement was instituted that year. For a decade, both Presidents Ronald Reagan and George H. W. Bush had extended a trade policy known as most-favored-nation (MFN) status to the Chinese government. Indeed, until 1991, the yearly renewal of MFN status for China's trade had been a formality. This policy allowed China to receive the same trade benefits with the US as any other country. But in 1991, George Mitchell and I drafted legislation that would condition these MFN benefits until the Tiananmen Square victims were accounted for and those who had been imprisoned were released, and until "significant progress" was made on human rights in China and Tibet. At the time, I argued that passing the legislation would send the right signal to the younger generation of Chinese politicians who would soon take the reins of power from the country's aging leaders. The bill passed the House by an overwhelming vote—409–21—and later passed the Senate. President Bush vetoed it and set back the effort when we could have exerted real pressure and strengthened the hand of reformers. Looking back, it is even more clear that it was missed opportunity after missed opportunity during these crucial years that changed the course of history and set the stage for the challenges and threats that we face from the Chinese government today.

That same year, on September 5, a few months after the second observance of the Tiananmen massacre, I traveled to Beijing as part of a bipartisan delegation. For two days during private meetings with Chinese officials, our delegation was repeatedly told that there was "no prohibition on freedom of speech in China." Three of us put that to the test by visiting Tiananmen Square. The site was like a magnet for us; there was no way we could visit Beijing without being drawn to the vast, iconic square.

Together, Rep. Ben Jones, Democrat of Georgia, and Rep. John Miller, a Republican from Washington State, and I stood in Tiananmen Square and unfurled a small, hand-painted black fabric banner emblazoned with the words "To those who died for democracy in China," in English and Chinese characters. It was a simple, silent protest, but there were journalists present to cover and film what we did. The banner had been given to us by Martin Lee and other pro-democracy leaders when he hosted our delegation in Hong Kong. Chinese police officers quickly moved in to surround the three of us, and chased us out of the square. The police officers even detained the journalists who were there to record the moment and punched one cameraman. While Chinese officials were angry, that didn't affect me. They also were not the only government officials who were angry. That evening, we were entertained at a Chinese government official banquet with good food and grim faces. J. Stapleton Roy, then-US ambassador to China and a distinguished Foreign Service Officer, had to bear the brunt of our insistence on supporting the Tiananmen protesters.

When our delegation returned to Hong Kong, which was still under British control, residents applauded us. Workers in the hotel and transportation industries, shopkeepers, all kinds of people came up to us and told us how grateful they were that we had remembered the victims of Tiananmen Square.

After 1989, in both Asia and the US, I got to know many of the Chinese student dissidents who had shown such bravery at Tiananmen and were forced to flee. Some still cannot return home— and we lament that so few of the reforms that they fought for have led the Chinese government to change for the better.

In the early years of their forced exile, sometimes the students would call me in the middle of the night to ask for advice. They explained to me that they didn't know how to disagree and ultimately arrive at a compromise—and they were eager to learn. I told them it was okay to disagree—that's democracy. They were deeply committed to building a better country. They were fabulous and brilliant individuals, an explosion of light and hope, and they deserved our support.

In Congress in 1992, Democrats and Republicans tried to stand up again, legislatively, for the Chinese dissidents, but with the same result. Our bill to condition China's MFN status passed both houses of Congress, only to be vetoed by President Bush. Yet China remained a big issue, because that year was a presidential election year. The Clinton campaign invited pro-democracy Chinese students to the Democratic National Convention.

We made some progress in 1993 when President Clinton used an executive order to set conditions on China's MFN status renewal. Among the requirements that China had to meet were: compliance with a US-China prison labor agreement—again, because many Chinese goods for export were made by forced prison laborers, working in appalling conditions; adhering to the Universal Declaration of Human Rights; permitting international radio and TV to be broadcast; releasing citizens who were being detained as political or religious prisoners; and allowing international human rights and humanitarian organizations to have access to prisoners. The executive order also called for the protection of Tibet's religious and cultural heritage. George Mitchell and I were the sponsors of the legislation to condition MFN, and we both thought that the conditions and protections in the executive order could help. The president had also promised that he would hold China accountable before expanding trade. As George Mitchell told me, "The president has given you his word."

THE ART OF POWER

I was still hopeful when, in April 1994, I squared off against Montana Democratic senator Max Baucus at the National Press Club. Senator Baucus was a strong supporter of MFN for China. He acknowledged that human rights abuses were occurring inside the country, but he argued that economic reform would drive political reform. As Senator Baucus said, "There are human rights abuses," but then he added, "That's not the point," claiming that with "MFN in place, China will become the great, respected, democratic nation that we all hoped to see." Senator Baucus and his side espoused a principle of "peaceful evolution"—where increased economic relationships would lead to more democratic freedoms. However, the Chinese government opposed the peaceful evolution approach.

My view was quite different. During my remarks at the Press Club, I noted that believing economic reform would be a catalyst for political reform "was by no means inevitable," adding, "There is no such thing as 'trickle-down liberty.'" I quoted Chinese dissident Fang Lizhi, who had said that "the Chinese authorities clearly like this theory because they can use it to cover up their record of human rights violations." And that was exactly the case. I went on to quote Deng Xiaoping, who had said that political reforms would take "generations," and his vow that the Chinese government would "crush any attempts to hasten the process."

China also wasn't eager to open its markets to US goods; it had enacted multiple barriers to keep our products out. In fact, in 1993, US exports to China were only 2.12 percent of our total exports around the world. But our trade deficit with China—how much we were importing compared to our exports—would rise from less than $6 billion in 1989 to $26.1 billion in 1993, a fourfold increase. And it wasn't simply lower-cost goods such as toys and clothing that were coming to our shores in container ships from across the Pacific. It was guns, specifically deadly assault rifles, manufactured by the People's Liberation Army (which had conducted the Tiananmen massacre) and sold in the US at rock-bottom prices of $55.95 for the SKS semiautomatic.

From 1987 until 1994, of all the rifles imported by the United States, 42 percent came from China. In fact, when the numbers were added together, China was responsible for exporting almost one million rifles to the United States—more than the total number of such weapons built by all US manufacturers combined in 1992. I stated that with China policy, the US was facing a choice—"ideals v. deals"—and I believed that the US had to hold firm. At the end of the lunchtime discussion between Senator Baucus and me, when the Press Club president gave each of us our "thank-you" ceramic coffee mugs for participating, he joked, "You can either throw [them] at each other or toast each other." That summed up the divide.

At the end of May 1994, President Clinton suddenly reversed course and decided to de-link trade and progress on human rights, which was a tremendous disappointment. President Clinton renewed China's trade privileges, despite the fact that there had been next to no progress on human rights (although he did ban the importation of Chinese-made guns and ammunition). But outside of weapons, he did not even single out products that were clearly being made by prison labor, which was wrong and unfair to American workers.

Everything, it seemed, was fair game when it came to trade. In addition to the president's economic advisors having argued that trade and human rights should not be linked, they persisted, wrongly, in saying that, in essence, further opening US markets to Chinese goods would promote free markets and democracy and decrease Chinese militarism. We were told that having better trade relations would lead to less theft of intellectual property, even though the Chinese government still was one of the biggest violators of those laws. We were told that China's leadership would be helpful in containing any threats from the hard-line, closed Communist nation of North Korea even as it became a nuclear power. Thirty years later, it is all too clear that these prospects of fundamental change were little more than self-serving rationalizations on the part of corporate America.

What the supporters of unrestricted China trade missed was that the trade was very one-sided. China's manufacturers were dominating our markets; the US was paying China in US dollars to purchase goods—and the Chinese government was then turning around and using that foreign exchange to buy support from other countries. For example, the Chinese government used US dollars to buy European products. Then, after getting the European nations "hooked" on Chinese trade, China's government reversed course and started selling far more to Europe than it bought from European nations, creating a ballooning trade deficit with those nations as well. By contrast, when Japan's foreign trade with the US was at a deficit of a 2- or 3-to-1 ratio, critics were hollering about Japan's unfair dominance. But as China started running a far bigger deficit throughout the 1990s—from 4- or 5-to-1—the silence from corporate America was deafening.

The most recent trade deal, negotiated by the Trump administration, committed China to purchase an additional $200 billion in exports by December 31, 2021. But according to the Peterson Institute for International Economics, none of those purchases happened; instead, China ultimately bought less from the US than it had before Donald Trump's 2018 trade war.

In Congress, year after year, our coalition continued to push for trade consequences for the Chinese government's treatment of its citizens, including the people of Tibet. We introduced multiple forms of legislation to do so. We also wanted to shine a spotlight on Chinese dissidents. One of the things that repressive regimes and authoritarians like to tell political prisoners is that no one remembers you, you do not matter, just give up and confess to our fake charges. We wanted the Chinese dissidents and the world to know that we had not forgotten them. Those of us who cared passionately about Chinese human rights would say the names of the dissidents on the House floor and in public venues to give them visibility and to say, We care. And we never failed to give lists of prisoners' names to Chinese government officials, when we visited or when they came to the US.

Despite the ongoing human rights abuses, the embrace of China by key sectors of official Washington continued. In 1998, Congress, encouraged by the administration, voted to change the name of China's trade status designation from most-favored-nation to "normal." Part of the argument made was that each year, when MFN came up for renewal, I had continued to win congressional support for repealing MFN in part because of its special privilege–sounding name—so changing the name of this trade status would help neutralize the yearly congressional opposition. "Normal," after all, was a far less intimidating word than the term "most-favored." Two years later, in 2000, a majority in Congress was persuaded to give the Chinese government "permanent normal trade relations" (PNTR). This new designation meant that there would no longer be a yearly debate on the country's trade status. The issues of human rights for Chinese citizens and an end to repression in Tibet would be ignored.

This change in trade status did more than simply try to diminish any emphasis on human rights, however. As multiple economists and analysts have argued, the granting of PNTR began the process that allowed many US manufacturing supply chains, from pharmaceuticals to electronics and technology, to move out of America and into China. PNTR linked greater swaths of the US economy and businesses directly to China. At the same time, rather than enrich the average Chinese person, many of the economic gains from these new markets and this new wealth went to a small, privileged, and politically connected class in China. And, again, the openings and liberalizations that had been promised and predicted did not occur.

The Sad Suppression of Hong Kong

One of the sad parts of this tale is what happened to the territory of Hong Kong, which the British delivered into Chinese governmental control in 1997 after their ninety-nine-year lease on most of the territory expired. The Chinese government had promised to maintain one nation, two systems, in Hong Kong—allowing the British-initiated liberties to remain and upholding what was known as Basic Law. But instead, China's leadership cracked down, limiting freedom of speech, freedom of the press, and freedom of assembly—and targeting anyone who attempted to dissent. As Chris Patten, the last British governor of Hong Kong, said in an interview with Radio Free Asia in 2022, "The Chinese had promised that it [Basic Law] would continue for fifty years. They've broken their word, as I'm afraid they do regularly. They break their word. They break international treaties whenever it suits them."

Ultimately, it was clear that China's leaders sought to diminish Hong Kong, particularly as a center of commerce. Instead, it was thought that the leaders wanted that role to go to its mainland city of Shanghai, as a source of national pride. But the impact was a brain drain from Hong Kong to Singapore and other parts of the world. Even those who have remained in Hong Kong often keep a foot somewhere else.

In 2019, the situation for Hong Kong residents deteriorated even further. As many as two million residents took to the streets to protest Chinese changes to their laws. Police deployed tear gas and rubber bullets and beat the protesters with batons. As the protests mounted, President Donald Trump was slated to meet with President Xi in Japan during the G20 Osaka Summit for industrialized nations. For another purpose, President Trump called me when he landed in Asia. I asked him, "Have you seen what's happening in Hong Kong? Twenty-five percent of the people of Hong Kong are in the streets." (Donald Trump has always been interested in the size of crowds.) I knew better than to directly ask him to raise the protests in Hong Kong with Xi, but I did ask the president to tell Xi that in the House and the Senate, Democrats and Republicans were united in their concern about the Uyghur minority in northwest China. About one million Uyghurs had been rounded up and detained in camps to be ethnically cleansed by the Chinese government. After the meeting, President Trump reported back to me that when he asked President Xi about the Uyghurs, Xi had responded, "Those people like being in those camps." To which I replied, "That's what authoritarians always say."

By 2020, in Hong Kong, the Chinese authorities had silenced the protesters. Under Hong Kong's new national security law, you can be deported to Beijing for trial if you are accused of a crime. The law is sweeping and impacts the most basic tenets of freedom of expression; violators are held in solitary confinement. (In March 2024, the authorities amended the law to increase the restrictions and punishments, including life imprisonment. The promise of "one country, two systems" continues to be obliterated.)

The Chinese government wasted no time in putting the harsh new laws into practice. In January 2021, fifty-three pro-democracy politicians were arrested for the "crime" of "subversion." They had been involved in a public opinion poll. I have a difficult time even referring to the national security law as a law—it is as bad as an edict can be, and its impact on Hong Kong is chilling. I often think of the ordinary citizens who in 1991 thanked our congressional delegation so profusely for honoring the Tiananmen Square protesters, six years before the British turnover. In just twenty years, the Chinese government had betrayed the international community and dismantled the rule of law and respect for human rights that the territory had long enjoyed. But make no mistake, the spirit of democracy remains strong in Hong Kong, as so many brave people continue to protest in small ways at great risk, including with candlelight vigils to commemorate the victims of Tiananmen.

Championing Tibet

The suffering in Hong Kong is, sadly, not surprising to those of us who have followed Chinese government repression in Tibet. When I was a new member of Congress, I had the deep honor of meeting the Dalai Lama, the spiritual leader of the Tibetan Buddhists. The story of Tibet is heartbreaking.

More than seventy years of military occupation have left Tibet fighting to save its culture, language, and religion. In 1959, when he was only twenty-three years old, the Dalai Lama was forced to flee Tibet for India as Chinese troops closed in on the Potala Palace, the winter residence of the Dalai Lamas since 1649, perched at 12,139 feet, the highest palace in the world. In the years that followed, thousands of Tibetan monasteries were destroyed. More than one million Tibetans were killed under Chairman Mao during the Cultural Revolution, and today, Tibetan monks and nuns are heavily monitored by the Chinese state. Those who disagree with the official party line are subject to torture and arrest.

After Tiananmen Square, we brought together Chinese student dissidents and Tibetan dissidents so that they could find allies in each other. The Chinese students had not been raised to understand Tibet, but after they met, many student activists found that they had common ground with the Tibetans. Both were seeking the same goal: freedom of expression. Notable actors and musicians—Richard Gere, the Beastie Boys, and others—took up the cause. I remember being on an Air Force One flight with President Clinton when I overheard him say, "We have to do something about Tibet—Hollywood is really on my case." Starting in 1996, the Beastie Boys (particularly Adam Yauch, the band's late singer) galvanized other top musical acts to join them at concerts around the world for freedom in Tibet. "FREE TIBET" T-shirts were seen on college campuses, and Tibet was a significant issue of conscience in many parts of the US, with Washington's corridors of power and the White House as the notable exceptions.

US presidents have a long tradition of meeting with the Dalai Lama, and President Clinton was no exception. The president promised His Holiness that he would set up a meeting for him with China's leaders. In return, he wanted him to abandon any support for conditioning the Chinese government's preferential trade status on human rights in China. The Chinese student dissidents were deeply disappointed by this development, and it was a devastating blow to attempting to hold China accountable. Also deeply disappointing was that this promised meeting between the Dalai Lama and Chinese leaders never happened. Instead, the

Chinese engaged in some low-level discussions that have gone no-where so far.

I am proud that in October 2007, after I had become Speaker, Congress awarded the Dalai Lama the Congressional Gold Medal, the highest civilian award we can bestow. Sen. Dianne Feinstein, my dear friend and colleague from California, sponsored the reso-lution. President George Bush came to the Capitol Rotunda to join in the presentation of the award. We were so pleased that he at-tended, especially because he was joined by First Lady Laura Bush. In his remarks, President Bush noted that "as a young boy in Tibet, His Holiness kept a model of the Statue of Liberty at his bedside. Years later, on his first visit to America, he went to Battery Park in New York City so he could see the real thing up close. On his first trip to Washington, he walked through the Jefferson Memorial." He added, "All of us are drawn to a noble and spiritual leader who lives a world away. Today we honor him as a universal symbol of peace and tolerance, a shepherd for the faithful, and the keeper of the flame for his people." President Bush spoke with true respect and drew the wrath of the Chinese government. He has told me that for years afterward, he has "taken heat" from China for at-tending the medal presentation. Thank you, President Bush.

In Tibet, Buddhist monks who celebrated the Dalai Lama's award were detained by the Chinese.

The award carried extra meaning because it came in advance of the 2008 Summer Olympics, which China was hosting in Bei-jing. Rep. Tom Lantos, chair of the Foreign Affairs Committee, Rep. Chris Smith, and I had opposed the choice of location. We wanted our statements, speeches, and resolutions around the Olympics to stand as a reminder that we would not be taking the focus off China. To underscore that point, in March 2008, I trav-eled to Dharamshala, India, where the Dalai Lama and some one hundred thousand Tibetan refugees lived in exile. Although this visit had been planned for months, the Friday before I arrived, protests had broken out in the Tibetan capital of Lhasa; the protesters were ruthlessly crushed by the Chinese, leaving as many as 140 dead. The Chinese premier blamed the Dalai Lama for the "unrest" and was furious with my subsequent visit to the Tibetan refugees' "capital in exile" in India.

When I became House Speaker, the Chinese leadership reached out to say that they wanted a fresh start. I was invited to visit. (I had insisted upon traveling to India to see the Dalai Lama before I traveled to China to meet with Chinese leaders.) I accepted the invitation in 2009, traveling to China a week before the twenty-year observance of the Tiananmen massacre. The primary topic of our meetings in Beijing was climate change and the importance of US-China cooperation. Our hosts treated our delegation as if it were on a head-of-state visit, closing streets and extending exclusive hospitality into the walled Forbidden City, the vast imperial palace complex and lush gardens built for the Chinese emperors in the 1400s. I hand-delivered a letter to then-president Hu Jintao, calling for the release of political prisoners, and I met with dissidents in Hong Kong. And in the meetings with Chinese leaders, I brought up Tibet.

But as the Chinese government began to draw tighter restrictions on Hong Kong, it also did much the same to Tibet. By 2010, the Chinese government had begun overhauling the school curriculum in Tibet and trying to erase the Tibetan language. The next step to further eradicate the culture was to promote intermarriage between Tibetans and Han Chinese, whom the Chinese government was sending in large numbers to Tibet. In protest, Tibetan monks began setting themselves on fire. China's leaders responded by sending more troops into the region.

In 2015, when President Xi traveled to the United States, he met with a group of leaders in the Capitol. Senator Feinstein and I were in the meeting, and we brought up the subject of Tibet.

President Xi told us that things were going very well in Tibet. He said that the Tibetans were very happy with what was going on. Perhaps wanting to preempt additional criticism, he suggested that I visit and see for myself how great things were. I replied: "Mr. President, thank you. I've been trying to get a visa to Tibet for twenty-five years. I'm happy to go."

The term "Potemkin village" dates from the 1700s and the rule of Russian empress Catherine the Great—Grigory Potemkin was a Russian military commander and Catherine's lover. When Empress Catherine and a group of diplomats embarked on a tour of "New Russia," Potemkin ordered that the villages they would go to be decorated and made to look outwardly beautiful to impress the dignitaries. In many ways, my visit to Tibet was the equivalent of stepping into a Chinese Potemkin village. When we visited a family home, one of the first things we saw was a massive picture of President Xi that took up nearly an entire wall. We listened politely as the older couple who presumably resided in the house told us how "wonderful" everything was in Tibet. Around the home, we also saw photos of grandchildren. When the couple's grown daughter came home and we asked about the children in the photos, her response was, "What children? I don't have any children." The pictures were fake. Those photos were an apt metaphor for the entire visit. Xi was very proud when he told me that the authorities had regilded the roof of the Buddhist temple in Lhasa. What Xi perhaps did not appreciate was that I don't care about how shiny the roof of a temple is. I care about the hearts and minds of the Tibetan children. It was heartbreaking to see this beautiful region and culture be so undermined.

Inside the Potala Palace where His Holiness grew up, and in the temples and monasteries where we saw the lamas, Tibetan monks, studying, there was not a single book by or about the Dalai Lama. Our Chinese minders followed us closely; nevertheless, everywhere we went, we made it a point to mention the Dalai Lama. Later, Congressman Jim McGovern of Massachusetts, whom I called the spiritual leader of our visit, thanked President Xi and told him that we had been shown "a lovely Potemkin village."

Years earlier, during one of my visits to Beijing, the foreign affairs committee of the People's Congress (China's unitary governing body) hosted an official lunch in honor of our delegation. The location they chose was the Tibet Room inside the Great Hall of the People. Every inch of the available wall space is covered with some facet of Tibetan culture. During my remarks, I mentioned how this room praised and honored the culture of Tibet—and how ironic it was that outside of this beautiful room, the government was attempting to destroy Tibetan culture. It would be an understatement to say that my words did not go over well, but my point was made. My rift with the Chinese leadership over Tibet is a long-standing one.

Why has the Dalai Lama inspired such devotion around the world for more than six decades? As he approaches his ninetieth birthday, I think of a visit to India in 2017. We had a large bipartisan delegation in attendance. His Holiness invited me to sit with him while he listened to reports of Tibetans who had fled that week across the border into India. Together, we heard reports of the torture of nuns and monks, and listened as these new refugees cried and bore witness. When I spoke to the crowd assembled outside, I expressed criticism of China. I discussed how moving it had been to listen to the testimony of the Tibetans who had fled to safety in exile. Then our delegation headed inside for a private lunch with more than one hundred young lamas.

At the lunch, the Dalai Lama spoke: "We have a conflict with China, but we respect even the hard-core Communists—we look at them with compassion. We can set an example to the world that nonviolent struggle can work. If we had fought our struggle with violence, we would not have as many friends as we do now." He introduced me, and I repeated some of my remarks about the Chinese government's cruelty, introduced our bipartisan delegation, and promised that we would help the Tibetans. Again, I said to them: If we do not speak out against human rights abuses in China because of commercial interests, we lose all moral authority to speak out against human rights abuses anywhere.

After my speech, His Holiness thanked me and added, for everyone in the room: "We must pray for Nancy so that we rid her of her negative attitudes." That one act speaks volumes about why so many around the world continue to embrace the Dalai Lama's message of peace: he believes in peace and compassion even for adversaries. He wants actions to be motivated by positive associations, not negative ones. But try as I may to follow his guidance, to rid myself of negative attitudes, to be a positive warrior for Tibet, I cannot stay silent about how the Chinese authorities use economic leverage and brutality to silence the voices of Tibet's friends.

As I said during that visit, "We're not going away. We can do this slowly. We can do it long. We will not be silenced. The Dalai Lama will not be silenced."

This is why, despite all the pressure, I knew it was so important to go to Taiwan in 2022, the first time a Speaker of the US House of Representatives had traveled to the country in twenty-five years.

Standing Firm on Taiwan

Taiwan is truly beautiful. It is a dynamic, young, vital, fabulous place whose residents have great concern for the environment. It has also struggled to overcome its own dictatorial past and build a representative democratic government.

I remember my first visit, in 1999, for the twentieth anniversary of Congress's passage of the Taiwan Relations Act. It was particularly memorable for the incredible food, because so many of the great chefs had fled the mainland to escape the iron rule of Chairman Mao. When I returned to the US, I held a press conference. I was shocked at the number of media outlets in attendance. But the press was not there because they cared about the well-being of the Taiwanese people after a recent devastating earthquake—instead, their questions centered on when factories and key manufacturing would be fully up and running again.

The factories did return, and today Taiwan is a vital economic powerhouse. This small country produces more than 90 percent of the world's most advanced semiconductor chips. In fact, after Congress passed the CHIPS Act in July 2022 to bolster our domestic technology production, the Taiwan Semiconductor Manufacturing Company pledged to invest some $40 billion in a US chip "fab," or factory, led by entrepreneur Morris Chang, who was a special guest at a luncheon that then-president Tsai Ing-wen hosted for our delegation.

President Tsai graciously welcomed our entire delegation and presented me with a lovely award, the Order of Propitious Clouds with Special Grand Cordon. She is so strong and remarkable, and she has been undeterred by Chinese government threats. She arranged meetings for us on security and the economy. And we also met with the opposition. Some of Taiwan's democracy advocates wanted our delegation to see the National Human Rights Museum. In the beginning, Taiwan had its own challenges with the suppression of democracy. The island spent thirty-eight years under martial law. We saw the prison cells where the authorities kept people who spoke out for democracy. Our guides gave me books and talked about the fight to democratize their government. At the museum, I also had the opportunity to see my old friend Wu'er Kaixi, one of the student leaders of the 1989 Tiananmen Square protests. I also met with Lam Wing-kee, a Hong Kong bookseller who had published works critical of the Chinese Communist Party; Lee Ming-che, a Taiwanese activist who had spent five years imprisoned in China; and Chen Chu, who was imprisoned in a 1979 crackdown and would rise to become chairwoman of Taiwan's Human Rights Commission and president of the Control Yuan, a branch of the Taiwanese government.

It is important to recognize that, as with human rights in China, support for Taiwan has bipartisan backing. When President Tsai visited the US in 2023, Kevin McCarthy, then the new House Speaker, invited her to meet with him. He held a bipartisan event at the beautiful Ronald Reagan Presidential Library in Simi Valley, California. Once again, China's leaders rattled their sabers, complaining, threatening, and issuing sanctions against the event.

But those of us in Congress who care about Taiwan know how important our voices and support are. On that August 2022 trip to the island, every member of the delegation was grateful for and appreciative of how we were received. A bipartisan delegation of senators had traveled to Taiwan a short time before us. But the Chinese authorities were fixated on my group, in large measure because I had been opposed to so many of their actions and policies for decades. After my efforts to keep the spotlight on them, China hoped it could turn the tables and stare me down.

In January 2024, Taiwan demonstrated the vitality of its democracy by holding a free and fair election. There was a large turnout, and voters chose Lai Ching-te as their new president. Taiwan's importance and value can also be seen in the many contributions of Taiwanese in America, including Morris Chang and Nvidia cofounder Jensen Huang, a leader in artificial intelligence.

Some in the foreign policy establishment still consider me a thorn in their side when it comes to China. The DC lawyers and lobbyists—many on the payroll of the Chinese government—have thanked me for sending their children to college. But if I do say so immodestly, my knowledge of China is second to none in Congress: I've spent at least an hour every day for three decades doing my homework on China, reading and consuming information on issues from human rights to nuclear proliferation to trade. At one point, my dear colleague Jack Murtha even suggested that I do my reading in the morning and not at night because I was losing too much sleep over what I was reading. But every statement our coalition has put out, every speech we have made, every piece of legislation we fought for, every trip we took, and every dissident's name we have ever spoken—it all makes a difference.

I just didn't fully appreciate how much until I was invited to a dinner in San Francisco in November 2023. The night before, a large banquet had been held for President Xi. That banquet had been arranged for Xi's California visit to participate in the Asia-Pacific Economic Cooperation summit, and its guest list read like a who's who of the US titans of tech and industry, some of whom paid $50,000 to sit at Xi's table.

But this San Francisco dinner took place after Xi departed the city. It was attended by many of the same industry leaders and was hosted by Marc Benioff, the head of the software company Salesforce. The evening's speaker was Stanford University's

Dr. Fei-Fei Li, a Chinese-born American and a highly respected expert on artificial intelligence.

As she stood to give her presentation, much to Marc's and my surprise, she began by saying, "Before I present, I see that Speaker Pelosi is here, and I want to note that I would not be in the US and be here tonight without legislation passed by Speaker Pelosi." She went on to explain that my legislation to welcome and protect Chinese people in the US after Tiananmen had allowed her and her mother to emigrate to join her father when Professor Li was sixteen. "Our family is so grateful to her," she said.

When her presentation was over, I went up to thank her and asked her if she would like to meet Secretary of State Antony Blinken. She told Secretary Blinken her expanded story, and how pivotal my support for Chinese exiles and human rights has been, adding again, "We are constantly grateful." I turned to Secretary Blinken and said, "Now you know why the Chinese don't like me."

And I've never been prouder to have earned an entire government's scorn, because that means I've made a difference in the lives of individual people who deserve to speak, write, gather, think, worship, and most of all live without fear.

The Tiananmen Square massacre is a moment that challenged the conscience of the world and, thirty-five years later, continues to do so. The spirit of Tiananmen, of June 4th, endures—in the hearts and minds and actions of those continuing the struggle, both in China and around the world. We know that the spirit of Tiananmen is alive and well, in part because China's leaders live in fear of it every day. That's why they have their security cameras, censorship of the internet, and obsession with trying to prevent the Chinese people from learning the truth.

Tiananmen gave us one of the most enduring images of the twentieth century, one that will forever be seared into our collective consciousness: the picture of a lone man standing before a tank on June 5, the day after the massacre. His was an unforgettable act of courage, of sacrifice, of defending human dignity. In my congressional office, I have a large posterboard photograph of "Tank Man" that I regularly use during floor speeches to commemorate Tiananmen. It was signed by the dissidents I met with during my time in Congress, and it is one of my most cherished symbols of our work together on human rights in China.

Leadership to Meet Domestic Challenges

"We Won't Have an Economy on Monday"

"Why Am *I* Calling *You*?"

The House Democratic leadership usually met on Monday to discuss important bills coming to the floor and issues for that week: health care or tax policy, or the wars in Afghanistan or Iraq. But on Thursday, September 18, 2008, we convened a special meeting. Our eyes were relentlessly trained on the turmoil on Wall Street.

Just four days earlier, on Sunday, September 14, two major Wall Street firms had collapsed. Bank of America had formally agreed to buy and save Merrill Lynch, the world's largest retail brokerage, for $50 billion. Merrill was overburdened with debt and had lost more than 40 percent of its value in three months. But Lehman Brothers, the fourth-largest investment bank in the United States, unable to secure a buyer, had filed for bankruptcy in the early hours of September 15. By Tuesday afternoon, the Federal Reserve was offering to extend a two-year, $85 billion bailout to the insurance giant AIG, hoping to stave off its bankruptcy. That bailout would ultimately cost more than $180 billion.

By the time I gathered with my team in the Speaker's Conference Room, a stately corner suite on the second floor of the Capitol, the only topic on everyone's mind was the latest financial news. With the Department of the Treasury leading the response, everyone in the room wanted to hear directly from Secretary of the Treasury Hank Paulson.

Secretary Paulson had joined the Bush administration a few months before the 2006 election, which handed control of the House and Senate to the Democrats. When I was elected House Speaker, he briefed me regularly, providing updates on the financial markets and the overall financial system, and we had also worked together on a comprehensive tax reform package, which addressed the needs of very-low-income Americans. We had built mutual trust during that process. In the deliberations surrounding the 2008 financial crisis, I always knew that Hank Paulson was speaking for the president, which I welcomed.

Seeing how rapidly the financial situation was deteriorating, and knowing the potential risk that an offhand comment by a member of Congress could further undermine the stock market, I told our party leadership team that I would call the secretary and ask him to brief the entire Democratic leadership the next morning. As I placed the call, I looked at my watch—it was exactly 3:00 p.m. Given the chaos and everyone's busy calendars, I decided to arrange a meeting for 9:00 a.m. the next day.

The secretary immediately took my call, and Hank's response was nothing short of stunning: "Madam Speaker, tomorrow morning will be too late." To which I replied, "Then why am *I* calling *you*?"

Why hadn't he called me? My impression from his response was that the White House was not eager or ready to inform Congress of how severe the country's financial situation had become. Perhaps they believed they could contain the damage and ride out the problems quietly, possibly not revealing the true extent of the collapse until after the November presidential election.

To his credit, Secretary Paulson did not duck my question. "You're the Speaker of the House. I'm the secretary of the Treasury. You're asking me, and I'm telling you what's happening." He said that we were facing a meltdown of our entire system. Where I had begun our conversation thinking that the worst-case scenario was maybe one bank failure, I instead left knowing something far grimmer.

It was clear that we needed to convene a meeting—immediately.

Hank and I agreed that he would come to Capitol Hill at 5:00 p.m. Next, I called the chairman of the Federal Reserve, Ben Bernanke, who immediately agreed to attend. Apparently the White House was less than pleased. Soon after, I heard that the internal reaction at 1600 Pennsylvania Avenue was: "Who said *she* could call a meeting?"

I let the White House know that the Speaker of the House said she could call the meeting—and that they could send whomever they pleased. In Washington, the unwritten rule is that the leader who hosts the meeting controls the agenda. If we were to meet at the White House, members of Congress would mostly speak only when called upon. But in the halls of the Capitol, members would have a stronger voice.

As the meeting took shape, the list of participants grew. The administration added Chris Cox, chairman of the Securities and Exchange Commission, and also staff from the Treasury, to report on their rapidly evolving plans. Congress would be represented by the leading Democratic and Republican leaders. Given what Hank had told me, I knew we would need to pass legislation ASAP, and for that to happen, we would need bipartisan support.

So congressional leaders on both sides were in attendance. But I did not want participants to attend simply because we needed votes. We needed far more—bipartisan input from representatives and senators with years of experience and expertise in crafting key legislation: Leaders John Boehner and Steny Hoyer and, from the Senate, Harry Reid and Mitch McConnell. We had key committee chairs and ranking members, including, from the House, Barney Frank and Republican Spencer Bachus, and, from the Senate, Democrat Chris Dodd and Republican Richard Shelby.

To accommodate the additional participants, we changed our start time to 7:00 p.m. The stakes could not have been higher.

After calling the meeting to order in the Speaker's Conference Room, I first recognized Secretary Paulson and asked him to give us a report on the meltdown. I knew the news that was coming and wanted the members to hear directly from Hank, just as I had. His description was of a financial crisis from the depths of hell. Dante himself could not have imagined or named a circle so deep and so horrible. We were not talking about the failure of just one or two banks but a meltdown of the entire system.

I turned to Chairman Bernanke and asked what he thought of the secretary's characterization. He replied: "If we don't do this tomorrow, we won't have an economy on Monday—including no commercial paper." Commercial paper is a short-term debt instrument with multiple uses, including allowing businesses to fund their payrolls or cover inventories and short-term bills. It is frequently purchased by money market accounts and is essential to the "Main Street" economy. If companies cannot move money, we have no economy.

Ben also gave us the grave message that it was only a matter of days before a global financial meltdown.

Personally, I felt like I had been kicked in the back by a mule. This was a crisis of almost incomprehensible proportions, one that would be catastrophic not only for Wall Street investment houses but also for millions of Americans and many others around the world.

Remember, this was Thursday evening. And the "Monday" message was coming from Ben Bernanke—the chairman of the Federal Reserve and a highly regarded expert on the Great Depression. In fact, it has been written that, in a meeting at the White House that afternoon, Chairman Bernanke told President Bush: "In terms of the financial system, we've not seen anything like this since the 1930s, and it could get worse."

Until that moment, I had kept my eyes largely fixed on Hank and Ben, but now as I surveyed the entire room, I saw the stunned and ashen faces of my colleagues. After hearing such explosive statements about our economy, no one interjected to offer a different opinion on the crisis. This was not the time for second-guessing or recriminations. The only question we could ask was, What do we do to move forward?

For almost two hours, that was the question we all wrestled with.

Warning Signs

It was unprecedented to hear the secretary of the Treasury speak of a system-wide meltdown and the Federal Reserve chair explicitly say that we risked "not hav[ing] an economy on Monday." But in fact, this financial collapse did not happen overnight. Multiple autopsies would be conducted in the wake of the 2008 financial crisis. The fuller story of its origins is jaw-dropping.

The first part of the story begins in the housing market. After the Great Depression and World War II, homeownership became an increasingly fixed part of the American dream. In the early

2000s, millions of homebuyers were targeted by predatory lenders who convinced them to take on debt they could not afford to repay, much of it in the form of adjustable-rate mortgages, whose interest rates and monthly payments were subject to substantial increases. Some mortgages were designed such that borrowers would make "interest-only" payments to lenders in the early years rather than paying down the principal they owed on the homes they had purchased. Many of these loans fell into a category known as subprime mortgages. They also contributed to this stunning statistic: the total debt loaned to and held by American households between the years 2001 and 2007 was nearly as large as the entire mortgage debt that was accumulated by US households throughout the previous history of our nation, from the time when mortgages first appeared in 1766 up to 2000. It took the US more than two hundred years of existence to pass $5 trillion in outstanding household mortgage debt in the late 1990s. By 2007, total US mortgage debt had reached $14.62 trillion, and it was still rising.

In the lead-up to 2008, many mortgage lenders also changed the way Americans bought homes. For years, when someone bought a house, they ordinarily applied for a mortgage locally, where they often knew their banker. But now these loans had been turned into commodities and were being sold to unknown buyers. As a result, some homeowners had no idea who their bankers were, and the bankers, lacking roots in the community, simply wanted a high rate of return on their purchase—or to get out if they weren't making enough money. Defaulting on a mortgage and foreclosure were problems that only impacted the bankers' balance sheets.

Predatory lending practices put homeowners at substantial risk, and the risk was magnified across the financial system when more and more Wall Street firms started buying these risky mortgages and bundling them together in financial instruments called mortgage-backed securities. The banks resold these products to investors in the US and around the world, deceptively peddling what they were selling as "high-yield, low-risk"—when in truth the defective underlying mortgages made these assets low-yield, high-risk. Wall Street worsened the problem by creating what they called collateralized debt obligations (CDOs). CDOs bundled separate, lower-rated mortgage-backed securities into one product—and sometimes this bundling miraculously resulted in AAA-rated securities. As Michael Mayo, a former Federal Reserve employee and a financial services analyst, later explained to the Financial Crisis Inquiry Commission: it was "a lot of cheap ingredients repackaged to sell at a premium."

But the reckless behavior did not stop there. Wall Street created and sold separate products known as credit default swaps. In theory, they represented protection against a decline in value, but they also allowed for speculation—betting against these mortgage securities—which ultimately only further compounded the risk.

As this high-wire financial act began to teeter, people lost their jobs—and thus their income to pay their mortgages. And the cost of many of those mortgages had risen because from 2004 to 2006 the Federal Reserve had raised interest rates, a standard practice to counteract inflation. But rising interest rates made adjustable-rate mortgages more expensive, which triggered defaults. Banks were left holding properties they could not sell, and this led to losses and a constant tightening of loans and credit, which further weakened the economy.

Cynically, once the housing market faltered and mortgage defaults began, some of the major promoters and sellers of these instruments pivoted. Goldman Sachs was a leader in this bad, and perhaps unlawful, behavior. They began to take the short side on credit default swaps—in other words, betting on mortgage securities to fail, often against their own clients. The prevailing mindset on Wall Street was IBGYBG—"I'll be gone, you'll be gone." Grab the big gains up front and get out before the big losses of the future.

How were these deceitful practices allowed? Under what has been called the blind eye of government regulators and financial industry leaders, a widespread ethos of deregulation had entered the financial system. In retrospect, one of the most catastrophic changes occurred in April 2004, when the Securities and Exchange Commission loosened something called the net capital rule.

Previously, financial institutions classified as broker-dealers and investment banks had to maintain a ratio of 12-to-1 debt to equity on their investments—meaning that they could not have a balance sheet of debts that exceeded twelve times their assets or equity. Now, firms with more than $5 billion in assets were leveraging themselves an unlimited number of times. Five of the firms that took advantage of this new rule were Bear Stearns, Lehman Brothers, Merrill Lynch, Goldman Sachs, and Morgan Stanley— and they began to routinely raise their leverage ratio to 30-to-1 (or even higher) on their investments. Those numbers might have worked if the investments had been sound, but they weren't. High-risk and highly risky investments were an unsustainable combination. Ultimately, none of these five firms would survive as independent investment banks. They collapsed, were sold, or became commercial banks.

So, come the fall of 2008, the risky choices made by multiple financial institutions and the slow dismantling of key pieces of meaningful regulation had corroded the integrity of our financial system, putting America on a collision course with crisis. Overnight, lenders began pulling the plug on short-term loans to financial institutions holding these assets. Banks were told they needed more collateral—or the loans would be called.

What many of us learned only much later was that in the days and even weeks leading up to our meeting on the night of September 18, the Federal Reserve had been quietly pouring money— tens of billions of dollars—into the financial markets to keep the markets sustained and to prevent further stock-value collapses. Congress was unaware that the Fed even had funds of that magnitude available for that purpose, as well as for the AIG bailout.

Though Secretary Paulson described it as a meltdown of the financial sector, everyone gathered in the Speaker's Conference Room knew that the upheaval on Wall Street would wreak havoc on communities and neighborhoods across the country—landing right on families' kitchen tables. And while the crisis stemmed in significant measure from the regulatory failures of the Bush administration, Democrats knew we had to solve this crisis in a bipartisan way, and as quickly as possible, to avoid further harm to America's working families.

Eventually, we would also need to take steps to make sure it never happened again—but first, we needed to deal with the catastrophe at hand.

"Break the Glass"

As the members and senators began to fully process what they had heard, they responded with many questions. In reply, Secretary Paulson told us that Treasury Department officials had studied various models and put together what they termed the "break-the-glass" plan. Because the plan's very title indicated a dire emergency, I was compelled to ask: Why hadn't they done this already? That's when the administration team incredibly told us that they were "saving it for the next president." In less than two months, voters would head to the polls, and on the Democratic side, we were overwhelmingly certain that Senator Barack Obama would win the election. I grew deeply concerned that the Bush administration was merely hoping to keep the economy on life support for six more weeks—and when the walls came tumbling down, it would be attributed to Obama's victory. The administration's answer injected a level of political negativity into a discussion that had up to now been bipartisan.

Nonetheless, we set politics aside and listened to Hank and the others present the administration's break-the-glass plan. Well-respected economist Alan Blinder, who had served on the Board of Governors of the Federal Reserve in the 1990s and is a professor at Princeton University, would note in his own book on the 2008 crisis that the break-the-glass plan was in fact drafted by an economist and an investment banker and finalized in April 2008. It was commissioned as a "contingency" plan after Bear Sterns nearly failed. But the Bush administration appeared to treat each new crisis more as an individual issue; Hank Paulson would later admit as much, writing that they were "using duct tape and baling wire to try to hold the system together." As Secretary Paulson explained the break-the-glass plan to us, he said that the Treasury needed both the money and the power to rescue the failing banks. It proposed to do so by buying hundreds of billions of dollars' worth of their toxic assets.

"Toxic assets." Those words struck me as the worst oxymoron I'd ever heard.

I opened the meeting up for additional discussion, beginning with Harry Reid. Harry's first question, and one he would continue to ask at regular intervals, was simply: How much will this plan cost—$100 billion? No, he was told. Ten minutes later, he asked, Will it be $200 billion? The answer was still no. By the time Senator Reid had reached a figure of $400 billion, Hank Paulson said that he was getting warmer.

"With all due respect, Mr. Secretary," I interjected, "'getting warmer' is how I speak with my grandchildren. That is not how the secretary of the Treasury responds to the leader of the United States Senate."

The secretary told us that he would give us the figure later. It would ultimately be far more than $400 billion.

Congressman Spencer Bachus raised an important question: Why couldn't we simply buy shares in the banks directly instead of purchasing their toxic assets? This proposal, known as capitalization, was supported by Barney Frank, the House Financial Services Committee chair, and had broad bipartisan support in the room. Given what Hank and Ben had said, it was clear that Congress would have to pass legislation as quickly as possible. I said that I was going to put it in our draft bill—not as a requirement or a prescription for how much the Treasury Department must do but as an authorization to use the money Congress was going to appropriate in that manner, should capitalization be the final decision.

The secretary's response to me was curt: "I don't want it in the legislation. I am not going to use it." I never did understand why Hank Paulson was so resistant to capitalization. Ironically, capitalization would be exactly the approach the administration eventually used. Significantly, others present raised questions about foreclosures and what could be done for homeowners.

Speaking for the Democrats, Barney Frank expressed support for restrictions on top executive pay for companies that would be receiving government money. Top investment banking executives were receiving millions and even tens of millions of dollars in salaries and bonuses. Barney did not want hard-earned taxpayer money to be used to subsidize the salaries of the individuals who had largely created this mess in the first place, and I agreed. He also pointed out that if members of Congress and the administration were going to persuade the public of the need for a rescue plan, there had to be recognition that CEO and executive compensation was a big problem.

To our disappointment, Secretary Paulson resisted the request, saying that if we restricted executive pay, some of the banks would refuse to participate in the rescue plan. In my view, this attitude was not necessarily the secretary's but a reflection of what he thought he could achieve. Barney would later say that the secretary's response was one of the worst statements about the personal values of the leaders of the financial community that he'd ever heard.

For everyone at that table, the purpose of that meeting was to arrive at a solution. Whatever our private reservations, that Thursday night, we knew we needed to have unity—and we did. There was near-unanimous agreement among the congressional leaders, and we stood together before the news media to deliver a brief, joint message. With the lone exception of Sen. Richard Shelby of Alabama, the ranking member on the Senate Banking Committee, the Democratic and Republican leadership agreed: we were going to move forward.

When it was my turn at the microphones, as the assembled media photographers' cameras clicked nonstop in the background, I said, "We just had what I believe was a very productive meeting where we heard from the administration and from the chairman of the Fed, an initiative to help resolve the financial crisis in our country. Our purpose is to do that and in doing so, to insulate Main Street from Wall Street and recognize our responsibility to the taxpayer, to the consumer, and to the people all across our country." All of us knew that, at the end of the day, we had to succeed. The only question was: When would the end of the day come?

The Administration's Proposal

About twenty-seven hours after our meeting had adjourned, at around the stroke of midnight on Friday, Secretary Paulson sent us a three-page draft proposal for the legislation that would eventually be called the Troubled Asset Relief Program. It came with a price tag of $700 billion.

This figure was astounding, nearly twice the amount we had been led to believe might be involved Thursday night. In 2008, the entire annual non-security-related, discretionary domestic budget of the federal government—including education, housing, agriculture, commerce, labor, some health care, scientific research, transportation, judiciary, energy, environment, and more—was about $346 billion. The administration was asking for double that—two years' worth of domestic investments. Democrats had no intention of handing over a $700 billion blank check to Wall Street and simply hoping for a good outcome.

Along with the massive dollar figure, the proposed legislative language from the Treasury Department gave the Treasury secretary sweeping and unprecedented power to disburse this funding at his discretion. One sentence made Secretary Paulson's decisions "non-reviewable"—"by any court of law or any administrative agency." This seemed more like an act of arrogance than a serious plan. Despite our respect for Secretary Paulson, we were not going to pass legislation that could not be reviewed by the courts or Congress. That was against the basic provisions of the Constitution.

After receiving the proposal, we set nearly all of it aside and began actual bipartisan conversations between Congress and the White House. One-hundred-page bills are routine for Congress—three pages represented a woefully incomplete effort. Democrats were committed to insulating Main Street from the crisis on Wall Street and to keeping people in their homes. For that reason, we insisted that the final legislation include greater accountability and oversight for any proposed spending—so that a bailout didn't give bankers a chance to cash in.

At one point, I thought back on the last two days: until I had called Hank Paulson, no one in the administration had shared the full extent of the crisis. Less than forty-eight hours later, they were more than requesting—they were saying that they must have $700 billion to prevent collapse. When had they intended to ask us for this money? What were they thinking? Barney and I have often wondered about the what-ifs from that September.

That weekend, I was back in California. Paul had undergone a hip operation at Stanford University Medical Center, and I had flown home to be with him. But the legislative work could not and did not stop. My task was to negotiate with administration officials and members of Congress and take calls from stakeholders while sitting in a hospital room that, like most, was busy and noisy, with nurses constantly coming in and out and an endless chorus of beeps and whirs of the machines in the background. Thankfully, Paul was asleep the whole time—as the House began the process of assembling a package to rescue the global economy.

Eventually I sought refuge by pacing the halls and outdoors, clutching my cell phone. I was deluged by calls from multiple titans of the financial world, each with differing views on the proposals being suggested for the draft bill—especially capitalization. Word had gotten out about my comments at the Thursday meeting—that I had said I would include, but not require, capitalization authority for the Treasury secretary in the bill. Some in the financial community agreed that capitalization should not only be in the bill but also be the recommended or even required course of action. Others argued that it would be a mistake to include it at all. Ironically, what both sides always seemed to agree upon was that the other side had its own agenda and was not acting in the public interest. Whichever party I was on the phone with at any given moment invariably said that they were thinking of the broader financial good. I listened respectfully to all points of view, amused that each caller thought the other side had an agenda while maintaining that they did not.

Four banks had serious challenges, including two investment banks, Morgan Stanley and Goldman Sachs. Over that weekend, they moved from being investment banks to bank holding companies. This change would afford them various protections under the law, such as a shield against certain financial losses and access to quick cash at the low interest rates available to commercial banks but not to Wall Street investment banks. It also put them under the broader supervision of the Federal Reserve and other government regulators, not the Securities and Exchange Commission. As the *New York Times* put it: "It was a blunt acknowledgment that their model of finance and investing had become too risky." When the banks were making big returns on risky investments, they were happy to avoid scrutiny and play by a very lax set of rules. But once they found themselves in a big financial hole, they came running to Washington to have the federal government, backed by the taxpayers, bail them out and protect them from their high-flying behavior. These were major financial institutions running and hiding from their mistakes and their exposure at tremendous cost to the rest of the economy and us.

Nor was it the first time Wall Street had engaged in this type of behavior, although the scale was unprecedented. As a member of what was then called the House Committee on Banking, Finance, and Urban Affairs, I had seen, again and again, that a self-serving Wall Street found a way to privatize gains while nationalizing risk. I don't want to paint every bank and banker with the same brush, and the financial services industry is important to America's economic well-being. But it is always imperative that we also protect depositors, taxpayers, and constituents—whose economic security has always been and will always be essential to America's economic strength and integrity. Being deemed "too big" should not automatically be a guarantee that, no matter how badly you mismanage your institution and your balance sheets, the system will not allow you to fail. Regrettably, the refrain for these banks became: too big to fail, too big to jail.

Legislating in a Time of Crisis

As the 2008 crisis grew, our legislative teams and staff were determined to draft a bill that would provide both funds and management. I'm a legislator at heart. For me, the only way to reach a sustainable solution is through collaboration as we legislate. There would be no break-the-glass solution to stanch the fallout from the collapse without a genuine bill. Working in a bipartisan way, we were making progress. John Boehner and I stated that our shared goal was basic good government principles—including, as we stated, rigorous and independent oversight, strong executive compensation standards, and protections for taxpayers.

I reminded members that we were facing an unprecedented crisis—it meant the loss of jobs, household wealth, and homes, and it wasn't just impacting one segment of the economy, it was the whole system. As Barney Frank said, "We, none of us, had experience with something of this magnitude." But we were determined to find a solution—and even though it required the input of multiple committees, we knew we needed to act quickly. The markets were following our every move.

On September 24, President Bush gave a speech to the nation on the financial crisis. I was pleased that he acknowledged the improvements that Congress had made to his administration's original proposal.

But it wasn't just the current White House in the picture. Our legislative negotiations came in the midst of a presidential campaign between Senators Barack Obama and John McCain. Hours before President Bush's speech, Senator McCain publicly suspended his campaign and called for a high-level meeting at the White House on the financial crisis. McCain had already called me personally to request that I participate in the meeting—he'd said that he had some suggestions. John and I had worked together to pass the McCain-Feingold Campaign Finance Reform Act in 2002, in my first leadership role as House Democratic whip, and we were friends. While we didn't always see eye to eye, John truly appreciated the necessity of hearing all sides in a debate. Even when we were not publicly in agreement, he would regularly come up to me and privately encourage me to "keep fighting these guys."

But on the phone, when he began by addressing me as "Madam Speaker" and not "Nancy," I knew that the call would be cold—and I'd have to call him "Senator," not "John." I assured him that we were on a very positive path to a bipartisan agreement. When he raised the subject of the meeting, I was unwilling to attend. The meeting itself seemed unnecessary. But President Bush's chief of staff, Josh Bolten, called me repeatedly to say that it was important to the president that I come. So I reluctantly agreed.

The White House Meeting

The meeting was held in the White House Cabinet Room on Thursday, September 25. Harry Reid and I strategized beforehand about what our approach would be in order to maximize the prospect of passing the most responsible legislation. The Republicans had also been planning; they held a meeting in the Oval Office with President Bush directly before our larger bipartisan meeting in the Cabinet Room. In the Oval, the president had said bluntly to everyone, including John Boehner, "We've got to get this done"— but Boehner would note that he had to admit that he didn't have sufficient support among his members to pass the president's current proposal. Hank Paulson had realized something very similar when he'd met with Republicans on Capitol Hill. So much for a Republican strategy for responsible legislation. It would require the commitment of Democrats to pass this legislation.

Our meeting in the Cabinet Room included Vice President Dick Cheney, Secretary Paulson, John Boehner, and Mitch McConnell. The other participants included many of the same faces from our earthshaking meeting the previous Thursday, and of course the two presidential candidates, Senators Obama and McCain.

President Bush opened the meeting, as always, graciously: establishing that we had a common goal and needed to work as quickly as possible to get the job done. When he finished, he asked Secretary Paulson to describe the situation. Again, Hank described the devastating meltdown and the urgency of the situation requiring a solution.

As is protocol, the president then turned to recognize the Speaker of the House for comments. I thanked the president for holding the meeting—and added that, recognizing the urgency, and in the interest of time, Harry Reid and I had agreed that the Democrats would yield our time to Senator Obama. Everyone was stunned. Congressional leaders never give up a chance to present their views during a meeting with the president.

Surprised, the president asked: "Is that right, Harry?" Reid simply said, "Yes, Mr. President."

Senator Obama spoke briefly and eloquently. He was gracious to President Bush, and respectful of the urgency and responsibility, and he pointed out some thoughtful adjustments to the proposal that were needed to better protect taxpayers and homeowners. "But since Senator McCain called for this meeting," he said, "I think it's important to hear from him."

Senator McCain presented some points about executive pay and oversight, and he said he thought that consensus could be reached. But the overall impression was that he didn't have a plan or proposal to present in a meeting that he had called for. With McCain's hesitancy, the room's decorum crumbled. Attendees started talking over each other, trying to be heard.

Finally, the president stood up and said: "I think I've lost control of the room. This meeting is over."

A few minutes later, the Democrats gathered inside the nearby Roosevelt Room to review what had happened. Secretary Paulson approached our Democratic huddle hopefully. Whether to be humorous or in desperation, he walked up to me and dropped to one knee. He was, as he described, "genuflecting at the altar of the Speaker of the House."

"Gee, Hank," I quipped, "I didn't know you were Catholic."

"Please don't blow up the deal," he pleaded.

"It's not me blowing this up," I told him. "It's your side."

But even I did not fully realize at the time how prophetic those words were—as the House Republicans would vote overwhelmingly against TARP.

Senator McCain had expressed reservations about TARP earlier in the week, but responsibly, the following night, Friday, neither McCain nor Obama took aim at TARP as a political target during the presidential debate. As we continued our negotiations on Saturday, however, considerable challenges remained.

Much of the conversation on the Democratic side focused on our concern for providing relief for homeowners—especially to prevent foreclosures and their disastrous impacts on families, communities, and our economy. House Democrats, led by Barney Frank, included authorization for the administration to use some of the TARP funding for homeowner relief. Barney thought that he had convinced Secretary Paulson to include homeowner relief in the second tranche of TARP funding. Unfortunately, it was not elevated in importance by the Bush administration, which resisted attempts to modify the terms of residential mortgages.

Many of my members and I had also wanted to include bankruptcy protections in the text of the bill. We thought that the ability to declare bankruptcy would give homeowners leverage with their banks against foreclosure. Without it, lenders—now practically anonymous—could foreclose with ease and without care. Heavy opposition from the financial sector ultimately kept bankruptcy protections out of the final bill. To this day, it is still opposed by banks.

But we were seasoned negotiators, and we brought every skill we had to the table, knowing we had to craft a piece of legislation that would do the job and be supported by both sides—immediately.

Leaders from the House, the Senate, and the administration reconvened in the Speaker's Conference Room on Saturday, September 27. Our focus quickly centered on negotiating provisions related to executive compensation—including the infamous golden parachutes, which provided generous bonuses, perks, and benefits for departing executives—as well as determining how to conduct oversight of the entire TARP initiative, and the timing and tranches for how the funding would be distributed.

As negotiations continued over the weekend, the House still had other pressing legislative business, requiring us to leave for votes. We passed an important civilian nuclear cooperation agreement with India, which had been a priority for me as Speaker. Immediately after, everyone was back at the table, trying to reach an agreement. We stayed late into the night, huddled in the conference room and other venues. We were all tired. Hank Paulson even got sick—"the dry heaves again," as he would say.

Respectful of various approaches, I pushed our group to compromise because we had to continue to work for an agreement for the American people. The urgency of the situation dominated our decision-making. We agreed to a basic deal on the distribution of the funds, restrictions on executive compensation, and strong oversight measures, with language accepted by all sides.

I had proposed an industry tax—to make the banks, not the taxpayers, pay for the relief—but it did not receive bipartisan support. Instead, we included an alternative plan to recoup our tax dollars from the financial services industry if the TARP funds were not recovered and the program ultimately generated financial losses for the taxpayers—who were the ones saving the banks. With the last details resolved, triumphantly, the six of us—Harry Reid, Chris Dodd (chair of the Senate Banking Committee), Barney Frank, Chuck Schumer, Hank Paulson, and I—walked

together into the Capitol's famed Statuary Hall and officially announced our agreement to the press.

But that did not mean that either chamber had the votes required to pass the bill.

First Vote: Monday, September 29

Knowing we had to act fast to calm the financial markets and
consumers, on Monday morning, we immediately prepared to
bring TARP to a vote on the House floor. But I was skeptical of
our success. I have never brought a bill to the floor unless I knew
for certain that it had the votes. As part of our negotiations, we
had agreed that, because Democrats were in the majority, we
would produce 120 votes and the Republicans would produce 100,
to be sure to reach the 218 needed to pass. These numbers and our
agreement were essential, not only to pass the legislation but especially to keep our promises to our rank-and-file members that
this would be a bipartisan bill.

I knew that the Democrats would honor our commitment of
120 votes. As always, I had the names of our members who had
pledged to vote yes. I told the Republicans and the White House
that I needed to see the names of the 100 Republican members
who had committed to voting for TARP.

They never showed us the list of names, likely because they
knew they didn't have the votes. But even then, the president said,
"Who would possibly vote against this?"

The truth, however, was that TARP would not be a popular vote for members of Congress. Democrats viewed the
meltdown as the result of the failed policies of the Bush administration, while many Republicans were opposed to regulation and

supervision—and even when the walls came tumbling down, they opposed intervention. They viewed the $700 billion TARP legislation as a major intervention into the financial markets.

But that morning both President Bush and Barney said that even without the 100 Republican names, we should bring up the bill—because it would be worse not to bring it up. Before the vote, our Democratic members met and expressed the obvious concern—that TARP looked like a bailout of Wall Street at the expense of Main Street. Most of my 120 members insisted that they could not vote for TARP unless I went to the House floor and laid the blame at the Republicans' doorstep. I promised them that I would describe how we got there.

I began by telling the entire chamber that I was "proud of the debate." I acknowledged that the $700 billion figure truly was staggering. And I did not shy away from publicly defining, both on the House floor and after for the press, why this crisis had befallen us.

> This is a crisis caused on Wall Street. But it is a crisis that reaches to Main Street in every city and town of the United States. . . .
>
> The American people did not decide to dangerously weaken our regulatory and oversight policies. They did not make unwise and risky financial deals. They did not jeopardize the economic security of the nation. And they must not pay the cost of this emergency recovery and stabilization bill. . . .
>
> Our message to Wall Street is this: the party is over. The era of golden parachutes for high-flying Wall Street operators is over. No longer will the US taxpayer bail out the recklessness of Wall Street.

How sadly unattainable. Somehow, Wall Street always found a way to continue its private party, no matter the consequences for everyone else.

We called for the vote and held it open for an extra forty minutes—a long time on the congressional clock. Most votes are fifteen minutes to thirty at most. I spent the entire time in and out of the chamber, standing on the floor, making sure that our Democrats who were voting for the bill showed up. But the Republicans never materialized. The nays exceeded 218, meaning that the TARP legislation had failed. The split-screen images playing across the television monitors in the rooms around the chamber were horrifying. As the House vote failed, ultimately by 228 to 205, the Dow dropped 777.68 points: at that time, it was the single largest intraday drop in the index's history.

After TARP failed to pass, Republican leaders in the House—Eric Cantor was one—tried to blame my speech. But the truth is, they never had the votes to begin with. To their credit, some Republicans were honest, admitting that their vote of no had nothing to do with Nancy Pelosi. They were honest about the fact that they did not believe in supervision or regulation; again, when the walls were about to come tumbling down, they opposed intervention. In my view, they were just staying true to their anti-government beliefs.

Barney Frank made a wonderful statement to the press—accusing Republicans of killing a bill in the national interest just because Nancy Pelosi "hurt their feelings." But the vote was not only a defeat of the bill. It undermined the bipartisan commitment to a carefully crafted plan. Not only did House Republicans refuse to rescue the American economy—they and the party would use it to attack our candidates in the 2010 election. Responsibly, that Monday, we put 140 Democrats on record in support of

TARP—Republicans mustered just 65 votes, with 133 voting no, well short of their promise of 100 votes.

Senate Vote: Wednesday, October 1

As we reviewed the wreckage stemming from the failed TARP vote, we realized that the legislation had to be sweetened to garner the necessary votes for it to pass. Rahm Emanuel, a member of the House Democratic leadership who had been part of the negotiating team, began working with Harry Reid to encourage the Senate to take up the bill forty-eight hours later—and include in it additional provisions for tax extenders, a mental health parity bill, and an increase in the amount of bank deposit insurance available to consumers, raising the total amount to $250,000 per bank.

Recognizing that the bill could not fail a second time, Harry Reid demonstrated his highly regarded effectiveness by requiring all senators to remain in their seats while the votes were cast. The Senate passed the amended TARP legislation by a solid bipartisan margin of 74–25. All eyes were back on the House.

Second House Vote: Friday, October 3

After Harry Reid passed the bill in the Senate, we felt confident in proceeding again to a House vote. We knew we could not depend on 100 Republican votes—but ultimately, we did increase support from members on both sides of the aisle. Rep. Louise Slaughter noted on the House floor that the stock market had lost more than $1 trillion on Monday, after the failed House vote, decimating people's retirement and college savings accounts—and that this stock market loss was far greater than the TARP rescue request.

But nothing was assured until the vote closed. We all worked hard, and I was especially grateful to Barney and Maxine Waters for their strategic whipping. At 1:22 p.m. on Friday, October 3, the House passed the TARP legislation, 263 to 171—with 172 Democrats voting yes but only 91 Republicans. Let the record show: the Republican side never was able to convince 100 members to vote yes, in either the first or second vote.

Within hours of its passage, the TARP legislation was placed on the Oval Office's Resolute desk, where President Bush signed it into law.

We knew TARP was only one step. Much more would be needed to stave off economic disaster, even in the short time before President Obama would become president. As Barney Frank told us: "TARP did not solve the crisis—but it did buy us time for a series of other measures to help keep the meltdown from being a worldwide depression."

Aftermath

Many financial institutions remained weak after the passage of TARP. And on Friday, October 10, the stock market bellwether, the S&P 500, recorded its worst week since 1933.

Late on Sunday, October 12—which was Monday, October 13, in England—I learned that the UK had decided to capitalize its banks: the very approach that we had raised in our emergency meeting on September 18, but which Secretary Paulson had rebuffed. After hearing the UK news, I thought, How long will it take for us to do the same?

Turned out it was not long. On Monday afternoon, I received a call from Secretary Paulson, who was informing congressional leaders that the United States was going to engage in a capital purchase program. He shared that he had carefully planned the capitalization program and, importantly, had convinced the big banks to accept it at a meeting that day—which was a major accomplishment. He never mentioned this proposal in our initial September meeting or the bipartisan support that it had then.

My members had wanted me to remind the secretary of this conversation—and our insistence on capitalization being included in this bill. And I did so. I never received any confirmation that the administration ever bought any toxic assets, but I am proud that our members provided a different break-the-glass proposal.

Members also wanted me to ask the secretary about the market collapse the week before. I told him that I had told them that if we didn't vote for the TARP bill, the market would collapse. They voted for it on October 3, and by October 10, the market had recorded the worst week since 1933.

Hank's answer was, "The market does that sometimes."

"Well, Mr. Secretary," I replied, "why is the market doing it *this* time?"

He said that Mitsubishi and Morgan Stanley were completing negotiations about a major purchase—21 percent of the firm— to help shore up Morgan Stanley's finances. It had taken several weeks, but the final agreement had been reached over the weekend. Sunday night, the secretary reported that he had received word that the deal was done. On Monday morning, Mitsubishi hand-delivered a check for $9 billion to Morgan Stanley in New York—likely the largest paper check ever written. With bank capitalization now finally on the table, the next change of course that we sought in response to the crisis related to housing assistance. A major disappointment for House Democrats in the enforcement of the TARP legislation was ignoring homeownership assistance. On November 17, Ben Bernanke and Hank Paulson came to my office. As Hank would later write, "Ben and I were once again sitting at Nancy Pelosi's long conference table surrounded by Democratic representatives and senators. Looking around the room, I saw no friendly faces." Given the level of cooperation that the administration needed—and received—from congressional Democrats, I'm not sure we were that unfriendly. But that was how Hank felt. And we did want accountability.

I got right to the point: "Don't you want to show those of us who voted for TARP that some of the money is going to foreclosure relief?" Hank didn't have a good answer, beyond saying that they would continue to work on loan modification plans to help reduce the number of foreclosures.

The next day, Hank appeared before Barney's Financial Services Committee—Hank himself recalled that while he had endured some "rough" hearings, "this was the toughest one chaired by Barney." Barney had many points he wanted to make and questions he wanted to ask, a strong example of House due diligence and oversight. His fellow committee members had questions too. Barney explicitly called for the Bush administration to use its authority to help homeowners facing foreclosures. He showed Hank four pages of excerpts from the TARP legislation—those pages authorized aggressive action by the administration on home foreclosures to provide true homeownership assistance. Maxine Waters added, "You, Mr. Paulson, took it upon yourself to absolutely ignore the authority and the direction that this Congress had given you."

Indeed, Democrats had repeatedly called upon the Bush administration to use the authority of the TARP legislation for homeownership assistance. But Hank took the position that this money was first and foremost for stabilizing the banks. After our work to pass comprehensive TARP legislation, that view was a big disappointment for us. And millions of American homeowners would pay a high price.

A New Day

In November, voters overwhelmingly chose Barack Obama to be their next president, and Democrats were poised to control the White House and both chambers of Congress. As I had said on the House floor during the debate before the first TARP vote: "And before long, we will have a new Congress, a new president of the United States, and we will be able to take the country in a new direction." Washington was infused with a new vision and values. In the House, we made it our mission to give leverage to workers, consumers, and taxpayers—not to the biggest corporations and the wealthiest few. And in January 2009, we quickly got to work.

Congressional Democrats were ready to deliver the stimulus package we believed our economy needed. The House Appropriations Committee—under the masterful, if often stern, leadership of Chairman Dave Obey—had already been working on a job-creation package, which would soon become the foundation of the American Recovery and Reinvestment Act (ARRA). It was significant in terms of scope—$787 billion—transformative in terms of policy, and essential in terms of the recovery of the country.

The recovery package passed in the House one week and one day after President Obama stood on the steps of the Capitol and declared, in his inaugural address, "The state of our economy calls for action, bold and swift . . . not only to create new jobs, but to lay a new foundation for growth." Less than two weeks later, it passed the Senate—with reduced investments from what we had designed in the House, but it was a strong package nonetheless. On February 17, President Obama signed the bill into law. Under his leadership, we enacted the ARRA in record time—because we knew that recovery was urgent.

The economic fallout had spread beyond the banking realm to the manufacturing sector, specifically the auto industry. Before Obama took office, Congress had been determined to rescue America's ailing auto industry. By December 2008, with the economy battered and fragile, two of the Big Three automakers, General Motors and Chrysler, needed $17 billion in loans to continue to operate. After the new Obama administration took office, Harry Reid and I worked closely with the Obama team for a more comprehensive rescue—not bailout—package. It was to be a lifeline for the industry to grow, not life support just to survive for a while. There were those who accused the government of bailing out the auto companies. But the fact was, we were not rescuing the Big Three; we were rescuing an important industry for our country.

In March, the new Treasury secretary, Tim Geithner, began an oversight program that included stress testing for the big banks. There were many lessons to be learned from the near collapse of our economy and the struggles with the TARP rescue plan, which could and would guide us going forward. And it was those lessons that we were determined to absorb so that we could fix the problems that had created them.

The Democratic congressional leadership wanted to ensure that another system-wide meltdown could never happen again. Barney Frank and Chris Dodd, who had played such important roles in TARP, took the lead in crafting the legislation that is known as Dodd-Frank. Its purpose was to address the root causes of the crisis. It was self-evident that the financial service companies had been recklessly investing money that they should not have been investing. As we surveyed the lasting damage from 2008, the assault from Wall Street on our economy and on working families was drastic.

We were blessed to have Barney Frank and Chris Dodd join forces on this initiative. They shared the same values, and their judgment was trusted by our members. We could count on them to understand the issues and strike the right balance. The goals of Dodd-Frank reforms were simple: protect the taxpayer, protect the consumer, and promote fairness and integrity in the financial system.

A significant provision of the bill was the Volcker Rule. Named for a former chair of the Federal Reserve, Paul Volcker, this rule prohibited FDIC-insured banks from engaging in risky deals when they were trading simply for their own profit. Naturally, the banks strenuously opposed the Volcker Rule—but Democrats delivered it into the bill nonetheless.

Soon after Dodd-Frank became law, the banks began their determined effort to undermine it: lobbying Congress to weaken or roll back some of its most important regulations, including the Volcker Rule. They were successful in watering down certain provisions.

The banks' opposition to Dodd-Frank was rooted in their compulsion to—as always—privatize the gains and nationalize the risks. They wanted to feel confident that the American taxpayers would bail them out again. Greed in certain parts of the financial services industry appeared to have remained insatiable.

The financial meltdown had a devastating effect on the entire economy—but it especially caused great collateral damage to America's families and homeowners. Wall Street had treated housing like just another commodity—but these were not just paper assets. Millions of foreclosures represented people's homes. And for most families, their house is also their most important financial accumulation of wealth. Homeownership is vital to building strong communities.

The value of protecting homes and the people who work and sweat and save to buy them has a special meaning to me personally. In fact, it's in my DNA. For my entire childhood, my father, Thomas D'Alesandro Jr., was the mayor of Baltimore. My mother, Nancy, made affordable housing her personal priority as First Lady of Baltimore. Early in her public life, she delivered remarks to the Baltimore section of the National Council of Jewish Women, making a passionate argument for providing housing. "How can we expect the parents to teach their children love, faith, and tolerance when they have no homes?" my mother declared. "When the home fails, the community fails, the nation fails." I have never forgotten her words.

During his tenure as mayor, my father pushed for improving the living conditions in low-income rental housing. He wanted better health and safety conditions, and grateful tenants welcomed his leadership. However, in some cases, slumlords fought back and told the tenants that if their units were improved, the rents would be raised to an unaffordable degree—meaning that they would have no place to live. That some real estate investors would put the greed of excess profit over respect and human decency in housing was a reality that I had seen firsthand. Then and now, that experience guided me in respecting everyone's need for a secure place to live. I was proud that my brother Tommy, who later served as mayor of Baltimore, made equal accommodation in housing his priority—an idea that had grown out of a discussion on civil rights that Tommy had with Dr. Martin Luther King Jr. before Dr. King's tragic assassination.

My view, as I have said, is that the financial crisis sprang from the Bush administration's fundamental failure to regulate and supervise the financial system. As we know from the vote on TARP, dislike of regulation was foundational to Republican philosophy: again, even when the walls came tumbling down, they did not believe in intervention. Sadly, Congressman Spencer Bachus summed up this view in remarks he made—after the crisis and the subsequent passage of the Wall Street reform bill—as the incoming chairman of the House Financial Services Committee: "In Washington," he said, "the view is that the banks are to be regulated, and my view is that Washington and the regulators are there to serve the banks."

Irresponsibility had led us into the crisis, and irresponsibility would be on display again as we struggled to solve the problem that had been handed to us. Inside the Democratic Caucus, many members felt rather betrayed that President Bush and the Republican leadership had been unable to convince even 100 of their members to support the bipartisan TARP legislation. Democrats had risen to the occasion, and then we had to shoulder the blame for public dislike of TARP, because we were in the majority and had delivered the overwhelming majority of the votes (almost 2-to-1).

The financial crisis of 2008 was a dark, difficult moment for our economy—the effects of which continue to reverberate to this day. And there's a lingering question as to why no one on Wall Street paid a price for the damage done to Main Street.

By 2010, more than 26 million Americans were out of work or without a full-time job, or had given up looking for work. Four million homeowners had lost their homes to foreclosure, and 4.5 million more were in the process of foreclosure or had fallen behind on payments. In the 2008–2009 stock market chaos, nearly $11 trillion in household wealth had evaporated, with retirement funds, college funds, savings, pensions for workers, and more swept away. Businesses small and large felt the harm of a deep recession, even though they played by the rules. Yet not one executive in the financial industry paid a price for the 2008 financial meltdown. We heard that these big institutions were "too big to fail," but that also began a policy of "too big to jail."

Why wasn't anyone held responsible? Why was there no cost in dollars or reputation to anyone in charge? In fact, in March 2009, just months after they had received a $170 billion federal bailout, the insurance giant AIG gave $165 million in bonuses. The public was enraged, and rightfully so. The anger unleashed by the grossly irresponsible behavior of these major financial institutions helped fuel the Occupy Wall Street movement on the left and the Tea Party movement on the right—intensifying a new level of polarization in our politics.

Clearly, there were no consequences for executives. To me, the central question is: How do we apply the concept of moral hazard—the principle that says if you let some questionable behavior go unaddressed, you are blessing that bad example for others? For those who say that we shouldn't prosecute these banks because they are too big to fail and therefore too big to jail, the attitude is that we should not hold somebody accountable because it might disrupt the business and the economy. My view is to hold individuals accountable and hire someone else. Otherwise, the message is that these banks and executives are above the law— and that cannot be the rule.

If a bank is weakened because of economic downturns, then

it may need help to prevent systemic consequences. If it is failing because of irresponsible behavior, that is a different story—
and that type of behavior is a major part of what was happening
by 2008. The banks' behavior was a betrayal of the public trust.
The standard of justice applied in those cases would certainly not
apply to any other industry, or any individual, who broke the law.

People ask why no one, not one person in the financial industry, paid a price in dollars or reputation for the financial
meltdown. I am very proud of the work of the Financial Crisis
Inquiry Commission, chaired by former California state treasurer
Phil Angelides. The bipartisan commission found some areas of
agreement on the root causes of the crisis. Nevertheless, some of
the Republicans on the commission unsuccessfully requested that
certain words be struck from the final report: "deregulation" and
even "Wall Street"—even though it was clear that responsibility
for the crisis lay in the poor decisions made by and the greed of
Wall Street institutions.

I am grateful that Congress, and especially House Democrats,
had the courage and ability to work together and stand together
to avert another Great Depression and complete worldwide economic collapse. But what leaves me sad still is that although on
the day of the TARP vote I said "the party is over"—in reality, it
wasn't. The struggle to build a more accountable financial system
continues, and I hope that the vital lessons of those dark days in
2008 will not be forgotten.

Again, "too big to fail, too big to jail" cannot be the rule.

Health Care Is a Right—
Not a Privilege

In March 1966, Dr. Martin Luther King Jr. challenged doctors and hospitals to abide by the Civil Rights Act, powerfully noting, "Of all forms of inequality, injustice in health is the most shocking and inhuman because it often results in physical death." In the spirit of Dr. King's message, Democrats have long declared that health care must be a right for all—not a privilege for the few. Yet by 2008 and 2009, structural and economic barriers, particularly around access to health insurance, were driving individuals and families into bankruptcy and despair.

For years, Americans' struggles with health insurance had been impressed upon me not only in my own district of San Francisco but as I traveled the country. One man in Michigan told me that his wife had been sick and bedridden for a long time. He said that he was at the end of the line in terms of his finances, especially with the cost of prescription drugs. That he might have to lose his home, that he was afraid of what would happen next. He cried when he told me that he was lovingly honoring his marital vows—in sickness and in health—but he couldn't hold out much longer. He was too proud to tell his children that he needed help, because they were raising families of their own. He pleaded: "When is something going to happen on health care in America?"

When indeed? A 2007 study cited in the *American Journal of*

Medicine found that health care expenses were "the most common cause of bankruptcy in the United States." A staggering 62 percent of US personal bankruptcies were due to health care costs—that number had been only 8 percent as recently as 1981. Unsurprisingly, most of these bankruptcies were being declared by middle-class Americans who already had health insurance. After illness or injury struck, they discovered that their insurance was "inadequate." The best estimates were that one in five Americans either lacked health insurance or had inadequate health insurance. But those numbers did not tell the full story—130 million Americans had what the insurance companies designated a "preexisting condition," meaning that they could be denied coverage or charged higher rates.

What constituted a preexisting condition? Often it was simply being a woman. If you had been pregnant, had undergone a C-section, or had survived domestic violence, you could be discriminated against in the insurance market because you were considered to have a preexisting medical condition. I was personally aware of these practices. I gave birth to five children—in a span of six years and one week. Because of that "medical history," my insurance provider deemed me to be weak. I was stunned: I believed that having five children only proved my strength.

But health insurers wrote the rules, and they ruled the roost. Insurance companies were allowed to cancel coverage in the middle of treatment for an illness; it did not matter if you had paid every premium in full and on time. Insurers put annual limits and lifetime caps on what they would pay. Young people frequently couldn't get insurance from their employers with their first job, and they could not remain on their parents' plans. An illness or an accident could be devastating. High co-pays and high deductibles on policies were also driving bankruptcies. So, while it was a highly profitable situation for the insurance companies, it could be a deadly situation for patients and families. The economic situation as a deep recession hit the US in 2008 elevated the health care issue to a full-blown crisis.

Health care access was not, however, a new issue for anyone in Washington. For a hundred years, US presidents had tried to achieve universal access to health care—without success. Teddy Roosevelt introduced the concept to the nation. Franklin Roosevelt was successful in implementing Social Security, and he also hoped to include national health care in his initiatives but was not successful. Harry Truman, who wanted health care reform as early as World War I when he saw the health conditions of US Army recruits, worked so relentlessly on Medicare that when it was finally passed under Lyndon Johnson, President Johnson traveled to Truman's hometown in Independence, Missouri, to sign the bill in President Truman's presence. Social Security, Medicare, and Medicaid became the three great pillars of health and financial stability for our seniors, our children in need, and persons with disabilities. However, they did not provide universal access to affordable health care. Strides were made in the Clinton years with the State Children's Health Insurance Program (SCHIP), a priority for First Lady Hillary Clinton, as she emphasized the importance of access for all.

Yet until this point, when Democrats had tried to produce transformative health care legislation that would honor our nation's founding promise of life, liberty, and the pursuit of happiness, those efforts had fallen short. But we refused to give up. When I came to Congress, I was among a generation of members who had embraced that challenge. I arrived in Washington as the AIDS epidemic was raging, and my San Francisco district was one of the most heavily impacted areas in the nation. The suffering of my constituents made me acutely aware of the need for universal health care, long before I ever thought that I might become Speaker and work to lead our fight. Personally, I was driven by my Catholic faith to honor the Gospel of Matthew, the hope of my constituents affected by the HIV/AIDS epidemic, and the charity of those who cared and advocated for health justice. My hope sprang from my faith in the goodness of others.

But in addition to hope, we needed the stars to align in Washington. We finally had that alignment when Barack Obama became president. He had campaigned on a promise of access to universal health care. Now, with both the House and the Senate having significant Democratic majorities, we had an opportunity to deliver for the American people. I believed that President Obama's visionary leadership and determination—and the courage and commitment of congressional Democrats—would make affordable health care not only a priority but a reality. In the House, our vision for passing health care was summed up as "Triple-A"—accessibility to quality care, affordability for consumers, and accountability for insurance companies. We believed it was our responsibility to create—alongside Social Security, Medicare, and Medicaid—a fourth pillar of health and financial security for all Americans. The idea of health care as a right, not a privilege, was in our Democratic DNA.

Our primary goal with our legislation was to ensure that when Americans faced a health crisis, they would not also face a financial crisis. Consumers would have more choices, so they could find plans without waiting periods for coverage to start and without high deductibles. There would be an annual limit on out-of-pocket expenses to be paid by patients and no lifetime limits on care. There would be no more co-pays or deductibles for preventative care. If someone changed jobs, or lost their job, or had a preexisting medical condition, they could no longer be denied coverage. And being a woman would no longer be a preexisting condition. Our goal was to ensure that insurance companies could not use any of these events or facts as an excuse to reject an applicant for health coverage.

In retrospect, it is difficult to imagine how health care reform was so controversial. If basic compassion was not enough of a motivator, the dismal economic numbers of health care should have been. By 2009, we as a country were spending 17 percent of our gross domestic product on health care costs, while 46 million Americans lacked coverage. By the year 2025, health care costs were projected to be 25 percent of the economy, rising to about 37 percent in 2050. I recall meeting with labor union leaders around the country to discuss pensions, and they also wanted to discuss prescription drug prices and health care. The status quo was simply unsustainable in terms of costs: costs to individuals and families—that is, taxpayers—and to small businesses and corporate America (both of which were providing a great deal of employer-based insurance). The government at every level—local, state, and national (again, the taxpayer)—was footing the bill for a large and growing share of health care.

In an early March 2009 conversation with President Obama in the Oval Office regarding health care legislation, I said that we would be faced with multiple opponents: insurance companies, big-dollar anti-government advocates, and those who strongly opposed a public role in health care. At the same time, some of these same opponents would be inconsistently shouting at rallies and protests, "Keep your hands off my Medicare!" Ironically, they were saying that they wanted the government to "keep its hands" off the very successful government-run health care program for seniors.

House leaders who were committed to health care reform already knew firsthand how difficult the battle would be, because we had taken on these foes before. We bested the strong resistance to secure early funding to combat HIV/AIDS. We overcame President Bush's two vetoes of SCHIP (now called the Children's Health Insurance Program, or CHIP), which supports children's health needs. Our fight to triumph against President Bush's Social Security privatization effort was vital in helping Democrats win back the House majority in the 2006 election.

I told President Obama that our opponents would pursue a strategy of shock and awe, carpet-bombing, take no prisoners, and scorched earth—nothing would be off-limits. (Ultimately, it would be even worse than we and many other supporters had imagined. It would be more vicious and more aggressive.) I said we would need a clear message to inoculate against their lies and educate the public about what health care reform would mean for America's working families; that we would need to make sure our explanations were delivered clearly and repetitively.

In reply, the president said, "I know something about messaging. You will see a message machine coming out of this White House like you've never seen before." With the promise of air cover from the administration, I could engage House Democrats.

"Let's Get to Work!"

On March 5, the president hosted a very comprehensive meeting at the White House—Democrats and Republicans, House and Senate; outside stakeholders, including leading health advocates for cancer, heart disease, and other illnesses, health care organizations, labor unions, and academics, along with representatives from the insurance and pharmaceutical industries—to launch an initiative for health care for all.

At the meeting, the president said:

We're here today to discuss one of the greatest threats not just to the well-being of our families and the prosperity of our businesses, but to the very foundation of our economy— and that's the exploding costs of health care in America today. . . .

Let me be clear: the same soaring costs that are straining families' budgets are sinking our businesses and eating up our government's budget, too. Too many small businesses can't insure their employees. Major American corporations are struggling to compete with their foreign counterparts. And companies of all sizes are shipping their jobs overseas or shutting their doors for good. . . .

[T]here is no debate about whether all Americans should have quality, affordable health care—the only question is, how?

And the purpose of this forum is to start answering that question—to determine how we lower costs for everyone, improve quality for everyone, and expand coverage to all Americans. And our goal will be to enact comprehensive health care reform by the end of this year. That is our commitment. That is our goal. . . .

So let's get to work!

The president wanted our legislation to be unifying, bipartisan, and enacted into law soon. And we did get to work!

In a major departure from past efforts at health care reform, the legislation would not be written by the White House; rather, it would be drafted in Congress. What made this health care bill likely to succeed was that the central objective was a congressionally written bill, the product of a consensus among the House, the Senate, and the White House. This was our best path forward.

One of the great strengths that our Democratic leadership team brought to the table was longtime experience. We understood how the battlefield works in Congress. If you are going to do big things, that takes a full understanding of the minute details of policy and congressional processes. And that's what my team and I had. Our Democratic leadership quickly tasked the three committees with jurisdiction over the issue—Energy and Commerce, Ways and Means, and Education and Labor (also called, before and after, Education and the Workforce)—to involve our entire caucus. This would enable us to establish our priorities for quality health care reform legislation.

At the same time, we wanted to hear from as many outside voices as possible, starting with patients, patient advocates, and health care providers and hospital professionals. We reached out to a wide constituency of seniors, women, children, persons with disabilities, and multiethnic grassroots health advocacy groups. We called upon our friends in the labor movement, who had been in the fight for health care from the start. In doing so, we reactivated the formidable coalition that came together to defeat President Bush's ill-considered attempt to privatize Social Security. Our success then and our success now for health care would depend on a savvy combination of inside maneuvering and outside mobilization.

But more than a strong coalition was needed. Our biggest challenge lay in the Senate. When we started our health care work, Harry Reid did not have a sixty-vote majority, the required number to stop a filibuster that would prevent the legislation from moving forward. He had fifty-eight Democrats; Al Franken had not yet been declared the winner of his seat in Minnesota, and Arlen Specter of Pennsylvania had not yet switched parties from Republican to Democrat. We knew from the outset that we needed multiple legislative tracks if our efforts were to succeed. While the House committees worked on a stand-alone bill, the House Budget Committee prepared and passed a budget reconciliation bill that would enable us to proceed with legislation that combined both health care and higher education reform. According to the rules of Congress, passing a budget bill would enable us to use a process called reconciliation—which lowers the number of votes needed to pass a measure in the Senate from sixty to fifty-one.

We accomplished that necessity in April. So, from the start, congressional Democrats were prepared, if needed, to turn to reconciliation to achieve health care for all.

On May 13, I joined Steny Hoyer and the leading House committee chairs responsible for the legislation for a pivotal meeting with President Obama in the Oval Office. During our discussion, the president asked if I would immediately make a statement to the press and announce that the House would pass a health care bill by July 31. I said yes, but added that I was predicating my timeline on the Senate Finance Committee passing its bill by June 15, as the president had also called for, and which Max Baucus, its chair, and Harry Reid had reportedly committed to. I was confident that the House could meet this timeline, because health care legislation has always been a priority for us. In turn, I wanted to assure House Democrats that they could proceed confidently because President Obama was intellectually, politically, and personally committed to achieving our shared goal.

I was also confident we would succeed because of our key House committee chairs: two Californians, George Miller of Education and Labor and Henry Waxman of Energy and Commerce; and New York's Charlie Rangel of Ways and Means.

I tasked these three chairmen and their members with jointly writing one bill and passing it through each of their committees. In this way, we would have one draft and be speaking with one voice. They in turn had assembled a talented and knowledgeable staff who would serve our country well. My own health care staff in the Speaker's office was led by Wendell Primus, without whom we would not have succeeded.

Because health care legislation involved these three committees, nearly half of the House members were already included in the process by virtue of the fact that they served on a relevant committee. Thus there were multiple opportunities to hear from a wide range of voices and for individual members to participate in an informed and lively debate.

We knew this was our shot, and we were not going to pass up the opportunity to get the job done. As we sat around the negotiating table crafting the Affordable Care Act, we were always mindful of what America's families think about when they sit around their kitchen tables. Democrats have always believed that what we do in Congress must be relevant to our constituents' lives. House Democrats made every decision in favor of quality, affordable health care for all. That was our vision. And we viewed every obstacle as a challenge to be overcome, not as a barrier to success. Of course there were naysayers who said that we should wait. That the bill was too ambitious. That it was too hard to pass. But I have never placed a high value on naysayers.

Path to Success

In the House, the process started with collaboration. I had excellent rapport with each of our three extraordinary committee chairmen. George Miller was one of my closest friends in Congress. He worked very closely with Sen. Ted Kennedy—because George's House committee, Education and Labor, was responsible for many of the same issues as the Senate Health, Education, Labor, and Pensions (HELP) Committee, which Ted chaired. Both men were regarded as lions of Congress: highly respected and committed to universal health care as a right, not a privilege. George was also co-chair of the Steering and Policy Committee, so he had the ear of the caucus—and they had his.

Henry Waxman was the new chair of Energy and Commerce. He had been elected by the members, replacing the stalwart, long-serving representative from Michigan, John Dingell. Henry ran for committee chair in part because he wanted to be able to help shepherd the health care bill. He was extraordinarily talented and knowledgeable, and he had been a tremendous early leader on HIV/AIDS. I knew his work firsthand. When I arrived in Congress in June 1987, following a special election, it was a few months into the new term, and all the committee assignments had been taken. I wanted to find a place where I could work on HIV/AIDS, which, again, was the primary reason I ran for Congress. Henry offered to give up his seat on the Committee on Government Operations Subcommittee on Health so I would have a venue to help my constituents impacted by the crisis. It was a highly unusual and very generous move for someone to give up his place on a committee, particularly for the most junior member of the caucus, but that was Henry.

Charlie Rangel had years of experience in the House and

excellent credentials. He was passionately focused on issues relating to health care for all, community health centers, primary care doctors, and disparities in care for the underserved health—lending his powerful voice to support the poor and the uninsured. All of us in the House shared those concerns, but Charlie was very commanding in our ongoing negotiations with the Senate.

I wanted to be respectful of the chairs and their roles, but I told them from the start: "You're doing the work of the Democratic Caucus. This is not a personal thing. It's not my personal thing. It's not your personal thing. You are representing the caucus. Our caucus members elected us to these positions, and they expect us to produce a product that is not the lowest common denominator—but the boldest common denominator."

Our health care bill was not hatched by a few people. Our committee chairs worked with members to come up with one plan. House Democrats all got along pretty well because we listened. Members shared their wide-ranging observations—philosophically, regionally, ethnically, gender-wise, and generationally. I considered my role to be that of a maestro—I was guiding great musicians who kept our shared values at the forefront while giving space to recognize and understand regional differences.

I also knew that being a member of Congress was a hard job, particularly challenging when we are working on a major, transformative piece of legislation. From my time as the Democratic whip, I learned that if I fed my members, it put everyone in a good mood and made them feel welcome. I'm Italian, so offering food is also in my nature; our motto was "First, we eat." While I was Speaker, we had breakfasts, lunches, and dinners. We ran the gamut from roast beef and chicken to salmon and vegetarian and vegan options. Occasionally, we started with ice cream—especially chocolate, my favorite. I saw it not as a tactic but as an expression of love, a way of saying we care about you, you are special to us, and we want this to be a positive experience. But sometimes, when it came to the health care debate, if the meetings got contentious or long-winded, I'd have to consider: Do I supply food to improve the mood—or deny food to bring the discussion to an end?

One of the most passionate ongoing discussions we had in the House was around single-payer health care. When I first arrived in Congress, there was a movement for a single-payer system: the progressive vision for access to universal care. For years, Representatives Jim McDermott of Washington State and John Conyers of Michigan were leaders in proposing this legislation. They had an ardent but insufficient crew of supporters—of which I was one.

When it came to developing a single-payer plan for the 2009 health care reform, there were several visions: For some members, single-payer meant simplifying the system of how health care providers are compensated. One payer, a single payer: the federal government. Others pushed for a single-payer health care system like that used in Canada or the United Kingdom, where the government is both the health care provider and the payer.

During discussions on the health care bill, I invited the single-payer advocates to gather in the Speaker's office one day. It was a long meeting, and at one point, I was called away to speak with George Mitchell, who, as the US government's special envoy for Middle East peace, was sharing a report on an administration initiative. (George and I had worked closely on China issues after Tiananmen Square.) Everyone was proud of George's work on the Good Friday Agreement between Great Britain and Northern Ireland in 1998 and hoped that he could achieve some success in the Middle East.

During our conversation, spirited shouting could be heard coming from the adjacent conference room. George and I found ourselves trying to talk over the noise. Multiple members were boisterously competing to be identified as the author of the single-payer legislation, which they knew would not prevail; nonetheless, they wanted to have pride of authorship for posterity. While the record of senior members on single-payer was clear, newer members also wanted to claim credit. The smaller the prize, apparently, the bigger the fight.

Everyone emerged from the room thinking that he—just guys, of course—had prevailed. Despite the commotion, I was proud of the enthusiasm of my members. I will always remember that ruckus with a smile. But that meeting was also the end of a single-payer component in the Affordable Care Act. It lacked enough support beyond the members in that room. Ultimately, even House stalwarts declined to offer a single-payer amendment to our consensus bill. Instead, House Democrats focused on what was known as the public option.

The public option is a government-run insurance program that would not eliminate but would compete with private plans. In March 2009, President Obama stated: "The thinking on the public option has been that it gives consumers more choices and it helps keep the private sector honest, because there's some competition out there."

We agreed with the president. There was strong support in the House for a public option. In the House, our bill in all three of our committees contained a public option—as did the bill from the Senate HELP Committee, advanced by Senator Kennedy. I said at the time that the public option was the best way to lower costs, improve the quality of health care, ensure choice, and expand coverage. The public option would bring real financial reform over a ten-year period, and I was glad to see it in our final bill in the House.

Proudly, on June 19, right on schedule or even slightly ahead, the three committee chairmen released their single, unified draft legislation for health care reform. It is important to note that this legislation was historic—not only because it happened but because it was largely written by Congress, not the executive branch.

After they had written the bill, the chairmen had to shepherd it through each committee, where all the members, on both sides of the aisle, would have an additional say. We had scores of hours of bipartisan committee hearings and hundreds of amendments— some offered by Democrats and some by Republicans. All the amendments received the same treatment: some were adopted, some modified, and some turned down. So the Republicans had plenty of opportunities to make their own modifications to the bill and have them considered by the committees.

The House passed our bill out of committee. This effort was in stark contrast with the Senate—indeed, health care severely tested the House's relationship with the Senate. We endured months of delays waiting for the Senate to act. During these months, Rep. John Dingell frequently reminded us of the old adage for House Democrats: the Republicans are our opposition, but the Senate is our enemy.

Ted Kennedy's HELP Committee passed his bill on time. The Senate Finance Committee did not move until October. Chair Baucus said that he didn't believe in schedules, ignoring the June 15 deadline that President Obama had called for—and to which the senator himself, as we have seen, had supposedly committed.

House members were very unhappy with the Senate's timing. While the Senate bill remained tied up in committee, Republicans and industry opponents had an unprecedented opportunity to go to the public and misrepresent our House bill. They claimed that it restricted care and created "death panels" designed to deny care at the end of life, that it funded "abortion," and even that it would be the end of private insurance or be nothing more than another "giveaway" that hurt the middle class. The Senate, by its process and delays, had given the other side ample time to undermine our work, simply because some Senate Democrats thought they could get a Republican vote on the Senate floor—which I knew they were never, ever going to get. I said to the senators: "It's like the Dance of the Seven Veils. These people are giving you this flirtation that they're going to give you a vote. And you are playing right into their hands."

Never was that truer than in August, when our members returned home to their districts. August 2009 was the worst month I could remember.

I always liked to "own August"—an opportunity for all of us to engage at home with our constituents on what we had accomplished. But this year was different. This August was just as I had forewarned: shock and awe, carpet-bombing, take no prisoners, scorched earth—and more. Day after day and night after night, cable news flooded the airwaves with images of people heckling Democrats during summer town halls in their districts—repeating Republican lies about our bill. House Democrats stayed in the fight and saved the bill, even though we were very disappointed not to have the previously promised messaging air cover from the White House. We had hoped that the White House would heed House Democrats' warnings about the brutal attacks.

In June, Rosa DeLauro proposed a plan to use the stories we had collected from Americans about what the health care bill meant to them and their families. We had created a story bank filled with them. Rosa asked for $9 million from the president's political operation to counteract the negative messaging and tell the truth about what was in the health care bill—to tell the stories of why we were promoting this bill and the patients who needed it in a focused way. The answer was no. As the summer dragged on, it was clear that we were on our own. Instead, Democratic members were largely left to make the case for the health care bill themselves, while facing millions of dollars in attack ads. We had to save the bill.

We had a number of House members who were young military veterans. One, Patrick Murphy from Pennsylvania, gave us the best analogy for how to move forward. He described what it was like to be in the theater of war. "It is," he explained, "one-hundred-plus degrees, you are carrying a fifty-pound pack, you haven't had a shower in days, you are in close quarters all the time, and you could be shot at any moment. You cannot complain about the heat, the weight, or the lack of a shower. Instead, there is only one thing you can do: remember why you are here and 'embrace the suck.'" None of us may like it, but we have to deal with it, he explained. That summer and throughout the fall, across the country, Democratic members of the House "embraced the suck."

One fighter at the grassroots level was a new member from Virginia, Congressman Tom Perriello. In his own words: "I held more than twenty-three town hall meetings, in every county of my district. More than eighteen thousand Virginians attended these events. Thousands more dialed in to participate in conference calls." Tom would lose his reelection campaign in 2010 in a heavily Republican district—but his courage would have more meaningful rewards. He has told the world: "I can attest that the handshakes and hugs from thankful parents over the years have meant far more to me than a couple more years in Congress ever would."

House Democrats fought back against the assault on what we were trying to accomplish on health care—and better than the senators did. I may be biased, but it looked to me as if the Senate didn't seem used to dealing with people on a grassroots basis, unlike those of us who stand for reelection every two years. The attitude in the Senate, compounded by the Senate's delaying tactics, could have ended our health care reform prospects in August—it was the determination of House Democrats that kept the process afloat.

Then, on August 25, tragedy struck. Senator Kennedy, the health care champion in the Senate, passed away. The American people had lost a great patriot, and the Kennedy family lost a beloved patriarch. Over a lifetime of leadership, Senator Kennedy's statesmanship and political prowess produced a wealth of accomplishments that improved opportunities for every American. Sadly, Senator Kennedy left us one year after he had inspired the nation with his optimistic, vital, and courageous speech at the Democratic National Convention in Denver, where we nominated President Obama.

Knowing that the passage of true health care reform was at stake, as a final, gracious act, the senator left a beautiful letter for President Obama:

Dear Mr. President,

I wanted to write a few final words to you to express my gratitude for your repeated personal kindnesses to me—and one last time, to salute your leadership in giving our Country back its future and its truth.

On a personal level, you and Michelle reached out to Vicki, to

*our family and me in so many different ways. You helped to make
these difficult months a happy time in my life.*

You also made it a time of hope for me and for our Country.

*When I thought of all the years, all the battles, and all the
memories of my long public life, I felt confident in these closing
days that while I will not be there when it happens, you will be the
President who at long last signs into law the health care reform
that is the great unfinished business of our society. For me, this
cause stretched across decades; it has been disappointed, but never
finally defeated. It was the cause of my life. And in the past year,
the prospect of victory sustained me—and the work of achieving it
summoned my energy and determination.*

*There will be struggles—there always have been—and they
are already under way again. But as we moved forward in these
months, I learned that you will not yield to calls to retreat—that
you will stay with the cause until it is won. I saw your conviction
that the time is now and witnessed your unwavering commitment
and understanding that health care is a decisive issue for our future
prosperity. But you have also reminded all of us that it concerns
more than material things; that what we face is above all a moral
issue; that at stake are not just the details of policy, but fundamental
principles of social justice and the character of our country.*

*And so because of your vision and resolve, I came to believe that
soon, very soon, affordable health coverage will be available to all,
in an America where the state of a family's health will never again
depend on the amount of a family's wealth. And while I will not see
the victory, I was able to look forward and know that we will—yes,
we will—fulfill the promise of health care in America as a right and
not a privilege.*

*In closing, let me say again how proud I was to be part of your
campaign—and proud as well to play a part in the early months*

of a new era of high purpose and achievement. I entered public life with a young President who inspired a generation and the world. It gives me great hope that as I leave, another young President inspires another generation and once more on America's behalf inspires the entire world.

So, I wrote this to thank you one last time as a friend—and to stand with you one last time for change and the America we can become.

At the Denver Convention where you were nominated, I said the dream lives on.

And I finished this letter with unshakable faith that the dream will be fulfilled for this generation, and preserved and enlarged for generations to come.

With deep respect and abiding affection,
Ted

Senator Kennedy's profound letter was a challenge to the conscience of America. On September 2, Harry Reid and I wrote President Obama, inviting him to address a joint session of Congress. We had done the grassroots work to build support, we knew we had the votes in the House, and now we wanted that soapbox power of persuasion that only the president commands to strengthen public sentiment and support. Senator Kennedy's letter, along with the unwavering resolve of the House Democrats, had convinced the reluctant elements in the White House that we were poised to win on our vision of health care reform.

One week later, in a nationally televised address to the joint session of Congress, President Obama made a forceful case for long-overdue health insurance reform. He declared that we were closer than ever before in history to making real progress on an issue that touches the lives of everyone and impacts our economy:

ensuring stability and security for Americans with health insurance, and affordable coverage for those without it.

As the president said, our health care system had placed an unsustainable burden on taxpayers: "Everyone in this room knows what will happen if we do nothing. Our deficit will grow. More families will go bankrupt. More businesses will close. More Americans will lose their coverage when they are sick and need it the most. And more will die as a result. We know these things to be true. That is why we cannot fail."

The president also made it clear that the public option—contained in our House bill—was the best way to create the competition needed to lower costs, improve quality, and preserve choice for all Americans. House Democrats welcomed his call for a public option. But there was a surprise embedded in the president's speech. It was the first time that the House Democratic leadership had heard of President Obama's decision to place a $900 billion cost limitation on the legislation. It was never clear where this cap came from.

Ultimately, not wanting to jeopardize this opportunity, the House accommodated the president's spending cap—but unfortunately, the Senate did not accommodate his clear call for a public option. Despite our continued fight—and the overwhelming support among the public—the Senate bill did not include a public option. It was clear that the insurance companies had too much influence when the bill's passage required sixty votes in the Senate.

Nevertheless, in the overall political environment and the strong fight being put up by the legislation's opponents, the president's public commitment to health care reform was essential for moving forward. He said that he understood that the politically safe move would have been "to defer"—but that was not what the moment called for. "We did not come to fear the future. We came here to shape it."

A great message from the president!

That fall, House Democrats continued to hold meetings with all stakeholders. We had meetings on "family, doctor, and clergy discussions"—what the GOP erroneously called "death panels." We had ongoing meetings on regional disparity, a key issue. Reimbursements, treatments, and spending differed from state to state; addressing how resources were best allocated and ensuring that there were no winners or losers was a major issue. We had meetings on medical devices. We discussed the many disparities in health care.

At the same time, we held universal readings of the final House bill. Those readings were mandatory for our caucus. Every member had to be present. Chair John Larson of Connecticut presided, calling the caucus to order. Rob Andrews of New Jersey—who served on the Education and Labor Committee—took us through the reading. Rob was fantastic, and he was trusted by the members. He could clearly explain each provision, walking members through and drilling down on the smallest detail.

We were determined to hold these mandatory readings so that everyone had read the bill, had it explained to them in full, had their questions answered, and could discuss it with confidence. We took it piece by piece by piece, covering every single word—and that took days. By the end, members not only knew what was in the bill, but they could participate in enriching it.

In our readings, questions arose. For example, members asked if smokers should be charged more. Our members were well versed in nutrition, wellness, and prevention; we always maintained that our legislation was not just about health care but about a healthy America. We decided to hold a meeting to discuss whether insurance companies could charge more for smokers. Democratic members from tobacco-growing states came loaded for bear.

We gathered a panel of leaders from the American Heart Association, the American Cancer Society, and other organizations who highlighted the health risks of smoking. We wanted our efforts to not simply be about paying for health care but also to identify ways to build a healthier America—and smoking is a major risk factor for many serious illnesses, including cancer and heart disease. But in response to our question—should insurance companies charge smokers higher premiums—to a person, each of the leaders of these anti-smoking groups said no. Everyone's first thought was, Holy smokes! (Pun intended.) The response shocked us, because it was not what we were expecting, but the groups were adamant: "You cannot give these insurance companies any instance where they can charge more." They did not want to open the door to allowing insurers to charge certain groups of consumers more or to try to exclude some Americans from coverage. As much as these health leaders wanted to discourage smoking, they did not trust the insurance companies to do the right thing for patients.

There were other follow-up meetings—sometimes to dispel misrepresentations that the Republicans were putting out, and sometimes to explain what the Senate was doing and where they were in the legislative process. Another dynamic at work during the fall was when would we get the important Congressional Budget Office (CBO) cost estimates. The CBO determines how the legislation is "scored"—meaning what the ultimate cost will be—and the CBO score is essential to our fiscal decisions. Sometimes the CBO would be more or less optimistic than our projections—and we would have member meetings to reconcile the overall cost of the bill.

Some meetings were very personal: individual members would come in, either a few from a state or even one at a time, just to talk about everything. On health care legislation, I always believed that every person, every constituent, was an expert. Former House Speaker Tip O'Neill is famous for saying, "All politics is local." With health care, all politics is not just local, it is personal.

All of us in leadership spent considerable time working with our individual members. I'm still bothered by Republican accusations that we had not read our own bill—the meetings we held were not a secret. Perhaps in accusing us, the Republicans were simply projecting their own poor practices in policymaking and procedural shortcomings.

I was continually reminded of the Republican and industry propaganda that produced a steady stream of mistruths and misrepresentations, seeking to undo the entire process. One night, I was eating dinner with our team at a restaurant in Washington, and a man came up to my table holding his beautiful baby girl. When I congratulated him on his beautiful baby, he said to me: "For her sake, I wish you had read the bill."

I replied: "For her sake, we wrote the bill." And I added, "We read the bill, too." Again and again, Republican lies to help corporate America.

Negotiating with the Senate

After months of uncertainty and delay, the Senate finally moved its bill out of committee in October, which reassured us that it could produce a final bill. We passed an improved version of the

House bill on November 7, and the Senate passed its bill on the Senate floor on Christmas Eve. To reach that point, our country was blessed to have the leadership of Harry Reid, the Democratic leader of the Senate. He was a champion of America's working families, and he was committed to helping get the job done.

But the Senate as an institution is very different from the House, and many House Democrats were deeply disappointed in the Senate bill, which they saw as a missed opportunity. House Democrats had courageously voted for stronger measures in our Affordable Care Act, and many refused to support the weaker Senate bill, which we viewed as wrong on so many scores: not only because it did not include a public option, but because it also weakened the mandates for employers to offer—and individuals to purchase—health insurance. And it reduced plans to expand Medicaid to cover more low-income Americans. Now both sides would have to go to conference, which is the congressional vehicle to resolve the differences between the House and the Senate— with the goal of arriving at a compromise between the two bills.

Our internal debate in the House regarding the Senate legislation was heated. There were several areas of major disagreement, beyond the lack of a public option and changes to the health insurance purchase mandates in the Senate bill. Another area of disagreement in the course of the negotiations was how the legislation would be paid for. The House had included a surcharge for those making more than $500,000 per year—which was clean, ironclad, and constitutionally clear. But the Senate didn't like that provision. They instead wanted a "dogs and cats" solution, as House members often call smaller funding proposals in legislation. That's not to denigrate dogs and cats. We all love our pets— just not as a way to pay for legislation. One of the "dogs and cats" that the Senate came up with was a $40 billion tax on medical devices over ten years. When our members who represented areas with medical device companies heard about this idea, they objected vehemently. Their objections produced a lively debate in the House Democratic Caucus. Indeed, the debate inside the Speaker's Conference Room could be heard around the Capitol. The pitch was high, and the tone was fierce.

In response, I said to them, Here is what we will do. I will cut the medical device tax down from $40 billion to $20 billion—if you go to your medical device people and say, "We will not cut it any further. This is the agreement." Then I told Harry Reid, "Cut the tax by twenty billion. This is it. I won't lower it ten cents more, but you can't raise it ten cents more."

That proposal infuriated Harry. He and I always had a beautiful relationship—except for this one exchange, which was not a good one. He said, "How dare you take away our Senate pay-for! This was a very thoughtful measure on our part. How dare you!" I replied: "Harry, you don't have any 'pay-for,' because our members aren't going to vote for it at all. Now you have twenty billion. Just because you want forty billion doesn't mean you get forty billion."

Again, he said: "I can't believe you would do this to me—that you would take away our pay-for!" Ultimately the $20 billion cap was left in.

At the same time, the Senate's rejection of the public option had been a personal disappointment for many of us in the House. The public option would have saved $100 billion in federal government spending over ten years. Sadly, we just could not get it to be accepted in the Senate. However, the legislation did ultimately allow for individual states to design something approaching their own public option in how they organized their state health care exchanges and marketplaces. In our final legislation, we also worked together to make accommodations for the consumer, which approached what a public option would have provided. For example, Covered California, the state's official health insurance marketplace, works beautifully there.

Another moment of deep disagreement occurred when Senator Baucus and my dear friend Rahm Emanuel, the president's chief of staff, secretly negotiated a deal with Pharmaceutical Research and Manufacturers of America (PhRMA), the pharmaceutical industry's top lobbying group, limiting Big Pharma's financial obligations. Big Pharma was happy because they would not be paying their fair share. (In addition, as the Sunlight Foundation would point out, Rahm's deputy chief of staff was Jim Messina, who was a former chief of staff for Max Baucus.)

The revelation of such a deal was a severe blow to House Democrats. Members felt betrayed because of the priority we had placed on lowering drug prices and because of the secret nature of the agreement, which was outside the integrity of our House-Senate commitment to jointly write the ACA. During the 2006 election year, when we retook the majority, House Democrats had, in our "Six for '06" agenda and "New Direction for America" platform, a promise of legislation enabling the secretary of Health and Human Services to negotiate lower prices for prescription drugs. The proposal passed the House but not the Senate. The relationship between the Senate and the pharmaceutical industry had been too cozy for too long, and now Big Pharma was laughing all the way to the bank. It also was disheartening because if Big Pharma had paid more of its fair share, we could have covered the costs for more primary care doctors to meet the needs of low-income and rural Americans.

The disappointment was terrible, and the latest proof of what we in the House had known for some time: there had been a Senate bias in the White House that did not serve us well in the health care debate. This bias was intensified because both President Barack Obama and Vice President Joe Biden had served in the Senate, and their staffs were largely drawn from the Senate. House members suspected—with justification—that the White House was giving deference to the Senate bill. Even though the leader of the White House health care staff had said that the House bill was as close to perfect as a bill could be, it appeared that others in the White House preferred the path of least resistance. Some wanted a smaller, "Kiddie Care" approach—and still others wanted us in the House just to accept whatever the Senate was able to pass. This group of White House staffers included Rahm Emanuel, who even proposed what was dubbed the "Titanic plan," with benefits only for children and some women.

But I made it clear—in the Oval Office and in our leadership conference calls—that the approach was not acceptable. House Democrats were not going to support a piecemeal, incrementalist, eensy-weensy-spider plan. That was not going to happen. We were not going to take baby steps.

So in January, when we went to conference, everyone knew where the House Democrats stood.

The End in Sight

The January conference was remarkable: it was presided over by the president of the United States, the House was led by the Speaker, and the Senate was led by the majority leader. Other committee chairs and members participated, and the staff was divided into fifteen subgroups to address specific areas. The ACA conference appeared to be the first of its kind in history. And despite those who wanted to surrender the opportunity of a generation, President Obama stayed true to a grander plan.

We worked through mid-January. However, our final bill would not be voted on as a conference report—because on the nineteenth, Republican Scott Brown won the US Senate seat in Massachusetts, the seat that Teddy Kennedy had held for decades. While Massachusetts replacing Ted with a Republican was hard to believe, it could not have happened at a worse time, because now we no longer had sixty Democrats in the Senate.

With Scott Brown's election, the press insisted that the ACA was dead and would never pass. In reply, I told the reporters that we would never abandon our generational responsibility and opportunity to achieve universal health care. That was our decision. That was our only possible path.

I told them we wouldn't allow anything to stand in our way. No matter how high the barrier. First, we would push open the gate. If that didn't work, we would climb the fence. If that didn't work, we would pole-vault in. If that didn't work, we would helicopter in, but we would not let anything stand in our way.

In early February, President Obama called for a February 25 meeting of the most senior congressional leaders from both parties for the highest level of discussion at one of the most prestigious venues in Washington: Blair House, usually reserved for foreign dignitaries and heads of state. It was a history-making occasion, and President Obama called it the White House Health Care Summit. Nearly one year after he held his opening health care forum at the White House, he was still sincerely seeking Republican ideas—and, he hoped, votes.

House Democrats hoped for that same success, too—not because we needed Republican votes, but because we wanted bipartisanship. Many Republican provisions had made their way into the final House bill, but ultimately, we did not receive one GOP vote.

Sadly, that same lack of support was exactly what transpired at Blair House. It became clear that even with Republican provisions already included in the bill—and even if the president accepted some additional GOP proposals—Republicans would never support the ACA.

Recognizing that this would be a party-line vote, some in Washington again suggested that the House just pass the Senate bill. To that, I responded: "This is not anything that my members will vote for. I'm not even bringing it up. It will not pass." Indeed, our members were unhappy with the suggestion of settling for the Senate bill. I could see the anger in their faces. My members were very strong. They said, We're just not voting for it, period. I told them, "I'm with you, I won't vote for it, and I won't even ask you to vote for it."

It was clear that our only path forward was through reconciliation: passing a second legislative package that would amend the Senate bill and only require fifty-one votes. However, even with the Senate agreeing to proceed under reconciliation, what emerged as a serious problem was that, in order for the process to work under the complicated parliamentary rules of reconciliation, House Democrats did have to pass the highly unpopular Senate bill first. My members were not happy with me when they learned that we had to pass the Senate bill separately and send it to the White House to be signed into law before we could amend it with our fixes in reconciliation.

My only option was to seek extra assurances from the Senate.

To his eternal credit, Harry Reid recognized our shared values and knew why we were fighting so hard. House Democrats made a list of what we needed to add from our bill and the most egregious items we could not live with that remained in the Senate bill, all of which we wanted to address in reconciliation. We insisted that the reconciliation package would make the following changes:

- Increasing the consumer subsidies for insurance premiums and cost-sharing that would be offered through the new insurance exchanges.
- Expanding Medicare's drug benefit by phasing out the "donut hole" in that benefit, which caused consumers to pay an increased amount for prescription drugs after they reached a certain level of spending, and also reducing overall payments to insurance plans under the Medicare Advantage program.
- Increasing the federal share of spending and changing the eligibility for certain Medicaid (the federal low-income insurance program) beneficiaries.
- Modifying the design and delaying the implementation of the excise tax on insurance plans with relatively high premiums.
- Increasing the rate and expanding the scope of a tax that would be charged to higher-income households.
- Increasing the penalties for employers that do not offer health insurance and modifying the penalties for individuals who do not obtain insurance.

It was clear that the House needed assurance from fifty-one senators that they would agree to our reconciliation fixes. I told the president and Harry Reid that we needed a letter signed by fifty-one Democratic senators stating their commitment. Some of the days during the negotiations were historic and advanced the ACA. The day that Harry brought the reconciliation letter to me in the Speaker's office was one of those days. He showed me the letter with fifty signatures, and he said that there was one more letter from Sen. Robert Byrd, who was in West Virginia but had signed his own letter. Fifty-one senators had committed to voting for the priorities that House Democrats were insisting upon in the reconciliation package.

This was no small feat—because not every senator shared Harry's commitment. As we would later learn, there was a cynical comment made by a Democrat in the Senate that Congress should not have focused on health care reform because it would largely benefit the poor, and the poor do not vote. Fortunately, Harry did not share this view.

Harry radiated strength and confidence when he came to my office with the letter bearing the fifty signatures. I said, "Harry, I'm not going to ask you for a copy. I want to say to my members that you showed me the letter and that I trust you." I wanted to demonstrate to him and to my members the trust and confidence I personally had in him—which anyone who knew him would agree was well deserved. Today, I wish I had a copy of the letter so that people could see an outstanding example of his integrity and effectiveness—and I hope that one day the letter will become part of the public record.

Now the House needed our own moment of decision and courage. The leadership and I shared our members' disdain for the Senate bill without changes. However, I reassured them that I would never have brought it up without a guarantee of securing the changes we sought. With the commitment of fifty-one Democratic senators—and the reputation of the trusted leadership of Harry Reid—our members reluctantly and with reservations prepared to vote for the Senate bill. The back-and-forth in our caucus had been intense—but now we had a path.

With a mixture of courage, pride, and a belief in our values as House Democrats, I asked our members to make a great decision for America. House Democrats knew full well the difference that health care reform would make and the role they played in shaping it—so I told them to "embrace the suck."

As we prepared to bring the Senate bill to the House floor, the trust of my members in the president, in the majority leader, and now in me was all on the line.

Final Negotiations

Before we could vote on any bill—Senate or reconciliation—we had to address two more contentious issues for House members. We had already dealt with these issues in the House in the fall, but they reemerged in our final negotiations in the spring: abortion and regional disparities.

While Republicans and naysayers were misrepresenting what was in the legislation regarding abortion, I was never frightened by that. I had confidence in our legislative language. Nothing in the legislation made new federal policy regarding abortion. Throughout the process, I remained particularly saddened by the misrepresentations of the United States Conference of Catholic Bishops (USCCB). As a devout Catholic, I respect the view of the Catholic Church against abortion—shared by members of my own D'Alesandro family—but I rejected the bishops' skewed view of our legislation.

Our meetings and calls with the Catholic bishops resembled something removed from reality. One particularly heartbreaking telephone call involved a USCCB representative. We were in one of the Speaker's rooms with members of the Pro-Choice Caucus, including Rosa DeLauro, Diana DeGette, Anna Eshoo, Jan Schakowsky, Lois Capps, and Louise Slaughter. We all shared our deep dismay that the bishops were opposed to the ACA, which would benefit so many.

It became clear that the bishops were using their misrepresentation of the bill's language regarding abortion to try to take down *Roe v. Wade*. To achieve that goal, they were prepared to undo the prospects of health care for all Americans. The comment that nearly brought me to tears—which was not only rare but unique for me—was spoken by the USCCB representative—someone with whom I had worked for years. He triumphantly said: "I have never seen the bishops so united as they are against the Affordable Care Act."

I was deeply saddened by the bishops' disregard for health care as a right for all and not a privilege for the few—and for their willingness to act based on misinterpretations, which we had repeatedly explained were not true. I have never been more disappointed in some of the Catholic bishops than I was during this fight—because their opposition was in complete defiance of everything they claimed to stand for.

One of the main misrepresentations centered around how the bill addressed the Hyde Amendment, named for the late Republican congressman Henry Hyde. The Hyde Amendment is a legislative provision barring the use of federal funds to pay for abortion, except to save the life of the mother or in the case of a pregnancy arising from incest or rape. Its author, a Democrat, Rep. Jim Oberstar, said: "I know what the Hyde Amendment is. I wrote it, and I support it. And this bill does not violate it."

Congressman Dale Kildee of Michigan, who had once studied for the priesthood, stood with Jim Oberstar. Together they gave their imprimatur: "This is okay to do." They really were statesmen—they gave us inspiration with their understanding of the details, the standing that they had on the issue, and their courage to speak out.

I was truly thankful to God for the nuns, who knew what was

in, and not in, the legislation. They were part of our first efforts to pass the bill. Later, they stepped up again to save the ACA when it came under assault. We would not have been successful without their work. I am particularly in awe of Sister Carol Keehan of the Daughters of Charity, the former head of the Catholic Health Association of the United States, who supported the legislation. Her leadership and that of many others across America, including Sister Simone Campbell, generated a letter representing more than fifty thousand nuns to initially support—and later to save—the legislation.

Important leadership throughout the discussion of our health care bill was also shown by Congressman John Dingell. His father, who had served with my father in Congress, had introduced health care reform in every Congress he served in. And John, as a junior member of Congress, had the privilege of gaveling in Medicare legislation when it passed. In fact, I would use John's Medicare gavel to gavel in the Affordable Care Act.

John worked with fellow Michigan congressman Bart Stupak, who needed reassurance that no funds in the bill would be used for abortion. Our bill never had any funding for abortion, which already would have been illegal under the Hyde Amendment. President Obama also assuaged concerns by putting forth an executive order reaffirming this policy—which was well received by our members and provided an additional level of comfort for the nuns.

The statement from the White House on President Obama's executive order explained that the ACA aligned with the longstanding restrictions on using federal funds to pay for abortion. The executive order was also written to underscore that there are "additional safeguards to ensure that the status quo is upheld and enforced and that the health care legislation's restrictions against the public funding of abortions cannot be circumvented."

While the abortion issue was always a matter of discussion until the very end, it was never an obstacle to passing our bill.

The one issue that was a real obstacle to passing the ACA was regional disparity, which was discussed ahead of the November 7 vote in the House and then again in March 2010.

Early in drafting the House legislation, members from the Midwest—Representatives Betty McCollum and Ron Kind in particular but others as well—began advocating for more attention to Medicare's geographic payment inequities. In some parts of the country, the performance of health services was high and the federal Medicare reimbursement rate was low. In other parts of the country, performance was low, and medical reimbursements were high—and most members who represented those low-performance/high-reimbursement areas wanted to keep the status quo and have their poor performers "grandfathered" into the legislation. It is important to note that, in addition to the unfairness of regional disparities, it was a bad health policy. A high number of patient hospital readmissions, while adding unnecessary costs, also indicated poor medical performance and a lower quality of care.

The shorthand for poor performance was "volume, not value," meaning that poor performance in health care outcomes was being rewarded with high reimbursement rates. However, the problem was far greater than simply dollars and costs for the patients and their families. "Volume, not value" meant that a hospital might discharge a patient too soon or with inadequate support, leading to readmission. Another hospital stay meant more money for the hospital, but it did not always mean a better outcome for the patient. At the same time, hospitals and health care systems whose patients were not being readmitted—who were getting it right the first time—were earning less money. We wanted a system of value, not volume—but Washington, sadly, is too often a status quo town.

Betty McCollum and Ron Kind's point was that they could not ask their constituents to subsidize low performance elsewhere in the country. In June 2009, Congresswoman McCollum authored a bipartisan letter to the House leadership, key committees, and ranking members urging them to make addressing Medicare geographic payments a priority in health care reform. We held multiple meetings and hearings on how to craft provisions to avoid regional inequities in Medicare reimbursement, and on how we could both lower costs and improve quality. Addressing the regional disparities was also essential to writing legislation that did not perpetuate the inequalities and differences in our system. My response to those who wanted to maintain the status quo was, "If you grandfather those areas in, you are not changing anything. You are perpetuating low performance, high reimbursement."

But it was essential that we stick together to craft a solution. Our work culminated in a July 24 announcement of a negotiated agreement between the House Democratic leadership and Representatives McCollum and Kind, along with then-representatives Bruce Braley of Iowa and Jay Inslee of Washington State. In my view, regional disparity turned out to be the biggest obstacle to passing our House bill. And we had to revisit the issue for reconciliation.

The debate on regional disparities continued throughout the remainder of our work on the ACA until Friday, March 19, two days before the ACA vote scheduled for March 21. Members asked informed and specific questions, which we addressed. I was pleased—to say with some immodesty—that my years on the Appropriations Committee enabled me to address key concerns. Ultimately, all members who expressed concerns greatly improved the legislation.

On March 20, the Obama administration weighed in. Secretary of Health and Human Services Kathleen Sebelius—who I am proud to say graduated from my alma mater, Trinity Washington University—had listened to, testified about, and understood the concerns about quality of care, and she sent a very strong letter about improving both the quality and the value of health care delivered in this country. The secretary referenced Sections 1157 and 1159 of the original House legislation as the basis for incentivizing high-value care across the provider system. She also announced that she would convene a national summit on geographic variation, cost, access, and value of health care later that year. Kathleen Sebelius's letter was essential in confirming the administration's commitment to better care in our country.

With that obstacle lowered, we could now proceed to finalize the vote count.

Final Count

As the final vote drew closer, I was confident that we would prevail. But I still wanted to ensure the bill received as many supporters as possible. I wanted to solidify our votes among the Illinois delegation, but both President Obama, who had been an Illinois senator before he became president, and Rahm Emanuel, who had been an Illinois congressman, wouldn't make two calls I thought we should make. So I acted. I called Chicago mayor Richard Daley for his advice on how best to persuade two representatives who were uncertain, Dan Lipinski and Jerry Costello. Both had voted yes for the crucial November 7 House vote, although only Jerry would vote yes for the bill's final passage in March.

The other call I made was to Cardinal Francis Eugene George of Chicago. I said, "Your Eminence, thank you for the honor to speak with you. I am calling to enlist your support for the Affordable Care Act, which will provide health care to tens of millions of Americans." He interrupted me by saying: "I'm only willing to talk if you're not calling about killing unborn babies." He had clearly ignored the support we had from pro-life members and the president's executive order. He was just focused on stopping the bill. With all the kindness and prayerfulness that I could muster, I determined that the call was a waste of my time. The attitude of some bishops was so contrary to our devotion to ministering to the needs of the poor and to my Catholic upbringing. These experiences were painful.

But the cardinal's views were not held by all the Catholic clergy. That Saturday, March 20, I called Father Ted Hesburgh, my hero of Catholic social justice and the longtime president of the University of Notre Dame. He was a champion of civil rights and had marched with Dr. King. I had visited him at Notre Dame and been regaled with his stories as he enjoyed his cigars.

"Father," I said, "I have to admit, we're having trouble with some cardinals, yet there is nothing in the bill that violates the Hyde Amendment."

He asked, "So who do you want me to call?" I suggested that he call Congressman Joe Donnelly, who represented the Indiana district where Notre Dame is located.

He said, "Got his number?"

I kept my call to Father Hesburgh secret out of respect for Joe Donnelly. Joe was a valued friend and colleague, later a senator from Indiana and subsequently appointed by President Biden to serve as the United States ambassador to the Holy See at the Vatican. But when I walked into the Democratic cloakroom in the Capitol, I heard members comparing stories of how I got their votes. Some with humor, some not.

As I entered, I heard Joe say, "You should hear what she did to me! She had Father Hesburgh call me and say, 'The Speaker and I need you to vote for the ACA.' What was I supposed to do?!"

God truly blessed America with the life, leadership, and legacy of Father Hesburgh. In my office, I have a beautiful statue of the Visitation of Mary sent to me by him. It represents the first time that Mary visited her cousin Elizabeth while they are both pregnant: Mary with Jesus and Elizabeth with John the Baptist. I deeply treasure this beautiful manifestation of motherhood from Father Hesburgh.

As House Democrats gathered for a final time ahead of the March 21 vote, we were prayerful and unified—and also vilified.

We came together in the Cannon Caucus Room, both officially and personally proud of the history we were about to make. Photographers captured our caucus proceeding down the steps toward the Capitol. Rep. John Lewis, our spiritual and intellectual leader, and John Larson, our caucus chair, led us.

But there was nothing peaceful about this moment. During the short walk, we were screamed at by protesters who waved flags and carried signs. For months, many of my members had been verbally assaulted by protesters. I recognized long ago that I had signed up for this; it doesn't bother me personally. I have thick skin. But as the health care debate unfolded, I saw that we were entering a new arena. It became common for protesters to march into my office, scream at my staff, and angrily throw their cut-up Medicare cards or even their hearing aids at anyone nearby—even when it was clear that they didn't seem to really know what they were protesting.

I have attended protests; before I was in Congress, I was an activist, out on the streets, carrying placards. I still have signs from more than thirty years ago leaning against a wall in my basement.

On other issues, I have said to angry citizens and even to angry members of Congress, "I'm with you, I've also protested, but this is a legislative body. Come back when you have votes to support your proposal, and we will talk."

But when it came to health care, we were witnessing a new level of disrespect. People with a different point of view thought nothing of getting right in a member's face, wherever that member might be. As Speaker, I had security, but most members did not. The level of venom also made many of us wonder if these were simply paid protesters. We had learned to recognize the difference between true grassroots activism and Astroturf. As we walked to the Capitol, our own voices were drowned out by the screaming and yelling, as many of the protesters called and heckled us by name. This was personal. Then the agitators started spitting. They spat on John Lewis, a hero of the civil rights movement. John later told me that he had not seen anything like it since the march on Selma, where he was among the peaceful marchers spat upon and attacked with billy clubs and bullwhips.

But despite the anger seething around us, we remained undeterred. We stood tall as I carried John Dingell's gavel.

As I walked to the floor, I was surprised to see that my daughter Alexandra had brought her two toddlers, Paul and Thomas, to witness history. Their presence deepened my appreciation for what our members were about to do—for the future and for all our children. Later, Paul and Thomas would sadly ask me why people outside were so mad at "Aunt Nancy"—having heard some of the horrible things being yelled about "Nancy," they thought that the crowd was angry at Alexandra's sister Nancy Corinne, one of their aunts. To them, I was simply "Mimi."

The House chamber is where our past colleagues abolished slavery, granted women the right to vote, and offered a hand to the weak, care to the sick, education to the young, and hope to the many—and when necessary had authorized going to war. And now it was here that we voted to establish the fourth pillar of health and financial security with the Affordable Care Act. To me, it was a blessed day in a blessed place.

Bringing the gavel down on the ACA was worth every sacrifice and every criticism. As Speaker, I was in awe of the courage of the House Democrats—none of our progress and eventual success on that day would have been possible without them. As a grandmother, I was overwhelmed by what the ACA meant for America's families.

We as a caucus had made the deliberate decision to honor our generational responsibility to provide health care as a right for everyone, not just a privilege for the few. Each member who supported the ACA and aligned with our commitment made every decision in favor of passage—no matter how difficult. We stayed together when it counted. As for the Republicans, one voted yes in November but none, as we have seen, in March. Once the vote was complete, Democrats from across the caucus embraced each other in triumph.

That night, President Obama called to congratulate and express his gratitude to our House Democrats. He shared that he was happier that night than he was on the night he was elected president. I replied, "I am pretty happy, too, Mr. President, but not as happy as I was the night you won—because without you as president, we would not have the Affordable Care Act."

Two days later, President Obama officially signed the ACA into law. It was a glorious day. Imagine being in the White House as the president signed a bill that would change the lives of millions of families. I was especially excited to be there with Secretary Sebelius. We asked the president if he would take a photo with the

"Trinity sisters." He replied: "Sure, where are the nuns?" Laughing, we explained that Kathleen and I were the Trinity sisters—and how proud we were that our faith and values had played a role in passing the ACA.

Reconciliation

On March 25, the Senate voted 56 to 43 to honor its commitment to pass the reconciliation bill, which officially amended the ACA and included every promise made to the House Democrats. Thank you, Harry Reid.

In the arcane rules of Congress, to have a reconciliation bill, the legislation must first be authorized in a budget bill. Our 2009 budget bill authorized reconciliation for both health care and higher education. While the health care debate continued for almost a year, we were also negotiating a higher education bill under the leadership of Chairman George Miller of the Education and Labor Committee. That bill made important changes to the funding streams for higher education. Our bill ended the practice of subsidizing private banks to provide student loans, made the loan system part of the Department of Education, and increased Pell Grant funding for college students in economic need. We were especially proud of the additional vital funding for minority-serving institutions (MSIs), historically Black colleges and universities (HBCUs), Hispanic-serving institutions (HSIs), and tribal colleges and universities (TCUs).

While the budget bill for health care and education was crucial in allowing us to proceed under reconciliation, it also became a flash point between the House and the Senate. Senators began requesting large financial set-asides from the bill for their pet projects, almost as if our budget bill had become something of a

Senate ATM machine. The House negotiators stood firm, and the bill's original financial priorities for higher education remained intact.

Unfortunately, whether to diminish our success on reconciliation or for some other reason, the White House decided to sign the reconciliation bill as if it were entirely a higher education bill, and not a vital part of the health care reform act. Once again, I had to express the dismay of House Democrats at the White House's indifference. The White House did not appreciate what it took to come to agreement in the House—and also with the Senate.

I told the president that George Miller was the reason the education bill passed in the House and also the reason that it was an effective bill, well received by the education and labor communities. The higher education community was greatly impacted, and appreciative of George's tremendous leadership. The president promised to thank George—but in public, the White House again failed both to understand the difficulty of passing a transformative bill and to acknowledge the House's role. Instead, political attention was directed at the Senate, and the White House overlooked its crucial allies in the House. Sadly, those of us in the House leadership found ourselves in this position constantly, with multiple administrations. In 2010, after all that George had accomplished and the victory he had helped deliver, this slight stung more than others.

Democratic courage on the House floor was not rewarded in the voting booth, either. When Democrats lost our majority in the 2010 election, several factors had helped to produce a perfect storm. In the fall of 2008—before the November election—House Democrats had voted, as we have seen, for TARP. While the initiative was intended to be bipartisan, the Democrats had been forced to save the day and the economy with tough, unpopular votes. Many voters had not approved of taxpayer money being used to bail out reckless Wall Street financial firms, even if that money would eventually be repaid. And voters had not always understood why Democrats had voted yes even as the Republicans reneged on their commitment to support President Bush's own proposal. With 9.6 percent unemployment and lingering unhappiness over TARP, Democrats were prime targets of criticism because we were the majority.

Members were inundated with negative messaging about the ACA, including the constant refrain that the legislation created "death panels" when it did nothing of the sort. Opponents also raised the specter of tax increases and other payment schemes that would result in job losses and kept stating that Medicare was at risk.

The timing was also particularly bad because, while we had passed the legislation, the promise of universal access to health care would not be realized for another three years: voters had no way to see the immediate impact of this historic bill. We had all the downside and none of the upside.

At the same time, the Supreme Court's infamous 2010 decision in *Citizens United v. FEC* had unleashed, as we have seen, a torrent of dark money (where the donor is unknown) to wreak havoc in the election. Our members—especially those in rural districts—were flooded by a tidal wave of negative advertisements spewing flat-out lies, including about the ACA. A report by Open-Secrets found that while less than $1 million in dark money was spent in 2009, spending skyrocketed immediately following the *Citizens United* decision: "topping $138 million before the 2010 Election Day."

After the joy of passing the ACA in March, 2010 turned into a tough year, with an awful result. We entered the next Congress in the minority, with the Republicans primed to take down the ACA—which they tried to do at least seventy times. For the remainder of the Obama administration, six more years, the GOP was clever in putting forth appealing resolutions designed to undo the legislation.

In my twenty years as either Speaker or House Democratic leader, my most difficult task was convincing Democratic members to sustain President Obama's anticipated or actual vetoes of these Republican resolutions. Personally and officially, I had to confront great, brave, and especially new members with stern objections to their possible bad votes.

They would say, "This Republican resolution is popular in my district, and I know my district better than you."

My response was, "I certainly hope so—but I know the Affordable Care Act better than you do. And the president's veto must be sustained." Graciously yet firmly, sometimes even harshly, I needed to convince these members, whom I loved, respected, and had helped get elected, that Democratic unity was more important, and that supporting the president on the ACA was essential. Many of them ultimately turned out to be strong supporters of the Affordable Care Act after they saw how far the Republicans were willing to go to destroy it. But I was saddened that I had to be so tough on insisting on these new members' votes at the outset when they had not been there for the fight of the generation to pass the ACA. Yet I knew that they had to vote with our party, even if it was hard to explain at home. That task was made more challenging by the ACA's rollout.

In August of 2013, I was approached by the White House. I was told that they knew I was unhappy about the previous shortfalls in their messaging—but that I would be happy to know that the "best message of all" would be the official rollout of the ACA in October. It turned out to be a disaster, with the website crashing within two hours of the launch and not all parts of it being fully operational. Coming from tech-sophisticated Northern California, I was stunned by the shortcomings of the "best message of all."

On the plus side, some of the problems that were initially encountered were due to the sheer number of people who had tried to sign up for ACA plans at once—and fortunately, no one whose sign-up was delayed lost any benefits because the website failed to work as hoped.

Saving the ACA

One of the main reasons I stayed in Congress after the 2016 election was to save the Affordable Care Act.

If Hillary Clinton—one of the best-prepared people in modern times to run for president—had won in 2016, I was prepared to leave Congress, knowing that the ACA would be safe with her in the Oval Office. Shockingly, Hillary did not win—and not only did she not win, but she lost to someone fully committed to repealing the ACA, Donald Trump. While the Republican slogan was "repeal and replace," they actually meant "repeal and replace with nothing."

After the election, I spoke with President-elect Trump and tried to convince him to spare the ACA: "I'm not going to ask you to do anything that is not in your interest, Mr. President. There is a way for you to make this better—we always want to make something better—or more to your liking and call it something else, but it will have the fundamentals."

As it turned out, he wasn't interested at all. We couldn't even have a reasonable conversation. And with unified Republican control of government, I knew I had to stay and fight. I feel very proprietary about the Affordable Care Act—and it was my mission to save it.

One of the first steps after the 2016 election was to establish our "First Stand"—to defend the ACA against the incoming Republican assault. We vowed not to let the other side make America sick again. We held a stakeholder call two days after the election with veterans, patient advocates, labor officials, women, and disability justice leaders—among others—to form a coalition to "Protect Our Care." A plan emerged from the meeting to host hundreds of community rallies across the country that started on Martin Luther King Jr. weekend. In my San Francisco district, three thousand people showed up. I said to them: "To stop Republicans from kicking millions of Americans off life-saving health care, we don't agonize; we organize. And we are not going back!"

We carried the momentum into Inauguration Day, when House Democrats wore Protect Our Care buttons. Then, on the Saturday after the inauguration, America was overwhelmed, in the most positive of ways, by the Women's Marches in Washington and around our nation. The marches were not partisan—people came not because of their affiliation with a political party, but because they shared a point of view. They were organic and had their own inspiration and momentum, demonstrating the value of showing up. Millions of women celebrated their power and were a joy to behold.

On Martin Luther King Jr. Day, we launched the First Stand effort of our Protect Our Care coalition—which uplifted and supported what would ultimately be ten thousand grassroots events across the country that were central to our success in saving the ACA. This effort and these events were effective because regular Americans told their stories. The stories weren't about provisions in the law; they were about saving lives. Early on, we could tell that our organizing was making an impact and would make all the difference in the end.

In March, House Republicans put forth a monstrous proposal to destroy the ACA. The Congressional Budget Office said that the Republican bill would have ripped health care away from 24 million Americans. And it would have denied protections for preexisting conditions for more than 130 million people. To make matters worse, Republican leaders bypassed the normal committee process to advance their bill, instead writing it behind closed doors. Paul Ryan, the new House Speaker, spent eighteen days on his legislation, and the so-called plan he put forward, the American Health Care Act (AHCA), was little more than a hodgepodge that cut support to low-income Americans and anyone with a serious health condition. Insurance premiums for others would skyrocket: a sixty-four-year-old earning $26,500 could expect a 760 percent premium increase, from $1,700 to $14,600. The only people the bill did help were the wealthy, by bestowing big tax breaks.

This misguided effort stood in sharp contrast to the many months we had spent meticulously debating and crafting the ACA—in our three bipartisan committees, within our caucus and the entire Congress, and in the public reading of the bill. Nevertheless, there were some who pushed us to cut a deal with the Republicans to save what ACA provisions we could, but to give up on keeping all of the act's vital changes that had helped expand Medicaid coverage. We said no—we wanted to save it all. The strongest voices for saving Medicaid were veterans, persons with disabilities, families of children with complex medical conditions—who named themselves the Little Lobbyists—and middle-income families who realized that much of seniors' long-term care was paid for by Medicaid.

Our Protect Our Care coalition marched, rallied, and mobilized across the country to ensure that families knew just how dangerous the Republican bill would be. Our efforts decisively won over the American people. Indeed, the one unifying theme of Paul Ryan's AHCA was that many people across the political spectrum hated it. Public polling data showed the Republicans' repeal bill to be the most unpopular piece of legislation in more than three decades. Only 17 percent of the public supported its provisions— and the Republicans were frantically changing major parts of the legislation the day before the scheduled vote. Talk about a bill that no one had read or had time to read. Because we made them feel the heat, Republicans suffered a humiliating defeat.

I remember March 24, 2017, with great clarity. The Republicans thought that they would repeal the ACA around the anniversary of the passage of the final legislation. But Democrats knew that Speaker Paul Ryan didn't have the votes to pass the Republican bill, because outside groups and patient advocates were reporting to us that the Republicans were still desperately seeking votes in and outside of the chamber.

As the AHCA was being debated, I told my members that I would seek recognition to request that the Speaker pull the bill from the floor. But before I could be recognized, Paul Ryan pulled his own bill—because he did not have the votes. One lesson in successful legislating that should be observed: the Speaker should only bring a bill to the floor when he has the votes—not simply on the anniversary of when I had the votes.

Speaker Ryan was forced to go to the White House and explain to President Trump that he could not pass the repeal bill. In response, the president declared that Speaker Nancy Pelosi and Leader Chuck Schumer would "one hundred percent own" the ACA.

Indeed, I was proud to!

That May, House Republicans thought that they had finally found a path to passing another version of their ACA repeal bill. I said at the time that the Republican members who voted for that monstrosity should have this vote tattooed on their foreheads— and that they must answer for this damaging vote to their constituents in their districts and to the voters at the ballot box. In a twisted celebration, Republicans even gathered in the Rose Garden to brag about ripping away health care from the American people. By the summer, Senate Republicans were advancing a measure to repeal the ACA—with no replacement. It was a gift to the health insurance industry and a cruel swipe at America's working families.

On the day of the Senate vote, I had the privilege of having a conversation with Sen. John McCain. We had become friends— and foes—working on many pieces of legislation over the years. I wanted Senator McCain to be aware of some questionable rule tactics being employed by the House GOP. Senator McCain said, "Nancy, I do not need you to tell me that. I know what is going on." He also told me that, under the circumstances, his vote would be no. I kept his comment a secret from everyone.

Later in the evening, as the debate in the Senate continued, I spoke to the peaceful and prayerful crowd of ACA supporters who had gathered outside the Capitol. The scene was quite a contrast to the gauntlet we had run the day we passed the ACA in March 2010, when we were subjected to our opponents' spitting, jeering, and crude obscenities. I told the crowd: "Let us all believe that we can succeed. We come here tonight because we believe we can make a difference." Some wondered why I was not attacking the Republicans or thought that I was not praising the Democrats enough. But hours later, as I watched Senator McCain give his thumbs-down during the Senate vote, I was beyond overjoyed. His was the thumbs-down heard 'round the world; his vote sank the repeal.

Senator McCain was always a person of his word—a true patriot. Every day, I wish he were still here. Ambassador Cindy McCain has carried on the family tradition of love of country and integrity in service as executive director of the UN World Food Programme.

As predicted, the voters remembered on the next election day. In 2018, Democrats took back the House, flipping forty Republican seats, a critical victory for both Americans' health care and American democracy. As the House Republicans learned that fall, ripping health care away from the American people is no cause for a Rose Garden celebration. At that time, people said to me, "Aren't you lucky that health care became such a prominent issue in the campaign?" I answered, "No. We made our own luck. We held ten thousand events on health care."

Impact

The ACA has survived. And consider this. Since its enactment in 2010:

- More than 40 million Americans have gained insurance.
- Nearly 130 million Americans can no longer be denied insurance because they have a preexisting health condition.
- Insurance companies can no longer cancel policies if someone gets sick, and there are no lifetime limits on care.
- Women can no longer be denied coverage—or be charged higher premiums than men—simply because they are women.

Until the ACA, many women were being charged up to 50 percent more than men.

- Millions of young adults can continue coverage under their parents' plans.
- Millions more seniors have benefited from extraordinary financial savings by closing the prescription drug "donut hole."
- Regional disparities were overwhelmingly reined in.
- More than 28 million jobs have been created in the Obama and Biden administrations since passage, despite Republican predictions that the law would be a "job killer."
- The ACA is proving to be the biggest deficit reduction bill in decades—saving over $1 trillion, despite Republican insistence that it would be a massive "budget buster."

Under Joe Biden, costs were lowered further because subsidies were expanded and extended—without one Republican vote. This remarkable record is largely ignored by the media. But it is a fact. That's why I'm so proud to have led the effort in the House.

When we sent the Affordable Care Act to the president in 2010, I encountered some of the same reporters whom I had told that, no matter what barriers were there—if there was a gate, we would push open the gate; if that didn't work, we would climb the fence; if the fence was too high, we would pole-vault in; if that didn't work, we would helicopter in—congressional Democrats would not let anything stand in the way of passage.

So, the reporters asked me: Which one did you do?

And I said that we pushed open the gate—succeeding with what we tried first. This was not only because of the magnificent leadership of President Obama at crucial moments throughout the debate and the hard work of members of Congress; it was also made possible by the outside mobilization of the public who supported us.

Before the ACA, we did not have an economy that allowed millions of people to freely change jobs, start new businesses, become self-employed, or pursue their artistic aspirations. Instead, many Americans were job-locked because they had a child or a family member with a preexisting condition and could not give up their health insurance. And we had chains constraining our businesses and their growth because of the rapidly increasing cost of health care.

But the Affordable Care Act is not just about health care for America. It's about a healthier America. It's about innovation and prevention. It's about wellness. In Senator Kennedy's magnificent words: "that what we face is above all a moral issue; that at stake are not just the details of policy, but fundamental principles of social justice and the character of our country."

With each year, I am grateful that congressional Democrats and the White House rose to meet Senator Kennedy's challenge. Although House Democrats did at times have doubts about the strength and courage of the Senate, those doubts did not extend to President Obama, Vice President Biden, and Majority Leader Harry Reid. From start to finish, President Obama brought vision, commitment, and knowledge to the debate. The president's vision was expansive, transformative, and a source of pride and trust to the members. When the ACA was derisively called "Obamacare" by the Republicans, we warmly embraced the name. However, I still call it the Affordable Care Act, because it was named to emphasize affordability—which also means accessibility. While we did not always get the messaging air cover that members needed in a timely fashion, the implementation of the ACA has improved the appreciation for it to this day.

Despite the low points, when even his staff was weakening in their resolve, President Obama stood strong. His knowledge of the legislation's broad possibilities and his awareness of the importance of specific provisions helped us. I will always remember when, during one discussion, he was called away to speak with heads of state regarding assistance to Haiti after the January 2010 earthquake. To observe a president deal with both situations simultaneously—with knowledge, confidence, and compassion—was remarkable. On the one hand, we saw President Obama's understanding of the need for new policy firsthand. And without being privy to heads of state calls, his judgment of what was urgently needed to address the catastrophe in Haiti made us reassured and proud.

While we did not always agree, we always respected President Obama's commitment to the strongest possible bill. It is essential to know, without doubt, that when members are asked to make what is for them a difficult vote, they need to know that the bill will be signed. There was never a question of President Obama's commitment.

Joe Biden's loyalty to the vision of President Obama was fortified and seasoned by his lifetime serving America's working families. He has always been a friend to the House Democrats—in campaigns and in legislation. Perhaps representing Delaware, a small state, with only one member of the House, made him better attuned than most senators to the needs of the people. House Democrats always knew we had a friend in the vice president.

Joe Biden's appreciation for the legislation was demonstrated by his characterization of it as a "big f****** deal." With full recognition of the law's complexity and scope; with a capital BFD. That knowledge served him and the country well when we expanded the ACA's subsidies and opportunities under the Biden-Harris administration. And we finally enacted the Inflation Reduction Act, enabling the secretary of Health and Human Services to negotiate for lower drug prices.

In the Senate, with appreciation for Senators Ted Kennedy and John McCain, the majority leader stands out: Harry Reid. In his life of leadership and service, Harry Reid acted with vision and integrity. These qualities served the American people well in the debate on the Affordable Care Act. His openness to receiving the House Democratic bill of particulars and delivering on the fifty-one Senate Democratic signatures made the ACA possible. Proud as he was of the Senate bill as the best the Senate could do, he knew it would not become law without the necessary improvements from the House. The trust his own Senate colleagues had in him was a boon to the nation—in this legislation and other challenges.

I enjoyed our very frequent phone calls, even though Harry was generally well known for ending calls abruptly. As soon as I started praising him for his leadership, courage, and occasional humor, that's when I would hear the line go click. Anyone who had served with Harry knew that his decisions were values-based and directly connected to the kitchen table of America's working families. His love for his wife, Landra, and their family was a great source of strength to him and a source of inspiration to those of us who knew them. Paul and I grew close to Harry and Landra, and our relationship with them and their family will always be one of respect, warmth, and love. We are grateful to Nevada for having sent Harry to Washington.

When Harry left office, he gave me, as a parting gift, a stuffed bald eagle that had graced his office in the Senate. I asked, "Harry, how did you get an endangered species?" He replied, "It was not captured or shot, but rather killed by being caught in electrical wires. Hence his name: Sparky."

With his permission, I changed the national symbol's name, appropriately, to Harry—a great American patriot and symbol.

Harry Reid's passing was a source of great sadness for so many of us. Personally, I lost a very dear friend whom I deeply miss.

Thanks to the courage and determination of congressional Democrats, we were able to accomplish a great deal. Speaking from a House perspective: our House leadership, with its beautiful diversity, served as a great sounding board on the three-committee, one-bill proposal: Steny Hoyer, our House majority leader; Jim Clyburn, our majority whip; Chris Van Hollen, chairman of the Democratic Congressional Campaign Committee; John Larson and Xavier Becerra, our caucus leadership; Rob Andrews; and George Miller and Rosa DeLauro, our Steering and Policy Committee co-chairs. John Spratt of the Budget Committee was essential, as was Louise Slaughter, chair of the Rules Committee, which brought the bill to the floor; and great thanks must go to our chairmen, George Miller, Henry Waxman, Charlie Rangel—and later, Sandy Levin—who all masterfully fought the fight. Rosa was especially relentless in her pursuit of priorities for women and children in the bill. As a senior appropriator who would go on to become Appropriations Committee chair, she understood the possibilities and the legislative language that was necessary. She was also a force in our debate with the bishops. However, our inside maneuvering would have only taken us so far. The outside mobilization propelled the ACA to success and survival.

I always quote Abraham Lincoln: "Public sentiment is everything. *With* it, nothing can fail; *against* it, nothing can succeed." And thanks to the patriotic outside mobilization demanding the ACA, we succeeded—and the ACA stands strong to this day.

Final Thoughts

On December 14, 2022, my portrait as Speaker was unveiled in the United States Capitol. I was so honored to have Democratic Senate leader Chuck Schumer, former Republican House Speaker John Boehner, and California representatives Zoe Lofgren and Lucille Roybal-Allard speak on my behalf, and the dazzling Denyce Graves bless us with her beautiful rendition of "The House I Live In (That's America to Me)."

But as honored as I was by the official guests, what meant so much to me were the comments by Elena Hung, a founder of the Little Lobbyists, one of the groups that had mobilized to save the ACA in 2017. Elena's daughter Xiomara had been born with a myriad of health problems, and she spoke from her heart:

> It is no exaggeration to say that my daughter Xiomara, the joy of my life, and countless children with complex medical needs and disabilities like her, are alive today because of the ACA....
>
> I often think of all the babies like Xiomara—whose five months in the neonatal intensive care unit totaled three million dollars in medical bills—who now have a chance at childhood because the Affordable Care Act banned lifetime limits on their care....
>
> [W]hat I hope everyone sees when they look at the . . . portrait is that Speaker Pelosi did it all For the Children.

What greater compliment could anyone receive?

Leadership in a
Time of Crisis

That Our Flag Is Still There

To this day, people still ask me how I remained so calm on January 6 as I watched the Capitol under assault. My answer is that I was already deeply aware of how dangerous Donald Trump was. He continues to be dangerous. If his family and staff truly understood his disregard both for the fundamentals of the law and for basic rules, and if they had reckoned with his personal instability over not winning the election, they should have staged an intervention. Whether because of willful blindness, money, prestige, or greed, they didn't—and America has paid a steep price. Not being calm on January 6 was a luxury none of us could afford.

For most of the afternoon on January 6, I was huddled inside a secure building on the grounds of Fort McNair, the third-oldest US Army installation in America, with the Senate majority and minority leaders—House Republican Minority Leader Kevin McCarthy was on the premises, but he did not join in our frantic phone calls to secure the National Guard and other responses.

I stayed calm because I knew what was at stake: the vision of our founders for a democracy, the sacrifice of men and women in uniform for our freedoms, and the hopes and dreams of our children. I knew of the fragility of it all. For a brief instant, I recalled how the last time I was whisked to a secure location with my colleagues was on the morning of 9/11, when we were attacked by a foreign enemy.

But on January 6, the attack was domestic. I knew Donald Trump's mental imbalance. I had seen it up close. His denial and then delays when the Covid pandemic struck, his penchant for repeatedly stomping out of meetings, his foul mouth, his pounding on tables, his temper tantrums, his disrespect for our nation's patriots, and his total separation from reality and actual events. His repeated, ridiculous insistence that he was the greatest of all time. It was the same for his subservient enablers.

It didn't take long for me to realize that I had more respect for the office of the president of the United States than Trump did. It has been clear to me from the start that he was an imposter—and that on some level, he knew it. Watching the insurrection, which Trump had instigated, begging him to provide the National Guard—as we did and which he refused to send—and taking into account my own worries about the basic security of Vice President Mike Pence, hiding inside the Capitol complex, and the important role he had to play, I knew we had to prevail.

My family was worried about my safety, but I knew that we had to defeat the mob. We could not let them prevent Congress from certifying Joe Biden and Kamala Harris's election as president and vice president of the United States. That's what mattered, and that's ultimately what we did.

Where did my calm come from? It came from prayers, strength, and the urgency to prevail. It also came from the courage of others. Our House Democrats and some Republicans were true patriots who, every day—but especially that day—were determined to protect and defend the Constitution against all enemies, foreign and domestic.

Prelude to the Assault on the Capitol

The road to January 6, 2021, began well before November 3, 2020, the long-awaited day of the presidential election. The plotting only intensified after November 7, when Joe Biden was officially declared the winner. After all the votes were counted, Biden had won by 7,060,140 votes (he was the first presidential candidate to receive more than 80 million votes nationwide). He had carried twenty-five states, plus the District of Columbia. For tens of millions of Americans, Biden's victory was a moment of great relief and great joy. The terrible, divisive presidency of Donald J. Trump was finally nearing its end. It was, quite simply, a victory for democracy and for decency.

In the final count, the numbers that mattered were how many states and which states Joe Biden and Kamala Harris had won—it had to be enough states to add up to a majority of votes in the Electoral College, because that is the constitutional mechanism by which the founders decided that the US would choose its presidents. As Hillary Clinton and Al Gore knew, having suffered the same fate in 2016 and 2000, respectively, it was possible to win the popular vote and still lose the presidency in the Electoral College vote count.

The House Democratic leaders also knew who we were dealing with in the now-lame-duck occupant of the White House. While we hoped he would abide by the results, we were prepared for the likelihood that he wouldn't and that the transition would be contentious. Months before, I had directed House members and staff to begin preparing for a potentially ugly, contested election. But even then, no rational person could have imagined the events of January 6.

As the votes were still being counted on November 3 and 4,

Donald Trump took to Twitter to make accusations about attempts to "STEAL" the election, adding, "Votes cannot be cast after the Poles are closed," apparently the first time the citizens of Poland—Poles, rather than the "polls"—had a role in US voting. Trump would later claim the election was "RIGGED," and his lawyers and allies mounted sixty-three separate legal challenges in multiple states. All except one were rejected by the courts.

On December 14, the electors of each of the fifty states and the District of Columbia met in their respective states to cast their ballots. There was chatter in some parts of the media about the possibility of "faithless electors"—Electoral College representatives who would change their ballots and not vote for Joe Biden. In fact, faithless electors are rare. To start, thirty-three states and the District of Columbia require their electors to cast their ballots to match the winner of their state; it was not possible for electors from those states to change their votes. Only roughly thirty-five electors in US history have been "faithless" in refusing to vote for the living presidential candidate whom they were designated to vote for, and Biden had a seventy-four-vote majority in the Electoral College. But in 2020, no one defected. The final Electoral College vote was a clear victory for Joe Biden, 306 to 232, similar to Trump's 304 vote count in 2016.

However, the Electoral College count failed to silence the man occupying the Oval Office. Recognizing that the other side was still refusing to accept the results, House Democrats began to construct a plan for how we would approach Wednesday, January 6, the day federal law states that the House and Senate, presided over by the vice president, are to certify the results of the Electoral College. The certification is an occasion of high drama with specific requirements, starting with ensuring the security of the special mahogany boxes containing the individual states'

Electoral College certificates. Then there is the timing of the joint session of Congress, called to order at 1:00 p.m., as well as the precise rules that spell out how the debate on objections to the count shall proceed.

Democrats knew that the debate on the House floor would likely become heated. Trump had long planned for the nullification of the election, sowing doubt about the results even before ballots were cast and challenging the results in the courts. So, before the joint session, we were prepared for the possibility of objections to the Electoral College votes by Republican members of Congress. It was clear that the results from Arizona, Nevada, Georgia, Pennsylvania, Michigan, and Wisconsin would be the targets. Ultimately, we learned that twelve Republican senators and dozens of Republican House members were going to object to certifying the Electoral College results.

Among the Trump election usurpers' demands was a commission to perform an emergency, ten-day audit of election results in contested states such as Arizona and Pennsylvania. But perhaps their biggest fantasy was to try to misuse a clause in the Constitution that says that if the Electoral College cannot decide who will become president of the United States, the House of Representatives will choose, voting state by state with one vote each. They were hoping to sow chaos by throwing the election to the House and then attempting to get to twenty-six states to vote for Trump. The possibility that Trump would attempt to carry these schemes through made our preparation so important, even as the Electoral College had made its decision.

In the House, we built a team of talented advocates and attorneys to prepare to dismiss Republicans' arguments: Jamie Raskin of

Maryland, a former constitutional law professor; Adam Schiff of California, a former prosecutor and chair of the House Intelligence Committee, who led Trump's first impeachment; Zoe Lofgren, also from California, a manager in Donald Trump's first impeachment, who had worked for a leading congressman, Don Edwards, on the House Judiciary Committee, when it prepared articles of impeachment against President Richard Nixon; and Joe Neguse of Colorado, who had served as one of the youngest state cabinet officials in the US. I told them that I respected their legal judgment, but I said, "I'm giving you one piece of guidance." It would take some of them by surprise. I explained, "You are not to mention Donald Trump's name. Just focus on the numbers and the law." For seven years, I had served on the House Ethics Committee, longer than anyone else in Congress (six years is usually the maximum, but I was asked to stay on an extra year to help update the rules). When the Ethics Committee investigated Speaker Newt Gingrich, our charge had been to consider three elements: the facts, the law, and the rules of the House. Someone's personality, the color of their hair, hearsay, and what type of insults they hurled were all irrelevant. The only thing that mattered was: What are the facts? And, in the case of the 2020 election: Were those facts consistent with the law?

I was confident that numbers and the law would again prove the integrity of the presidential election vote. I did not want this day to be about one man; it was far bigger than he was.

Knowing that the Trump attack agents would focus on Wisconsin, Michigan, Pennsylvania, Georgia, Arizona, and Nevada, we established a team from each state. The process for objecting is very clear: the House and the Senate come together in the 1:00 joint session. The vice president presides. When the electoral vote certification is announced for an individual state, any lawmaker could stand and object. Their objection must also be presented in writing, and it must have the signature of at least one member of the House and one member of the Senate. The written document must also state "clearly and concisely" the grounds for objection. The states are called alphabetically, and we knew that Arizona would be the first state to lodge an objection. (In 2022, Congress would enact the Electoral Count Reform and Presidential Transition Improvement Act to further clarify this process.) I tasked Democratic members from the individual states that were "in play" in the Electoral College to prepare the arguments needed. There would be no hearsay, no rumors, no disgust, and no focus on one person, only a strict focus on the voting numbers and the law, and on the Republican authorities in those states who had already validated the final numbers. Republican officials had signed off on the vote counting and the vote totals. In fact, Republican election officials would be central to our case.

We had the legal facts and patriotic, articulate members ready to make the case, state by state. We were confident that we had a beautiful, harmonious, and well-orchestrated answer to the chaos we expected to be unleashed when these dissenting members objected. As the end of December approached, we thought that the heavy-handed tactics of our colleagues across the aisle would be our biggest challenge.

Because of his constitutional law background, I appointed Jamie Raskin as our lead authority on the House floor. This day was about the Constitution. Following the discussion with our entire team and my insistence on no mentions of Donald Trump, Jamie stated that he was confident of what the narrative would be. He finished drafting his opening statement on December 31,

New Year's Eve. He was pleased with it, but thought it was a little drier than he wanted. So he decided to ask his twenty-six-year-old son, Tommy, to look at it. "He's a more inspirational writer," Jamie explained, "more inspiring than I am." Tommy, named for the American revolutionary Thomas Paine, was midway through his second year at Harvard Law School. He had just started as a teaching assistant, and he wanted to share his teacher's salary with those less fortunate, so he bought mosquito nets to protect Africans against malaria. After his students handed in their course evaluations, Tommy also made individual donations in each student's name to charities working to end global hunger.

Jamie went looking for Tommy. When he checked his bedroom, he found him on the bed. Tommy had died by suicide after years of struggling with depression. He left his family a note: "Please forgive me. My illness won today. Please look after each other, the animals, and the global poor for me. All my love, Tommy."

There are no words to describe Jamie's heartbreak when we spoke to him.

I didn't even want him to come to the House on January 3, for the election of the Speaker. But Jamie insisted, telling me, "No, Tommy loved you. Tommy would want me to." I finally asked him to "please vote and then leave. Go home to be with your family."

Jamie, Sarah, and the rest of the Raskin family buried Tommy in a small, private ceremony on January 5. Those of us involved in preparing for January 6, including Jamie, had already been receiving death threats. Reeling from the terrible tragedy and fearful for his safety, Jamie's family told him not to lead the January 6 debate on the Electoral College. They did not want him to bear the brunt of additional partisan attacks. But although he agreed not to take a lead role, Jamie still wanted to make a speech on the House floor before we began the official vote certification. His younger daughter, Tabitha, joined him, as did his son-in-law, Hank, who is married to Jamie's older daughter, Hannah. Prophetically, one of the questions both Tabitha and Hank had asked Jamie before they left for the Capitol that morning was "Will it be safe?"

We knew that a "Stop the Steal" rally had been planned for late morning on the National Mall. The man in the Oval Office had tweeted back in December, "Big Protest in DC on January 6th" and "Be there, will be wild." So we knew in advance that it would be a big day. The Capitol Police Board, a three-person body composed of the architect of the Capitol and the two sergeants at arms for the House and Senate, had reported that there would likely be crowds. But "crowds" is a fairly meaningless description. We have always had crowds at the Capitol. There were terrible crowds, often very hostile ones, during the health care debate and the vote on the Affordable Care Act. Those crowds had jammed the front and back of the Capitol Plaza as well as the parking lot. They were vocal, and though they had spat on congressional Democrats, they were not otherwise physically violent. For most of us on Capitol Hill, crowds mean a lot of noise.

No one conceived of anyone erecting a gallows and stringing up a noose.

At 9:00 a.m., when I arrived at my office, some protesters were already advancing toward the barricades, which looked like oversized bike racks. I held a Zoom meeting with the House Democratic Caucus and our Electoral College team, one final prep session before our busy afternoon and likely evening on the floor. At the end, I reminded everyone that this day, January 6, was also the Feast of the Epiphany, which marks the visit of the Wise Men to the baby Jesus. I told the members I wanted this January 6 to be "an epiphany for the American people" and added that maybe "the other side" would "have their own epiphany."

My daughter Alexandra had come to watch the events on January 6, and she had brought her two sons, the same boys who had been present for the health care vote. They were teenagers now, and she wanted them to witness history: a peaceful transfer of power. They did witness history, just not the history any of us expected. Early on, her son Paul had an inkling of how intense that history would become.

Before I left to go to the House floor, I was in the Speaker's office to review my notes and my statement. Paul was there. We had the TV playing in the background, hearing Trump's speech at the Ellipse, the park south of the White House and adjacent to the National Mall. We heard him say, "We will never give up," and telling the assembled crowd, "We are going to walk down to the Capitol." Then Paul was looking out the window and down the long vista of the Mall. "I think they are coming here, Mimi," he said, watching the crowd stream up. Alexandra, who is a documentarian, had her video camera and was recording these moments for her sons. That footage would become an important record of the day's events.

Paul was the first one to tell me that the people who had gathered for the rally were marching on the Capitol—that they were almost to the security perimeter.

Hearing Trump's speech as it was playing on the television in the background, I shot back, exasperated, "If he comes here, we are going to the White House." But soon the possibility of the president appearing at the Capitol, along with thousands of his loyalists, became a more serious threat. My chief of staff, Terri McCullough, told me that she had just received word that the Secret Service had dissuaded Trump from coming to the Capitol, telling him, "We don't have the resources." It was incredible that we were even in this situation. "If he comes, I'm going to punch him out. I've been waiting for this," I shot back. "For trespassing on the Capitol grounds, I'm going to punch him out. And I'm going to go to jail, and I'm going to be happy."

As I spoke, we could hear the protesters' chants through the glass windows as they gathered outside: "USA, USA, USA." I left to head to the House floor. The beautiful, heavy mahogany boxes containing the 538 signed electoral ballots were being carried by Senate staff into the chamber.

At 12:53 p.m., protesters broke through the outer police barrier around the Capitol, pushing back the officers who were protecting the building. At 1:05, I gaveled the House to order, and the vice president convened the joint session of Congress. It was an unusual session because of Covid. We had lawmakers spread across the chamber, some up above in the visitors' gallery, so that we could all follow physical distancing guidelines. There were strict Covid capacity rules: a limited number of members on the floor, a second limit on who could attend in the gallery, and others waiting in their offices to be called to the floor to speak or to vote. We also had very few staff present. Only one-third of my staff was at the Capitol. Other members were operating with a skeleton staff or no staff at all.

At the Ellipse, Trump's speech was ending as we opened our proceedings. Once again, the lame-duck president told the remaining crowd, with malice, "We're going to the Capitol. We're going to try and give them [meaning the Republicans in Congress] the kind of pride and boldness that they need to take back our country." At that same moment, the electoral count for Arizona was read out, and Arizona Republican representative Paul Gosar stood and said, "I rise for myself and sixty of my colleagues to object to the counting of the electoral ballots of Arizona." Texas Republican senator Ted Cruz joined Gosar's objection.

Following the prescribed rules, the senators who were present left the chamber to return to their side of the Capitol to debate the objection, while those of us in the House stayed behind to have our own debate. Outside, the mob had reached the steps of the Capitol and were clashing with law enforcement, but from inside the windowless, almost entirely soundproof House chamber, members were unaware of the mounting violence. (Members are not allowed to use cell phones on the House floor.) A few minutes after 2:00 p.m., the mob reached multiple entrances to the building. Windows on the Senate side were smashed with a stolen law enforcement riot shield and flagpoles, the glass was broken, and packs of rioters started streaming into the building, kicking in doors and bursting through openings wherever they could.

I was still in the Speaker's chair when several members of the Capitol Police rushed up and started to physically pull me off the podium, saying, "We have to leave." Initially, I argued with the team, telling them that I wanted to stay. Protesters and agitators were nothing new for me when I was presiding in the chair. I told the security team, "I don't care about that. I can handle it." Their response was curt. "This is different. No, you can't. We are going, now." I was pulled off the Speaker's platform so quickly that I didn't even have a chance to grab my cell phone or anything else. Only when I was racing down the hallway to the basement and then the depths of the garage did I learn that the people who had been outside, whom my grandson Paul had seen

THAT OUR FLAG IS STILL THERE

as tiny figures making their way down the wide paths and grass of the Mall, were now breaking into the Capitol.

As we raced down the narrow, dimly lit stairwell, I kept asking my security team and chief of staff, "Are we calling the National Guard?" I asked if anyone had called Senate Leader Mitch McConnell so he could agree to ask for the Guard. Terri, my chief of staff, told me yes. I balled my fingers into a fist when I said, speaking of the rioters, "We can't let them succeed. If they stop the proceedings, we will have totally failed." I climbed into a waiting vehicle and was rushed to Fort McNair. The Secret Service had already whisked Mike Pence off the Senate floor, where he had been presiding. The rest of the Senate and House leadership would also be brought to our secure location at Fort McNair, but Mike Pence remained inside the Capitol. He had refused to leave but did obey his security team's demand that he stay in a hiding place on the premises. Ultimately, Pence and his family spent hours concealed in the loading dock where his motorcade was parked.

"All We Want Is Pelosi"

Already the massive crowd was chanting, "Nancy, Nancy, Nancy," and yelling, "All we want is Pelosi," right outside my office and steps from the House chamber. The mob demanded of Capitol Police, Where is Nancy's staff? Later, I would see the security camera footage of my young staff hurriedly running into a side conference room and locking the door. Rioters insisted on speaking to "Pelosi" or "Nancy." One picked up the House phone, and when he wasn't put through to me, he told the operator to give me a message: "We're coming, bitch." Another rioter, who made it inside the Senate chamber, screamed, "Where the f*** is Nancy?" Someone else had left a large poster that said "PELOSI IS SATAN" on the windshield of a congressional vehicle parked outside. Another rioter, in a red knit "MAKE AMERICA GREAT AGAIN" hat, said she was looking for me "to shoot her in the frickin' brain."

Elsewhere in the hallways, the mob was screaming, "Hang Mike Pence." A bullet in my head and a noose for the vice president.

In his speech, Trump had just told his cheering supporters that "if Mike Pence does the right thing, we win the election," and "all Vice President Pence has to do is send it back to the states to recertify, and WE WIN." At 2:24, Trump tweeted, "Mike Pence didn't have the courage to do what should have been done to protect our Country and our Constitution." We were later informed that some members of the vice president's security detail called their families to tell them goodbye.

Inside our secure location at Fort McNair, Chuck Schumer and I watched TV coverage. We could see the live images of rioters breaking through the barriers, rushing the doors with flagpoles and baseball bats, and the police being overwhelmed. It was a melee, with rioters climbing the inaugural scaffolding, already erected around the Capitol in preparation for Joe Biden's swearing in. Chuck was hearing from senators who were trapped in their hideaway offices. I knew that members were trapped on the House floor. My daughter Alexandra was with me and was still filming—many of the raw events and emotions and the shock of that afternoon were all captured, as were the images and words of the Democrats and Republicans, Senators Schumer, McConnell, Dick Durbin, Chuck Grassley, and John Thune, and Representatives Hoyer, Jim Clyburn, and Steve Scalise—Minority Leader Kevin McCarthy remained almost entirely unseen. All of us were crammed into a lower-level space, which still had a lit Christmas tree displayed in the corner of one of the rooms. We were in constant touch by phone with our colleagues at the Capitol, while also trying to place calls to all of the key administration stakeholders to get them to dispatch the National Guard to put down the riot. As we spoke, we were watching the real-time news feeds of the rioters surging forward and the police being totally overwhelmed.

"Pleading for the National Guard"

Immediately, I began calling the Pentagon to reach Ryan McCarthy, the secretary of the army, to ask him to send the Guard detachment from the DC Armory, located two miles away from the Capitol. On the other end of the phone, everyone at the Pentagon, including Secretary McCarthy, could not have sounded less concerned. I felt like raising my voice and saying, *Turn on the TV. Do you see what is going on?*

I was told, in essence, by Secretary McCarthy, "Well, it's not an easy thing to call them up. There has to be some authority established at the Capitol." And I said in reply, "The authority is there, at the Capitol. You just need to let the troops go there." I added, "You aren't doing anything." Secretary McCarthy then told me, "Well, I have to go report to my boss. We have to go and tell him, and that takes time. I don't know what we can do." McCarthy's boss was Acting Defense Secretary Christopher Miller, and the response of both men was horrifying.

Here, I want to state clearly, because there have been so many mistruths, including, sadly, from Republican members of Congress: The National Guard is under the control of the executive branch. In my capacity as House Speaker, I had no authority to call up the Guard for anything, just as then-Senate majority leader

Mitch McConnell had no authority to call up the Guard. The only entity that can formally request—but cannot call up—the Guard is the three-member Capitol Police Board—the two sergeants at arms and the Capitol Police chief. Mitch, Chuck, and I repeatedly asked that the Guard be sent to the Capitol.

In the fifty states, governors can call up their individual state National Guards. But Washington, DC, is still unfortunately not a state. Thus the Guard is under the authority of the Department of Defense, and usually the authority to call it up is given to the secretary of the army. The true statutory commander of the DC National Guard is the president of the United States, but the best information that we had was that he was sitting in the Oval Office suite, watching the television coverage, and targeting Mike Pence on Twitter. Not until more than two hours after the Capitol had been breached did this occupant of the Oval Office directly ask the rioters to stop, again on Twitter: "I am asking for everyone at the U.S. Capitol to remain peaceful. No violence! Remember, WE are the Party of Law & Order—respect the Law and our great men and women in Blue. Thank you!" "Remain peaceful. No violence"? What a lying, shameful disgrace.

Around 4:00 p.m., Mitch McConnell, Chuck Schumer, and I were talking on Chuck's flip phone with Acting Defense Secretary Miller. Each one of us was still pleading for what was now a late but still very necessary response from the Guard. McConnell said the forces should be "getting there in one hell of a hurry, you understand?" Schumer told him, "This is an emergency, where life and limb are at stake." Completely exasperated, I said to Secretary McCarthy, "Just pretend that this was an assault on the Pentagon or the White House or some other entity. What would you do?" Secretary McCarthy kept saying that there was "no authority" to oversee the Guard at the Capitol or a plan. I told him again that there was, in fact, a designated authority at the Capitol, and that they could devise an operations plan while the Guard was on its way. It had reached the point where we were doing the thinking for the Defense Department personnel, telling them: Don't delay, move your Guard units, and plan as you go, knowing there is authority already on-site.

Chuck Schumer, Steny Hoyer, and I had also already called the governors of Virginia and Maryland and asked them to send reinforcements, which they did, dispatching their state police and local law enforcement. I had spoken to Governor Ralph Northam of Virginia, and by 3:15 p.m., Virginia law enforcement and National Guard troops had begun arriving in DC, while the Pentagon was still "deliberating."

Nearly all of us in the congressional leadership had also called across the administration to anyone we could get on the phone to say, "Tell the president to call these people off." Chuck and I had a heated conversation with the acting attorney general, Jeffrey Rosen. Chuck told him in no uncertain terms to intervene with President Trump to call off the mob. I said that the "rioters are breaking the law at the instigation of the president of the United States."

In the meantime, we were being told that it could take days to clear the Capitol building of the mob. The acting defense secretary said that he had no idea how many people were inside.

Taking Back the Capitol

It was a desperate feeling to be locked away inside Fort McNair for hours, but I knew that, above all, I had to remain calm. We had an unhinged president and an unruly, destructive, and dangerous mob. We had members, staff, police, maintenance personnel, and institutional workers at risk. We couldn't even afford the luxury of crying for the injured police officers. The line had to be: "This has to stop."

Still inside the Capitol, Mike Pence had also been calling the Pentagon, asking for the National Guard. I was particularly worried about Mike Pence. When I spoke to him, he was still concealed in the loading dock. I told him directly that we were "okay" but that I was "worried" about him. We also discussed the damage to the Capitol, and I told him that I had been told that there had been "defecation on the House floor." At the end of our call, I told the vice president again, "I worry about you. Don't let anybody know where you are." Pence told me firmly, "We're staying here." As he would later write, he didn't want anyone to see the image of a vice president fleeing the Capitol. I also had the distinct impression from our conversation that the Secret Service thought that it would be riskier to depart—that his motorcade would attract more attention and more threat. I was personally worried that his protective detail might not even allow him to return to the Capitol to finish our important work. I give Vice President Pence great credit for many courageous actions that afternoon and later that night.

Finally, after the acting secretary of defense relented and called up the National Guard, the troops were given their gear and began arriving at the Capitol. But it still took three hours from the time I was dragged out of the House chamber for the Guard to arrive at the Capitol complex, and another twenty-five minutes for them to begin operations. It took about three and a half hours to clear the rioters from the building, and smoke bombs had to be used on the Senate side, along with tear gas in the Rotunda, to drive out those intent on occupying the Capitol. Around 6:00 p.m., Vice President Pence called back to say that he was with the chief of the Capitol Police, and that it looked like the House and the Senate could reconvene in "about an hour." Around 6:30, I got in a vehicle to drive back to the Capitol. It was dark and strangely quiet on the roads; a six o'clock curfew was in place throughout the city. Only at 7:30 was the Capitol formally declared "secure."

In total, as many as two thousand rioters breached the Capitol and roamed the inside of the building. During the riot, 138 officers from the Capitol and DC Metropolitan Police were injured; fifteen were hospitalized. The violence was stunning. Rioters hit the officers on the head with lead pipes and sprayed them with chemical irritants; they beat the officers with stun guns, fists, sticks, poles, and clubs. Three DC police officers were dragged down steps and assaulted; a fourth was hit with a stun gun six times and suffered a mild heart attack. Among the Capitol Police, one officer had two cracked ribs and two smashed spinal discs; another lost an eye. A third was stabbed with a metal fence stake. One officer suffered injuries after being crushed between a door and a riot shield. Another officer was dragged by the leg and, a year later, still did not have full use of one arm. Officers reported slipping on pools of blood. Capitol Police Officer Eugene Goodman faced down angry rioters trying to reach the Senate chamber. He was assaulted with what was possibly bear spray, pelted with objects, and jabbed at with a flagpole. He later described the scene as being something "like out of medieval times." Five police officers died in the aftermath: Officer Brian Sicknick from a stroke the next day, and four others who died by suicide: Jeffrey Smith, Howard Liebengood, Gunther Hashida, and Kyle deFreytag. During the initial arrests of the rioters, police seized multiple firearms and found a cooler of Molotov cocktails in a car parked nearby. In the House chamber, the scene was complete chaos. Several representatives with military and law enforcement training had fashioned makeshift weapons out of upright wooden hand sanitizer stations, which they broke and turned into pikes. Outside, rioters used a sawed-off flagpole to break the door's heavy glass. The Capitol Police officers braced themselves around the damaged door, training their sidearms on the entrance, surrounded by a coating of shattered glass. Packs of rioters, who far outnumbered the officers inside the chamber, were roaming the hallways and streaming past the chamber's lower door. Periodically, some looked in through the broken panes and screamed obscenities while chanting, "This is our House."

One rioter tried to force her way through the broken glass on a door leading to the Speaker's Lobby, where some House members were trapped. The thinly stretched Captiol Police were trying to defend not only that entrance but the adjacent entrance to the House chamber with members trapped on the other side. They repeatedly told her and the advancing crowd to stay back. She did not. She broke the windows and tried to breach the door. A lieutenant in the Capitol Police drew his gun and was forced to shoot.

The lawmakers inside the chamber had truly harrowing experiences. Jamie Raskin, still on the House floor, had listened as fellow members called their spouses to tell them goodbye, as had the vice president's security detail. Jamie and other representatives had donned gas masks because tear-gas canisters were being fired in the hallways; the House chaplain said a prayer as members pulled out the plastic ventilator hoods outfitted with air filters that were discreetly hidden in pouches under their seats. Until that moment, many had no idea that the protective hoods were there; they had been added to the House chamber as part of the enhanced security precautions put in place after 9/11.

Rep. Jason Crow from Colorado, who had been sitting in the visitors' gallery above, had told his fellow lawmakers to remove their congressional pins, so the mob outside would have a harder time identifying them. After calling his wife to tell her that he loved her and to tell their kids that he loved them, Crow, a former Army Ranger, made a mental checklist and followed it: Lock doors. Move people away from entry points. Tell people to leave behind their bags and belongings so they can flee quickly. He also pulled a pen from his pocket and told his colleagues to be prepared to use their pens as weapons.

The members of Congress and reporters who were trapped in the House Gallery then lay down on the floor, trying to hide beneath the fold-up seats. Eventually, many would have to crawl on their bellies, combat-style, to reach a doorway that had been secured by the police, where they could at last escape; Jason Crow was the last member to leave. But before that, everyone inside the chamber could hear the mob outside pounding on the large double doors.

It sounded, Jamie Raskin said, "like a battering ram." Thankfully, the Capitol Police guided the members to safety.

A group of members who were in the gallery that day named themselves "the gallery group." They have formed deep friendships built upon their shared traumatic experience of January 6.

Prime Target: The Speaker's Office

Outside of the chamber, in the Capitol building itself, hundreds of staff and lawmakers were also hiding under furniture in various offices and conference rooms. Jamie Raskin's daughter and son-in-law hid under the desk in House Majority Leader Steny Hoyer's office while the mob pounded on the door. They quietly texted family and friends, saying their "I love you"s and goodbyes. As Jamie said, "They thought they were going to die."

Throughout the Capitol office buildings for the House and

Senate, lawmakers barricaded their doors. Staffers pushed furniture against office entrances, following the training they had received in active shooter drills, which many had practiced in high school. Then they crouched down and hid, not saying a word.

Hiding in the dark, eight members of my own staff could hear the mob chanting, over and over, "Nancy, Nancy, where is Nancy?" and, "We're going to get her." They heard the rioters break through the first locked door to the Speaker's conference room, splintering the heavy wood. My staffers were behind a second, locked door. They had taken refuge under a very long wooden conference table, contorted behind chair legs and thickly turned table legs, and that was where they remained, with the lights out and the curtains drawn, not making a sound, for two and a half hours. They heard the mob pound on the door to their hiding place, trying to break in. If that door was breached, each of them knew there was no way out.

My office was a particular target of the rioters' wrath. They ripped down the sign with my name and smashed it to pieces. Some entered my office. One man, who put his feet up on a desk, was carrying a 950,000-volt stun gun. Some stole personal effects and a laptop. A number of rioters rifled through papers on desks and pieces of mail. In my office, mail is sacrosanct and confidential. It is mostly sent by constituents and others who need specialized help. That the mob violated their privacy was particularly offensive to me. Not satisfied just to make a mess, the rioters also left behind nasty epithets scrawled on House stationery. They smashed a large antique mirror.

As more law enforcement teams finally began to arrive, gradually, hallway by hallway and floor by floor, the Capitol was cleared. What was left behind was pure destruction.

It was a scene of damage, disrespect, and disregard for the

people who keep the Capitol lovely. Around the building were masses of broken glass and splintered wood, and damaged paintings. "There's blood outside the Speaker's Lobby, ma'am," I was told. Some of those in the mob had taunted people who work to keep the Capitol safe and beautifully maintained with vile names. And in some places, including my office, members of the mob had literally defecated on the floors and the rugs. Smells of human waste, smoke bombs, pepper spray, and tear gas permeated the air.

What You Sign Up For

When I became Speaker, I knew that I was making myself into a target. It's a truth for anyone who holds the office. And it is a fact that you have to make peace with. I made my peace with it in 2007. I've made my peace with it whenever I have traveled to a conflict area or war zone. When I went to Kyiv in 2022, a little more than two months after the Russians invaded, I thought, I may well die here, and that's okay. I briefly thought the same on January 6. It is simply part of the job.

All members, to some degree, accept this risk. However, our accepting the risk is something that is fundamentally different for our families. I was fortunate that Alexandra and my grandsons stayed with me; I did not have to worry about their physical safety. I was deeply worried about my staff—particularly without my phone to contact them, although Terri, my chief of staff, kept in close touch.

Those of us sequestered in Fort McNair had individual protection—but the members still inside the Capitol did not. We worried for them and their safety. In many ways, those hours reinforced who each of us was. Chuck Schumer, Mitch McConnell, and I have known each other for years and have worked together for a long time. We joined together on calls for the National Guard, speaking firmly and with one voice. That afternoon, several media outlets called the first of two January 5 Georgia senatorial runoff elections for the Democrats. Upon hearing the news, Mitch walked over to Chuck to congratulate him on regaining control of the Senate. That was a gracious gesture amid so much turmoil. Others were true to themselves. Steve Scalise, the Republican whip, was with us as we made some of our emphatic calls for the National Guard. Yet he would later claim that no such calls were made, even though he stood next to us.

Fortunately, Alexandra filmed much of what happened, including those calls. Presidential historians have told me that they wish we had a similar record of other major events in American history.

Return to the Capitol

The security leadership initially did not want me or the other House leaders and Senate leaders to go back to the Capitol on January 6. They told me that the electoral vote certification would have to take place in a secure location off-site. I said no. It was clear that this decision would be wrong. We needed to show the American people and the world that we would finish the work of the Constitution in a timely fashion from the center of democracy, in the House and Senate chambers. Not behind closed doors in some hidden location.

Yes, on the afternoon of January 6, 2021, egged on by a selfish, thoughtless man, thousands of people rushed that beautiful building and broke its glass and doors, and a significant number of them tried to wreck it. The then-president of the United States was directing these people. He dishonored his oath of office. But that night, members of Congress would live up to their responsibilities and honor our oath. Every member of Congress and all of my staff returned and stayed until 4:00 a.m. on January 7 to complete our sacred constitutional duty of certifying the presidential election and ensuring the peaceful transfer of power.

One item that some of the rioters sought was the heavy mahogany boxes carrying the actual Electoral College ballots signed by the electors. The rioters presumably thought that if they could destroy them, it would end the certification process. Trump, who instigated the plot, didn't know enough about our government to realize that presidential electors sign a total of six ballots. Only one set goes to the Capitol; the other five are sent to a variety of locations, including the National Archives, to be preserved. Instead, the rioters tried to chase down the young staffers carrying those boxes, thinking they could end the count and the constitutional process. The ballots, however, were still safe at the Capitol, and that is where we, the Congress, needed to be.

To their credit, Mitch McConnell and Chuck Schumer in the Senate were in strong agreement. On the constant stream of calls that afternoon, they both said, along with me, "We want to go back to the Capitol." And again, "We must go back to the Capitol."

When I did return, the first place I went was the large Ways and Means Committee room, where many House members and staff had gathered. I asked to see my staff right away. There is no other way to say it: they were traumatized. It was easy for me to be tough and calm inside Fort McNair while they were hiding under tables in the dark, terrified that they were being hunted by an out-of-control mob with no escape.

Personally, I will never forgive the inciters and the mob for what they did to these young people. There was so much fright in their faces for what they had been through. Some of them left Capitol Hill for other jobs after January 6. Just as people who have been in an accident or who have been robbed can find it trauma-tizing to return to the scene where the event and the injury and the injustice happened, it was similarly traumatizing for these staffers to be back in the offices where this attack had taken place. The whole day was horrendous, but what happened to the staff was and is unforgivable to me.

Jamie Raskin put it eloquently when he described promising his daughter that it would not be like this again when she came back to the Capitol, and she replied, "Dad, I don't want to come back to the Capitol."

In the Ways and Means Committee room, after spending time with my staff and some of the members, I addressed them as a group. I reminded them that this was the Feast of the Epiph-any, adding that epiphany means "an awakening, an enlighten-ment," and I hoped that this day "would be an epiphany for all of us," showing respect for the Constitution. Instead, it became "an assault on our democracy," inside "our temple of democracy," seen around the world. I said that if the purpose of the mob was "to stop us from honoring the Constitution, that purpose will not be born." Now, it was time for us to come together to finish our work. I thanked Hakeem Jeffries, chair of the House Democratic Caucus, and Liz Cheney, the Republican Conference chair, for their joint support working together for the members who had been evacuated to the committee room. I added, "God has blessed America with the service of all of you to our democ-racy." Almost as soon as I started speaking, Republican repre-sentative Jim Jordan and others began sneering in the back of the room. When I told the members that "justice will be done," they laughed. It was appalling.

Next I made my way to the Speaker's office. One of the first things I saw was the ornate mirror that had hung over a fireplace in a gold frame through many speakerships. It had been broken and shattered; there was human waste on the carpet. Objects and signs had been stolen. Chairs were broken; one rioter had made off with a staffer's wallet, which the staffer, in his haste to escape, had left behind. Some of the staff had tried to straighten up the office a bit, so it wasn't so awful by the time I returned, but things were still a mess. I told them to stop and not to worry. It was more horrifying for me to see the trauma in the eyes of my staff than to see these signs of the physical disrespect shown the Speaker's office.

I don't care about things like the glass mirror; I care about people. I didn't want anyone trying to pick up the broken shards from the mirror when they might cut their hands. But while I don't care about a broken mirror, I do care about a desecrated Capitol, because it is a symbol of democracy to the world.

Honoring Our Constitutional Responsibilities

At 9:00 p.m., I returned to the Speaker's podium, took up the gavel, and called the House to order. I read a brief statement: "To those who engaged in the gleeful desecration of this, our temple of democracy, American democracy, justice will be done. Every four years, we demonstrate again the peaceful transfer of power from one president to the next. And despite the shameful actions of today, we still will do so—we will be part of a history that shows the world what America is made of."

I ended with a prayer: "Let us pray that there will be peace on Earth, and that it will begin with us. Let us pray that God will continue to bless America."

The House members began where we had left off, with the debate over the objection to the Arizona certification.

Then the most incredible thing happened. House members continued to object to the certification. I could not understand it. How could anyone who had been at the Capitol that afternoon—who had hidden under chairs and desks, who had heard gunshots or been rushed to a secure location—return and continue to affirm this lie? How could they attempt to end the electoral count after seeing all that trauma?

But 121 Republicans voted in favor of the challenge to Arizona—voting to object to certifying Arizona's eleven electoral votes—including the two top House Republicans: Kevin McCarthy and Steve Scalise. They had been in our safe location, Scalise even listening and watching as Mitch, Chuck, and I pleaded for the National Guard. Thankfully, 303 members of the House voted against the challenge, and it failed. And Republicans who spoke on the House floor in favor of the challenge to the Electoral College count were resoundingly booed. On the Senate side, Mitch McConnell had already called that chamber to order, and the senators had rejected the Arizona challenge.

Some House members continued to raise objections at other points in the count, but they received no support from any senators until it came time to certify the state of Pennsylvania. Then, seven Republican senators joined the House objection. But the full Senate rejected the Pennsylvania objection without any debate. The House, however, suffered through two hours of debate before the objection failed in a vote. At 3:41 a.m., with the vote count completed, Vice President Pence formally declared Joe Biden the winner of the 2020 presidential election.

But thirteen days remained until the inauguration. I and

many others wanted a consequence for the deranged, unhinged man who was still president of the United States.

Impeachments

The Democratic candidates had won both Georgia Senate run-off races, but these two new senators would not be sworn in until January 20, meaning that the Republicans were still in control of that half of the legislative branch. (The other newly elected and reelected senators had been sworn in January 3.)

This date mattered, because Democrats in the House were determined to pursue impeachment against Donald J. Trump—for the second time.

Impeachment is a serious decision; impeachment is and must be about the facts and the law. Any calls for impeachment must be subjected to strict scrutiny. To say that a president has committed "high Crimes and Misdemeanors" is a serious charge. I believe that impeachment should only be considered when there is a very strong and clear-cut case. A variety of early allegations against Donald Trump did not rise to that level.

But in the late summer of 2019, a whistleblower came forward with information about a phone call that Donald Trump had made in late July to the relatively new president of Ukraine, Volodymyr Zelenskyy. Every head of state call has various notetakers in the White House recording what is said; if not word for word, then a very close summation. This call was no different, and what the notetakers recorded was deeply troubling. After telling Zelenskyy that "we do a lot for Ukraine," meaning financially, and "I wouldn't say that it's reciprocal necessarily," Trump specifically said to Zelenskyy, "I would like you to do us a favor . . ."

During the call, Trump, in fact, asked for several favors: to have the US attorney general "call you or your people, and I would like you to get to the bottom of it." This request referred to Special Counsel Robert Mueller, who had been investigating allegations of Russian interference in the 2016 election. Trump was also looking to help one of his political allies, Paul Manafort, who was facing criminal charges. Multiple times, Trump raised the prospect of Zelenskyy working directly with Rudy Giuliani, the former New York City mayor, who would be a leader of Trump's claims that the 2020 election had been stolen. However, Trump's biggest ask was to move ahead with an investigation into the business dealings of Joe Biden's son Hunter in Ukraine.

Zelenskyy promised that a new prosecutor would look into "the company that you mentioned in this issue." Zelenskyy also referenced having stayed at Trump Tower when he visited New York, presumably to please the president. Trump again said to Zelenskyy that he would tell Rudy Giuliani, acting as Trump's representative, and Attorney General Bill Barr "to call you." In addition to this very damning phone call, Trump also delayed the release of $391 million in military aid for Ukraine, which had already been approved by Congress, making the entire series of his "favors" appear to be a condition for receiving US monetary and security assistance.

When word of this call reached Congress, including from a published report in the *Wall Street Journal* in September 2019, I agreed that it merited a formal impeachment inquiry. From the contents of the call regarding Hunter Biden, the son of Trump's likely political opponent in 2020, it was clear that Trump was trying to jeopardize the integrity of our elections. On September 24, I would announce the formal inquiry, saying that Trump had called upon a foreign power to intervene in the upcoming presidential election, which, I said, was "a breach of his constitutional responsibilities. The president must be held accountable. No one is above the law."

Trump called me that morning before I made the announcement. When I informed him of my decision, he responded indignantly, "Why are you doing that?"

I answered that it was because of his call with Zelenskyy. I reminded him that by then, I had spent twenty-five years working on intelligence issues. "I do not believe that the president [needs to directly] make a quid pro quo to intimidate a foreign leader," I said.

Trump responded, "I didn't do that," to which I answered, "You withheld aid, and there is an inference drawn."

We had about twenty minutes of back-and-forth. Trump's ultimate answer was, "It's come out in the media—the whistleblower doesn't have the facts. We have the call down in writing. Every word. It was flawless." I told him if that was indeed true, "we'll find out. Don't be afraid of it."

We ended with his continued complaints that "this is unfair . . . REALLY really unfair. . . . It is very unfair what you are saying. The call was perfect." And my final reply, "That call was perfectly clear. The truth will come out."

Neither Trump's bluster nor his phone call to me was going to change our necessary course of action.

The whole process of impeachment is very deliberate. In this case, the process needed to start with an inquiry, so the House could confirm the facts. Six committees had already been investigating issues related to Trump, so they had begun the fact-finding process, gathering testimony and documents. A month later, I called for a House vote to officially authorize the first impeachment proceedings, and in early December, the House Judiciary

Committee began drawing up impeachment articles against President Trump.

On Wednesday, December 18, the House voted to approve two articles of impeachment. Among the counts, the articles charged that President Trump had "betrayed the nation by abusing his high office to enlist a foreign power in corrupting democratic elections"; "President Trump, by such conduct, has demonstrated that he will remain a threat to national security and the Constitution if allowed to remain in office."

After the House impeached Trump, there was a trial in the Republican-majority Senate. Trump was acquitted of both charges, although Utah Republican senator Mitt Romney voted to convict, and we all praised his courage and patriotism. I was very proud of the House impeachment managers, led by Schiff, chair of the House Permanent Select Committee on Intelligence along with Jerry Nadler, Hakeem Jeffries, Zoe Lofgren, Val Demings, Jason Crow, and Sylvia Garcia. As Adam Schiff said to the Senate, Trump is "a man without character." He added, "He has betrayed our national security, and he will do so again."

Now, slightly less than a year later, we were again discussing impeachment—and the threat that Donald J. Trump posed to the Constitution and the country if he was allowed to remain in office. While the rioters were threatening members on January 6, Jamie Raskin and his fellow congressman David Cicilline, and Congressman Ted Lieu of California were already communicating with each other about bringing new impeachment charges, texting from their hiding places under desks and chairs. When I returned to the Capitol, I had made a promise that for those who damaged, undermined, and attacked our legislative branch and our rule of law justice would be done. Some on the other side, like Rep. Jim Jordan, as I have said, almost immediately began laughing the events of January 6 off. Others drifted to that position over the ensuing days and weeks.

But I believed that what had occurred on January 6 was a very serious situation for our country—and I was not alone. Most of us (previously, I had thought it was all of us) feel very privileged to serve in Congress, and we believe in upholding the dignity of the institution. It was very difficult to watch Republican lawmakers, so resolute on January 6 and clear in their horror at what had taken place, rapidly begin to fold on their principles and circle their wagons around Trump.

Following January 6, the Democratic leadership had discussed asking the vice president to invoke the Twenty-Fifth Amendment to the Constitution, which allows for the vice president and a majority of cabinet members to certify that a president is unable to discharge the duties of the office. Chuck Schumer and I had placed a call to Vice President Pence about this possibility. The vice president's office kept us on hold for twenty minutes. Thankfully, I was at home, so I could also empty the dishwasher and put in a load of laundry. Ultimately, Vice President Pence never got on the phone with us or returned our call.

I was so concerned by Trump's erratic behavior that on January 8, I called General Mark Milley, head of the Joint Chiefs of Staff. General Milley said he agreed on "everything" regarding Trump's very erratic state of mind. He assured me that the military, if given an order by the president to conduct a strike overseas, including a nuclear strike, was "not going to do anything illegal or crazy." It was reassuring, but it was also an awful question to be asking in the first place.

January 2021 was such a different moment from what had

happened nearly fifty years before, when Republican senator Barry Goldwater, along with the Republican leaders in the House and Senate, went to see Richard Nixon to tell him that he had lost a majority of his support in the Congress over his behavior in Watergate. Impeachment, they told him, would be next. The following day, Nixon resigned. That moral clarity of the congressional Republicans was sadly missing in January 2021.

On January 11, three Democratic representatives, David Cicilline, Jamie Raskin, and Ted Lieu, joined by 218 Democratic cosponsors, submitted House Resolution 24, which contained one article of impeachment against Donald John Trump, charging that he had "engaged in high Crimes and Misdemeanors by inciting violence against the Government of the United States," and concluding:

> President Trump gravely endangered the security of the United States and its institutions of Government. He threatened the integrity of the democratic system, interfered with the peaceful transition of power, and imperiled a coequal branch of Government. He thereby betrayed his trust as President, to the manifest injury of the people of the United States.
>
> Wherefore, Donald John Trump, by such conduct, has demonstrated that he will remain a threat to national security, democracy, and the Constitution if allowed to remain in office, and has acted in a manner grossly incompatible with self-governance and the rule of law. Donald John Trump thus warrants impeachment and trial, removal from office, and disqualification to hold and enjoy any office of honor, trust, or profit under the United States.

The resolution passed on January 13, by a vote of 232 to 197, with ten Republicans, including House Republican Conference chair Liz Cheney, voting in support. It was the most bipartisan impeachment vote in US history. It was also only the fourth vote to impeach a sitting president, with Donald Trump now having the dubious distinction of having been impeached twice. There were still a full six days left in his term, and if the Senate proceeded and voted to convict, Trump would be barred from ever holding office again.

We were ready to transmit the article of impeachment immediately, and under the Senate rules, once an article of impeachment is presented to the Senate, the trial must start the next day. But Mitch McConnell would not receive the article. He stalled, saying the Senate could not consider impeachment until January 19, its next scheduled business day, and the day before Joe Biden's inauguration.

On January 20, Joe Biden was inaugurated before an audience that, due to Covid restrictions, was smaller than usual. He gave a wonderful, healing inaugural address. Donald Trump did not attend. On January 25, I transferred the article of impeachment to the Senate, and Chuck Schumer, the new Senate leader, announced that the trial would begin on February 8 (opening statements were made on February 9).

While a few legal authorities and some Republican senators complained that a former president could not be impeached, more than 150 legal scholars from across the political spectrum, including Steven Calabresi, cofounder of the deeply conservative Federalist Society, and Charles Fried, Ronald Reagan's solicitor general, disagreed. They concluded that there was constitutional authority for impeachment, writing, "If an official could only be disqualified while he or she still held office, then an official who betrayed the public trust and was impeached could avoid accountability simply by resigning one minute before the Senate's final conviction vote. The Framers did not design the Constitution's checks and balances to be so easily undermined."

I appointed nine impeachment managers, led by Jamie Raskin, whose family had given him permission to proceed in holding Donald Trump accountable. He was joined by Representatives Cicilline, Lieu, Joaquin Castro, Madeleine Dean, Diana DeGette, Joe Neguse, Stacey Plaskett, and Eric Swalwell. They presented a criminal case, using FBI affidavits from those who had been arrested, video, and Trump's own statements. Rep. Jaime Herrera Beutler, a Republican from Washington State, also provided a statement, regarding a phone call between Trump and House Minority Leader Kevin McCarthy that McCarthy had described to her. She relayed what McCarthy had told her: "When McCarthy finally reached the president on January 6 and asked him to publicly and forcefully call off the riot, the president initially repeated the falsehood that it was antifa that had breached the Capitol. McCarthy refuted that and told the president that these were Trump supporters. That's when, according to McCarthy, the president said: 'Well, Kevin, I guess these people are more upset about the election than you are.'"

Every piece of evidence added up to the complete dereliction of duty by the president. On February 13, fifty-seven senators voted to convict, and forty-three voted against. Seven Republicans joined all fifty of the Democrats, but sixty-seven votes are required for a conviction. I cannot imagine how the Capitol Police and other law enforcement officers who defended the Capitol that day at such great personal cost must have felt watching that vote. Men and women whose lives the police are asked to give their own lives to protect were unwilling to vote to convict, and even went so far as to excuse the former president.

Mitch McConnell voted no, saying that he did not believe the Constitution allowed for the Senate to convict an ex-president. In a speech on February 14, during the impeachment trial, he called the events of January 6 "terrorism," adding, "Former president Trump's actions preceding the riot were a disgraceful dereliction of duty." He continued, "There is no question that President Trump is practically and morally responsible for provoking the events of that day."

But in the end, those were only words. They did not have the force of a vote. How sad for Mitch. What was he afraid of?

I believe the founders would have agreed with the House, not with the majority of Republicans in the Senate. When the founders wrote the Constitution, it was considered a compromise, and it was not perfect. The founders were not perfect. They gave us slavery in the Constitution, but they also gave us the ability to amend the Constitution so we could get rid of it. The founders could foresee a rogue president. And they gave the House the sole power to impeach, and the Senate the power to convict. But they could not foresee both a rogue president and a rogue Senate. On that February day, the Senate was unworthy of the confidence that our founders had placed in it. It's sad, because the most deliberative body in the world would once again become cowardly.

And we've all been living with the consequences of those raw political calculations.

January 6th Committee

With impeachment voted down, it was abundantly clear that the House and Senate needed to investigate what had happened leading up to and on January 6, much the way we had with 9/11. I wanted an outside bipartisan commission, with members appointed by both the House and the Senate. We had designed the commission to have an equal budget for both sides, Republican and Democratic, and equal staffing and equal subpoena power, which is unheard of when one party is in the minority in both the House and Senate. But I did this because I wanted the commission to be enacted by both houses. After much discussion about its role and scope, the House voted on May 19 to create the joint commission. The vote was 252–175, with thirty-five Republicans in support, even though the House Republican leadership, aside from Liz Cheney, was opposed.

In the Senate, Susan Collins, a Maine Republican, was very responsive and responsible. She said, "I've got to review this and make sure that the Republicans are treating it fairly and respectfully." I answered, "We won't have it any other way. You make whatever changes you want." Senator Collins reviewed it, spoke to her colleagues, and asked for the report to be completed by the end of 2022 before a new Congress was sworn in. We had the impression that there were thirteen Republican senators in support. We only needed nine Republicans to reach the filibuster requirement of sixty votes, because we had all fifty Democrats.

But despite his February statement blaming Trump for the insurrection, Mitch McConnell did not want the commission, and he made it his mission to kill it. He tracked down individual senators and some of these senators later told us that Mitch had asked them to do him a personal favor and vote against the commission. He flipped just enough that we did not have our sixty. The measure lost, 54–35, with eleven senators listed as not voting—nine of those eleven were Republicans. But Mitch was also told, "Do you think Nancy's going to let this go? This is not the end of it, Mitch."

Indeed, it was not. We put together our own committee in the House, the Select Committee to Investigate the January 6th Attack on the United States Capitol, and I invited the Republicans to make their appointments. Kevin McCarthy came back with five recommendations, three of whom had voted against certifying the election on January 6.

McCarthy's designated lead, Jim Banks of Indiana, immediately raised changing the focus to include demonstrations from the summer of 2020, following the death of George Floyd, and said that the commission was designed to "malign conservatives." Another pick, Jim Jordan, had repeatedly questioned the validity of the 2020 presidential election and had attended a meeting at the White House on how to challenge the election during the certification. Election deniers like Banks and Jordan had helped stoke the fires lit on January 6.

My answer to Minority Leader McCarthy was very simple: "Well, I can't accept all of those five, and I don't have to." Under the House rules, the Speaker makes the appointments in consultation with the minority leader. But the Speaker has the final say. Because of their possible involvement in the insurrection, I declined Banks and Jordan. In my statement, I said, "With respect for the integrity of the investigation, with an insistence on the truth and with concern about statements made and actions taken by these members, I must reject the recommendations of Representatives Banks and Jordan to the Select Committee. The unprecedented nature of January 6th demands this unprecedented decision." I still hoped that we could collaborate, but after that refusal, Kevin McCarthy pulled his remaining picks.

Instead, we moved forward with nine representatives, including two Republicans, Liz Cheney and Adam Kinzinger. Bennie Thompson of Mississippi would be the chair, and Liz would be the vice chair. They were joined by Democrats Zoe Lofgren, Adam Schiff, Pete Aguilar, Stephanie Murphy, Jamie Raskin, and Elaine Luria. Some people told me that by insisting on this committee, "because the stakes are so high, you have really gotten yourself a challenge." My reply was, "I don't think so. It will have authenticity and veracity, and it is necessary to help the public understand the narrative about what happened, both on that day and the events leading up to it." The January 6th Committee was ultimately an incredible success because of the leadership of Bennie and Liz, because of how it presented the information to the public, and because it also relied upon the testimony of people who worked in the White House and worked with Trump. It heard from a wide range of White House staffers, including Trump's daughter Ivanka and son-in-law Jared Kushner, who both were advisors in the West Wing. It heard from former attorney general Bill Barr and from multiple lawyers involved in the post-election debates. It heard from people who were designated as Trump loyalists, who had sat in on White House meetings. It received a list of members of Congress who wanted presidential pardons for their activities to invalidate the election. But first, we heard from the police officers who had suffered so greatly on that day and who courageously shared their stories: Washington Metropolitan Police Department officers Michael Fanone and Daniel Hodges, and US Capitol Police officers Aquilino Gonell and Harry Dunn, and, later, Caroline Edwards.

Every piece of evidence that the committee located was critical. The committee's work inoculated against further poison being fed into the veins of the American public. All those who were not pure Trump cultists could see what had happened. Similar to the 9/11 Joint Inquiry, the January 6th Committee issued a number of findings and also developed a list of recommendations: criminal referrals to the Justice Department, an overhaul of the Electoral Count Act of 1887, consideration of more serious sanctions on lawyers who were involved, and also ways to enable Congress to enforce its committee subpoenas in federal court.

It was among the most important work a congressional committee has done. Our members were outstanding. They were disciplined, they displayed clarity, and they told the story of January 6. For some who defended the Capitol, the cost of that day is unimaginable. We hold in our hearts the five police officers who died in the aftermath. Another Capitol Police officer, Billy Evans, would be killed less than three months later in a lone wolf–style attack on the Capitol checkpoint on April 2, Good Friday, compounding the grief of our officers and everyone who works in the Capitol. Officer Evans is, as I said at the time, "a martyr for our democracy." These terrible events made 2021 a particularly difficult year. And the trauma of January 6th experienced by those who were under assault that day—members, staff, press, institutional workers, and others—is still ongoing.

In 2022, for the one-year commemoration of the assault on the Capitol, we convened a conversation in the Cannon Caucus Room between historians Doris Kearns Goodwin and Jon Meacham, moderated by Dr. Carla Hayden, the Librarian of Congress. The event was attended by members, staff, and families. The historical discussion was a valuable presentation about division in our country around the time of the Civil War and the importance of unifying leadership to help the country heal. After their presentation, and for the rest of the day, attendees heard directly from members, who told their stories of their experience on that day and the trauma they continue to struggle with. Many had been reluctant to speak publicly until that day.

Members sharing their firsthand accounts was an inspiration and a source of strength in our efforts to ensure that the assault on the Capitol and our Constitution on that horrible day could never happen again.

As a token of appreciation to our three participants in the moderated conversation, I gave them pins and cufflinks that said, "ONE COUNTRY, ONE DESTINY." Those were the words embroidered in Lincoln's coat the night he died—and words we associate with John Lewis as we strive for a more perfect union.

On December 6, 2022, in my role as Speaker, I also had the honor to award the Congressional Gold Medal to the US Capitol Police and the Washington, DC, Metropolitan Police Department to recognize their service on January 6, adding, "We canonize these heroes in the pantheon of patriots."

"Our Flag Is Still There"

I still remember the first time I saw the Capitol. I was a little girl, six years old. I was with my whole family: my five older brothers, my mother, and my father. We had traveled from Baltimore to Washington so that Daddy could be sworn in for his fifth term in Congress. Tommy, my oldest brother, would have been sixteen. I remember my brothers saying, "Nancy, look, look, there's the Capitol. There's the Capitol." And I looked around and replied, "I don't see any capital."

We got closer, and they said, "Here's a better view. It's clear. You can see it from here. It's the Capitol." And I asked, "Is it a capital *A*, a capital *B*, or a capital *C*?"

By now they were both amused and exasperated. *"No,"* they said, "it's the Capitol of the United States, the big dome." Looking up and seeing that massive white dome, and especially seeing all the reverence my brothers had for this place at such a young age, so much so that they didn't want me to miss my first glimpse of the Capitol, and then going inside and seeing the tradition enshrined in the structure and experiencing the aura became a powerful memory for me. Every time I look at the Capitol, it is with the reverence I experienced as a child.

My father carried me in his arms as he was sworn in as a member of Congress, a ceremony I'll never forget. Fast-forward forty years and I was back on the House floor with my father, who was by then in a wheelchair, watching me be sworn in as a new member of Congress. Fast-forward another twenty years, and I was the newly elected Speaker, swearing in other members of Congress. From my stored memories over these decades of my life, I have a deep affection for the Capitol. For its place in history, for the work that has been done there, and for the courageous acts that people have undertaken inside its walls. It is truly hallowed ground.

The US Capitol is not only physically beautiful; the building is beautiful for what it represents. The Capitol and its dome have become symbols of freedom and democracy around the globe. George Washington laid the cornerstone in 1793, but the final work was not completed until 1866, after the end of the Civil War. When the Civil War began, the Capitol's dome sat half-finished. Some wanted all construction halted, but Lincoln overruled them, saying, "If people see the Capitol going on, it is a sign we intend the Union shall go on." In December 1863, as the Civil War still raged, the Statue of Freedom was installed atop the dome, accompanied by a full salute from the guns at the twelve forts protecting Washington, DC.

Nearly 160 years later, on January 6, we faced another perilous moment for our democracy, an attack not just on the Capitol but on our Constitution. The mob that ransacked the Capitol, that broke down doors, that fought against law enforcement, that terrified staffers and representatives, that went hunting for the vice president, for me, and for other members, displayed the opposite of citizenship. And some of the insurrectionists who carried out the assault were also carrying the Confederate flag under Lincoln's dome. It was incredibly sad for me to see the footage of the Confederate flag (as well as of other banners, including one modeled after a Nazi flag) being paraded and waved through those halls. One rioter wore a "CAMP AUSCHWITZ" sweatshirt. These were the January 6 insurrectionist cheerleaders.

But on January 6, on the Capitol, our shared American flag flew above them all.

Our flag has a special place at the Capitol. When I first glimpsed the Capitol dome as a six-year-old child, our flag was waving on top. At that time, it had only forty-eight stars; Alaska and Hawaii were not yet states. Inside Congress, at the start of each day in the House and the Senate, we open with the Pledge of Allegiance. I grew up in Baltimore, where Francis Scott Key wrote our national anthem, "The Star-Spangled Banner," after seeing the flag still flying over Fort McHenry at dawn following a fierce British bombardment during the War of 1812. My favorite line has always been, "Gave proof through the night that our flag was still there."

On January 6, just as I had done as a young girl all those years ago, I looked up at the Capitol dome and saw that our flag was still there. And on that dark January night, under our nation's flag, Congress came together to fulfill our oath of office and project America's strength and resolve.

The threat to our democracy is real, present, and urgent. The parable of January 6 reminds us that our precious democratic institutions are only as strong as the courage and commitment of those entrusted with their care. Today, Americans need to resolve to honor our higher purpose, as citizens of the United States of America, to ensure that our flag is still there, with liberty and justice for all.

Leading for the People

Why I Love the House

When Joe Biden and Kamala Harris were chosen by the American people on November 3, 2020, we understood that we were at a transformative moment with this historical opportunity. Ultimately, the record of legislative action and legislative accomplishment from President Biden and the Democratic Congress made the 117th Congress of 2021–2023 the most productive—and arguably the most impactful—legislative session since the eras of the New Deal and the Great Society.

The time between Election Day and Inauguration Day is usually one of responsible transition and excitement for a new president. Tragically, the time between November 3, 2020, and January 20, 2021, was fraught with Trump's deception and disrespect for the American people. Nonetheless, when Joe Biden and Kamala Harris were sworn in, they were ready! Ready to lead and prepared to serve alongside a Democratic Congress.

When President Biden took office, the situation was dire—and the numbers spoke volumes. Eighteen million Americans were unemployed. Twenty-four million people were going hungry. Twelve million children were living in households with food insecurity. Up to forty million people could not pay their rent and feared eviction. The time for decisive action was long overdue—and possible, with Chuck Schumer assuming the title of majority leader in the Senate and with a Democratic majority elected in the

House. Together, we supported the leadership of President Biden when he declared: "Help is on the way."

With the president's first initiative, the American Rescue Plan, we crushed the Covid-19 virus, we put money in people's pockets, helped parents get safely back to work, and helped children get safely back to school. The law gave money to states and localities to support frontline workers. And it gave middle-class families a deeply needed tax cut with the Biden Child Tax Credit, which cut child poverty in half.

Next came the Bipartisan Infrastructure Bill, which seized a once-in-a-lifetime opportunity to not only rebuild but reimagine our infrastructure for the twenty-first century. A centerpiece of the legislation was equity: the president's Justice40 Initiative required that 40 percent of the law's benefits flow to long underserved communities and demographics, so that more people could participate in the success of our economy and the growth of our society. Despite misleading Republican critiques, we made sure that the investments in the bill were paid for. While we did not get a unanimous Democratic vote in the House, we were able to get thirteen Republicans to join us, making it a bipartisan accomplishment.

But there were other challenges in dire need of addressing. For too many years our hearts have been shattered by mass shooting rampages at schools, grocery stores, and public spaces across the country. In June 2022, Congress came together to pass the first gun violence prevention legislation in a generation. This action is critical For Our Children: tragically, according to data from the CDC, guns are the number one killer of kids in America—more than car accidents or cancer. Lives have been saved by this legislation, but much more needs to be done.

We also wanted to look to the future and to a technologically secure America. As part of President Biden's big vision for America and for our future, we passed the CHIPS and Science Act to declare our economic independence, strengthen our national security, and enhance our families' financial future. Today, this bill is bolstering our nation's production of semiconductor chips, diversifying our STEM workforce, and creating good-paying communities throughout the country. I'm particularly grateful to our chair, Congresswoman Eddie Bernice Johnson, who worked with the top Republican member on the Science, Space, and Technology Committee, Congressman Frank Lucas, to craft this legislation. The night before the vote, Congressman Lucas made a great presentation of support for the bill to the Rules Committee. But sadly, by the next day, Republican leadership had instructed him to oppose the bill on the floor. We did end up getting twenty-four Republican votes on the floor—but they held their votes until they saw that Democrats had reached the required 218 to pass the bill on our own.

Two additional major pieces of legislation were passed and signed by President Biden in August 2022. The first cares for our veterans. Under the leadership of Veterans' Affairs Committee Chairman Mark Takano, we passed the Honoring our PACT Act, a bill that helps up to 3.5 million veterans exposed to toxic burn pits in the line of duty get the care they need. Our success was in part made possible by comedian and activist Jon Stewart and first responder champion John Feal's very direct appeals to Senate Republicans, making the case for the legislation.

Another legislative victory was the passage of the Inflation Reduction Act, a fitting capstone to President Biden's first two years in office. This law delivered the most consequential climate action in human history. It slashed the cost of prescription drugs for seniors by empowering Medicare to negotiate lower prices and capping insulin co-pays at just thirty-five dollars a month—a resounding victory for America's families.

But more remains to be done. In the House, we proudly passed the Build Back Better Act, a sweeping bill that included many transformative investments for America's working families. This legislation addressed childcare, universal pre-K, paid leave for all, home health care, the Biden Child Tax Credit, affordable housing, and climate action. But many of these initiatives were shamefully blocked in the Senate, which ultimately would only agree to pass a watered-down version of the original House bill. I look forward to the day when some of these priorities can be enacted by the full Congress and signed into law.

Indeed, when House Democrats held the majority, we followed through on our priorities. We proudly passed legislation to ban assault weapons, restore the essential protections of *Roe v. Wade*, strengthen the foundations of our democracy, and guarantee full equality for all, to name just a few. Together, these legislative initiatives represent President Biden's shining vision for a fairer, freer, safer, more inclusive America. And we must enshrine them into law.

But just as important: the victories that President Biden signed into law are under assault—by Big Pharma, by Big Oil, by the gun lobby, by extreme Republicans, and by Donald Trump. That's why, as President Biden has declared, we must "Finish the Job."

Looking Forward

I have won nearly all of the legislative battles that I started—and those that I haven't I characterize simply as "not yet achieved."

There are two fundamental areas of civil rights and equality legislation that I believe Congress must pass for the benefit of the

American people. We took action in the House, but we need to make progress in the Senate. The first vital piece of legislation is our For the People Act and the John R. Lewis Voting Rights Advancement Act. These bills were designed to make our democracy more democratic—with a small *d*. We passed both bills in the House of Representatives, but they were held up in the Senate by the filibuster—an antiquated rule that requires sixty votes to pass legislation.

My disappointment at their failure to win Senate approval was even deeper because slightly more than a decade before, the story was entirely different. The House, which at the time had a Republican majority, passed the 2007 Voting Rights Act with a strong bipartisan vote of 390–33—and with the important leadership of the Congressional Black Caucus. The bill was then passed unanimously by voice vote in the Senate. Senator Bill Frist, as the Senate Republican leader, and I, as the House Democratic leader, led a large procession of our members—Democrat and Republican, House and Senate—down the steps of the Capitol in celebration. President Bush proudly signed the bill.

But a few years later, in 2013, in its decision in *Shelby County v. Holder*, the Supreme Court decided to gut the legislation. I have proudly displayed a photograph of my speaking at the demonstration outside the Supreme Court during their deliberations; I was honored to be invited by the Congressional Black Caucus to join them. It was the same day that we unveiled a statue of civil rights pioneer Rosa Parks in Statuary Hall in the Capitol. Republicans attended the statue ceremony, and I had hoped—fruitlessly—that they would join our side if the Court ruled against the Voting Rights Act.

Some GOP leaders also traveled to Selma in early March 2015 to mark fifty years since Bloody Sunday, the day when civil rights leader John Lewis (who led the charge in Selma and later in Congress) and others crossed the Edmund Pettus Bridge. On that Sunday, March 7, 1965, the peaceful marchers were beaten, whipped, and doused with tear gas by state and county officers, who had been waiting for them on the other side. The marchers were subjected to this horrific attack only because they were speaking out for the right to vote.

Fifty years later, President Barack Obama and First Lady Michelle Obama led the commemoration, and the president spoke with great admiration for the courage of the marchers. Former President George Bush and First Lady Laura Bush honored the event and the cause with their presence. President Bush spoke with pride about signing the Voting Rights Act in 2007. I asked congressional Republicans if their presence in Selma meant that they would support a new voting rights bill. They said: "No, our going to Selma is all you're going to get."

It is shameful that they would show up while being unwilling to pass the Voting Rights Act, going backward in valuing the freedom to vote.

The other bill, the For the People Act, is a bookend in the fight for voting rights. Its first three hundred pages were written by John Lewis to end voter suppression, which is rampant. This act also creates a national commission to end political gerrymandering, so voters can choose their elected officials rather than elected officials choosing their voters through contorted legislative districts. The act also empowers small donors and grassroots activists with matching grants for small contributions, not paid for at taxpayer expense. And very significantly, it would counter *Citizens United*, which was one of the Supreme Court's most damaging-to-democracy decisions. That decision led to an explosion of what those of us in politics refer to as "dark money" in our elections. The numbers rose from $1 million in 2009 to $138 million in the 2010 election cycle, to target and defeat congressional Democrats. Dark money from fossil-fuel companies, the gun industry, and the pharmaceutical industry plays a disproportionate role in shaping agendas, policies, and legislation.

But I have not given up hope that my legislative regret will eventually become a legislative success in the House and Senate. In the 2024 election, many of us are working to elect senators who are committed to lifting the Senate filibuster rule and restoring faith in government by passing these pro-freedom reforms.

Another important legislative priority that I want to see become law is the Equality Act.

On my first day in the House, after I was sworn in, then-Speaker Jim Wright announced on the floor, "Does the gentlelady from California wish to address the House?" Some had cautioned me not to speak on the House floor as a new member—or if I did, to be brief. I went to the podium and began by recognizing Paul and my family and the D'Alesandros, my parents and family who were present, and the tradition of public service they had instilled in me. I thanked my constituents for electing me, and I said that Sala Burton sent me, and I was here to fight against the scourge of HIV/AIDS. (Sala's death earlier in the year brought on the special election, which I won.)

When I returned to my seat on the House floor, I glanced around, looking for some approving nods because I had been brief—not even two minutes. Instead, the expressions gazing back at me were riddled with dismay. As some of my fellow members explained, why would you want the first impression that all the members have of you to be that you were there to fight HIV and AIDS? Why would you say that? My response was, "I said I was here to fight HIV/AIDS because that's why I am here."

In the 1980s, I probably had more people I loved test positive with—or die from—HIV/AIDS than any of my congressional colleagues. At that time, San Francisco was sadly the epicenter of the AIDS crisis, and there were some weeks when I attended multiple funerals. I came to Washington to seek better policies and more funding to combat this deadly disease, and immediately I sought to get a seat on the committees responsible for federal AIDS policy. But while I was prepared to push for attention to and funding for HIV/AIDS, I was not prepared for the level of discrimination.

In Washington, people would say to me, it's so easy for you because San Francisco is so tolerant. My response was that I considered "tolerant" to be a condescending word. San Franciscans respected and took pride in our LGBTQ+ community. One of the most gratifying aspects of my service in Congress has been learning from the HIV/AIDS community—not just about science and medicine, but about courage.

Among those lessons was one from Cleve Jones, a gay rights activist in San Francisco. He asked me to meet with him and our then-new mayor of San Francisco, my dear friend Art Agnos. We met in my home, and Cleve explained that he wanted me to be part of a new idea: an AIDS quilt, with each panel dedicated to mourning someone who had died of HIV/AIDS. I said, Cleve, this is a great idea, but who sews anymore? I explained that in my Catholic convent school, our "recreation" was learning to sew, knit, and crochet. And, I added, I have five children and I don't sew. What makes you think this will work?

Cleve is a very goal-oriented, effective leader, and he had confidence in his vision, so much so that he persuaded me to sew two panels: one for Susie Piracci Roggio, who had been a flower girl at my wedding, and another for Scott Douglass, my dear friend who, at the end of his life, couldn't wait to go to heaven to see John F.

Kennedy. On my morning visits, he would say to me, "Why do I have to see you every day? I want to see JFK."

Nearly two years later, the quilt was gigantic—yes, people did, in fact, know how to sew—and Cleve came to me while I was a relatively new member in Congress with the request to spread the iconic quilt on the National Mall. The National Park Service had told him no but proposed that they display a few panels on a nearby street corner. With the arrogance of a junior member, I met with the Park Service with Cleve. I told them I spoke for the House Democrats—not all, I said with a smile, but most—and we wanted the quilt and its thousands of panels to be spread out on the Mall. The Park Service objected and subsequently contended that the quilt would kill the Mall's grass if rested on the ground for more than twenty minutes. No problem, we said. With Cleve's leadership, we promised hundreds of volunteers would lift the quilt every twenty minutes. Photographers and helicopters flew above the quilt, and its iconic image appeared around the world. And Cleve was declared newsmaker of the week.

In the spirit of San Francisco values, I was determined to bring knowledge and a can-do attitude to the work of crafting more en-lightened federal policies in Congress. Our solutions—developed in part with the University of California, San Francisco, and the angelic work of San Francisco General Hospital's Ward 86—were community-based prevention, research, and care. This innovative approach was the basis for the Ryan White CARE Act, sponsored by Congressman Henry Waxman and signed by President Bill Clinton with Ryan White's mother, Jeanne, present.

We were opposed at first, but over time and with persistence, we largely succeeded. We had three vital legislative priorities: on hate crimes with the Matthew Shepard and James Byrd, Jr., Hate Crimes Prevention Act of 2009, championed by Matthew

Shepard's mother and Barney Frank, who powerfully shared his personal story. Next, under the leadership of President Barack Obama, came the repeal of the military's "don't ask, don't tell" policy in 2010, which had barred LGBTQ+ individuals from openly serving our country in uniform. And then in 2022, under the leadership of President Biden, we codified marriage equality into law with the Respect for Marriage Act.

The fourth priority of our legislative pursuit of equality is the Equality Act, which was introduced by Congressman David Cicilline. This act would have officially ended discrimination against the LGBTQ+ community by amending the 1964 Civil Rights Act to explicitly prevent discrimination based on sexual orientation and gender identity. Our Congressional Black Caucus has always, proudly, been very proprietary of the Civil Rights Act, and was rightfully cautious of the assaults that might be made on the law if it were to be reopened. But John Lewis was once again a champion for ending all discrimination and became a lead co-sponsor of the act, saying at a 2016 House press conference that it was time to support the Equality Act, because "it is what justice requires" and "it is long overdue."

The Equality Act passed the House in February 2021, but it could not overcome the sixty-vote filibuster requirement in the slim Democratic-majority Senate. We had hoped that corporate America might be able to persuade some reluctant Republicans to support the bill, which President Biden was eager to sign. But while the business community bragged publicly about respecting LGBTQ+ rights, we learned it didn't prioritize advancing those rights in its political advocacy. The Equality Act's failure to become law remains a disappointment to me as Speaker, but with a strong Democratic Senate majority, an end to the Senate filibuster, a Democratic House, and, of course, a Democratic president,

I believe we will ultimately pass this vital civil and human rights legislation. And we will also pass the For the People Act and the John R. Lewis Voting Rights Advancement Act.

Because leadership means never being content with history, when you can and must make progress.

When people ask me why I haven't run for higher office or accepted a presidential appointment, the answer is easy: I love the House. The House of Representatives—known as the People's House—was designed to be close to the people. Our founders wanted us to run every two years to stay close to the people that we serve or be replaced. While the US Senate has its prestige and six-year term, its composition was also a compromise necessary to ratify the Constitution. For example, California has 40 million people and two senators—and several states have fewer than 1 million people and have two senators. In the House, however, California has fifty-two House members, and those other, far less populous states have one. There is power in numbers.

House numbers enable us to represent the beautiful diversity of America, which largely didn't exist at the time of our founding. What did exist was diminished by slavery, and by how Black Americans were counted—women weren't even given the right to vote. (Thank heavens the founders made the Constitution amendable.) Our diversity also includes differences of opinion, making the House more rambunctious in our debate and more collaborative when necessary.

One of the reasons I love serving the House is that I have the privilege of representing San Francisco. The song of our city's patron saint, St. Francis of Assisi, is our anthem. "Lord, make me an instrument of your peace. Where there is hatred, let me sow love.

Where there is injury, pardon. Where there is doubt, faith. Where there is despair, hope. Where there is darkness, light. And where there is sadness, joy." San Francisco is a great city and a true community. The beauty of San Francisco is in the mix. Every time I fly home and hear the announcement that we are landing, I feel the same rush of excitement that I did the very first time landing in San Francisco.

My district is physically small but mighty in people, covering most of San Francisco, with a current population of more than 750,000 living within roughly forty-seven square miles. My district is a celebration of the wonderful diversity of America: home to the oldest Chinatown outside of Asia and the oldest and largest Japantown in the US, as well as the North Beach Italian American community, the Latino families of the Mission District, the vitality of our Black leadership—the city's Fillmore District was known as the Harlem of the West—and of course the Castro, one of the first major urban areas to welcome and embrace the LGBTQ+ community, to name just a few. We are rich in nationalities, languages, and religions. We come together in rallies to protect our planet, in parades to salute our ethnicity, in celebrations with our sports teams, the Warriors, the Giants, and the 49ers, and in unity with a love of liberty, which is our heritage and our hope. God has blessed us with a beautiful city surrounded by the bay and the Pacific Ocean. We even have one of the most forward-looking national parks, the Presidio, which is not only a gorgeous nature preserve but a location where people can live and work. And what could be a more iconic image than our stunning Golden Gate Bridge?

When the people of San Francisco sent me to the House in 1987, I joined great members who were champions of civil rights, women's rights, the environment, social and economic justice, and more. I entered a room full of giants. Imagine joining a freshman class alongside John Lewis, with whom I had the honor of serving for over thirty years. Imagine standing on the House floor, where slavery was abolished and where voting rights were expanded to include Black men and then, much later, women. I was personally thrilled to serve where my father, Thomas D'Alesandro Jr., had served in the 1930s and 1940s. He was there when British Prime Minister Winston Churchill spoke on December 26, 1941, nineteen days after the Japanese attack on Pearl Harbor. Churchill had come to praise and inspire Americans as the two nations united to defeat Hitler's Nazi Germany and Imperial Japan. The House floor is a place where war has been declared, where opportunity was and continues to be expanded, and where presidents come to report on the state of the union.

When I came to the House, I did not regard it as a stepping-stone to another office, and that was why members trusted that I didn't have a personal political agenda when I advocated for a certain position on a vote.

I love the House because of the people who serve and the relationships that develop. I understand America better through the eyes of the members, recognizing that our job title and our job description are one and the same: representative. I have learned never to publicly question the motivation of someone's vote but rather to respect whom they represent. Soon, you know with whom you share values—or not—but at the same time, you also realize that tomorrow is another day and you may vote together.

My admiration for the House also springs from the fact that most of what I accomplished during my first dozen years—and what I saw my colleagues do—was as a rank-and-file member.

One very important initiative that I was able to accomplish while in the rank-and-file was the establishment of the Presidio public park in San Francisco. For more than two centuries—and under flags of three different nations—the Presidio stood as a military base guarding the Golden Gate. But in the 1990s, it was set to be shut down. Working with the San Francisco community, we first wanted to save it as a military post. But once it was clear that wasn't possible, we made it our mission to convert it from a post to a park.

It has been said that, in over two hundred years, a shot was never fired in anger at the Presidio. That became our motto and our determination as we worked toward this goal. Inside the Congress, our effort was always bipartisan—and in our community, it was a bipartisan effort to establish a Presidio Council. The Council ultimately developed the Presidio Trust, which became the basis for our legislation in Congress and a national model for military post-to-park initiatives.

My hero in all this was Jack Murtha, who helped fund the initial cleanup of the dilapidated military base, enabling its transition to a public space. Republican Representative Ralph Regula was very supportive as well—which helped us to secure bipartisan support for our legislation.

By late 1994, we had passed our bill in the House and were awaiting passage in the Senate when we learned that a Republican senator had put a hold on the legislation. Remember, ninety-nine Senators are not enough. Then, Congress adjourned for the upcoming elections—virtually eliminating the possibility of legislation. Concerned, I spoke with then-Republican Senate Minority Leader Bob Dole, who told me: "Don't worry, Nancy—when we come back in January, I will help you get this done."

As fate would have it, Democrats lost control of both the House and Senate in the 1994 "Republican Revolution." So, we had to start over trying to pass our bill in both a Republican-controlled

House and a Republican Senate. But Bob Dole was true to his word, and in 1996, Bill Clinton signed our bill into law.

Today, the Presidio is a spectacular, iconic, national urban park—with green spaces, entrepreneurial opportunities, educational activities, and amenities that are free and open for all to enjoy. The Presidio is precious to me, not just in terms of its beauty but as a model for bipartisan legislating.

Indeed, the House is a place where rank-and-file members are empowered to work with their colleagues to solve great challenges and meet the needs of their communities. It is truly the People's House.

Overwhelmingly, I have admired my colleagues and have regretted that there isn't a more positive view of them outside their own districts, particularly in the press and among the public. While some of us may have frequently disagreed over the years, there's generally far more mutual respect in our chamber than the public is aware of. That is, there was until recently, when Trump eroded that spirit and diminished bipartisanship.

I hope the American people will come to understand that the House's vitality and combativeness reflect the country and are consistent with the vision of our founders. Personally, politically, and, most importantly, patriotically, I have been truly honored to serve and lead in the People's House . . . for the People.

For the people, I am most proud of passing the Affordable Care Act. This success would not have been possible without the excellent inside maneuvering of our House Democrats and the vigorous outside mobilization. Again, I am thankful to them for their courageous support.

In the course of the passing and saving the ACA, Sister Joyce Weller of the Daughters of Charity shared with me how in 1993

she came across a beautiful prayer posted on the wall of a hospital in Sierra Leone: *When I die and happily meet my Creator, He
will ask me to show Him my wounds. If I tell Him that I have no
wounds, my Creator will ask: Was nothing worth fighting for?*

I am proud of my wounds, For the Children.

Acknowledgments

As I strive to acknowledge those who made this book possible, I want to convey what this book is not.

It is not a memoir; nor do I tell the entire story of how I went from housewife to House member to House Speaker. It is not an account of every challenge we face. It would take another book to record my political story, from Baltimore to San Francisco; to highlight my best friend in volunteering in politics, then-assembly speaker Leo McCarthy; to cover Governor Jerry Brown, whose presidential campaign thrust me into higher levels of political power; or to tell the story of my first race for Congress in 1987, chaired by John Burton, for which I had Sala Burton's endorsement winning the day for me. And it remains for another book to cover Covid, as well as the first two years of the Biden-Harris administration, the most productive legislative period since LBJ and FDR: the American Rescue Plan, the Bipartisan Infrastructure Law, the Bipartisan Safer Communities Act, the Honoring Our PACT Act, the CHIPS and Science Act, the Inflation Reduction Act, and more. More to come—including acknowledgment of the many members and staff who were instrumental in these legislative successes.

The best advice I received when I entered the political arena of congressional politics was: be yourself. So I'll begin by thanking the D'Alesandro family in Baltimore: Mommy and Daddy and

ACKNOWLEDGMENTS

our family, who infused me with values and respect for public service. Paul and our five children gave me the love and cooperation that allowed me to manage the joy of it all—and the energy to do so. The support of my San Francisco constituents gave me the confidence and pride to be "a voice that will be heard," as my campaign posters said.

Immense credit for all that has been accomplished during my career in Congress belongs to the House Democratic Caucus, which I often say is the greatest collection of intellect, integrity, and imagination assembled for the good of the American people. I am constantly humbled by the faith they placed in me as Speaker and leader. It took courage to break the marble ceiling and elect me to serve as the first woman Speaker. There are far too many members who have left their mark on the House to be able to properly thank them all by name, but there are a few members— and some staff, too—whom I recognize for their contributions to the stories I've told in this book.

In terms of the Iraq and intelligence sections, I am grateful to Sen. Bob Graham of Florida for his insistence on the truth and Congressman Tim Roemer of Indiana for his guidance— culminating in the 9/11 Commission and its work. On the staff side, Mike Sheehy and Wyndee Parker were superb. On the Joint Inquiry staff, Eleanor Hill and Rick Cinquegrana were spectacular. And on Iraq, Congressman John Murtha of Pennsylvania was my hero. He was a cherished colleague who provided wise counsel and deserves all the recognition in the world for taking a strong, principled stand against the war.

From Tiananmen to Taiwan, we have had decades of bipartisanship in Congress: Congressman Frank Wolf of Virginia and Congressman Chris Smith of New Jersey on the Republican side, and Congressman Jim McGovern of Massachusetts and

310

Congressman Tom Lantos of California on the Democratic side. On the staff side, Carolyn Bartholomew, Jon Stivers, and Reva Price led our efforts over time, and helped check my work in this book.

In the depths of the financial crisis, the fiery leadership of Chairman Barney Frank of Massachusetts championed taxpayers over corporate profits. In the wake of the crisis, he and Sen. Chris Dodd of Connecticut bolstered our financial system against future meltdowns with the Dodd-Frank reforms. Secretary Hank Paulson was central to brokering an agreement on TARP, which rescued our economy from free fall. He had the respect of the members because they knew he spoke for President Bush. Thanks also to Phil Angelides, whose authorship of the *Financial Crisis Inquiry Report* uncovered many of the systemic failures that caused the crisis. I am grateful for his insights and counsel as I wrote about TARP and its aftermath. On the staff side, we were ably guided by my senior advisor, Jaime Lizárraga, and then-chief of staff John Lawrence.

Envisioning, crafting, and enacting the Patient Protection and Affordable Care Act was a herculean task spearheaded by strong chairmen: George Miller of California, Henry Waxman of California, and Charlie Rangel of New York—and later, Sandy Levin of Michigan. Their fortitude, and that of the entire House Democratic leadership and the many members who participated in shaping the legislation, enabled us to aim high with health care reform. We must also salute Congresswoman Rosa DeLauro, a force of nature for women and children. I am grateful to our partners in the Senate—most of all my friend Harry Reid, who kept his word in a pivotal moment and helped get the final bill over the finish line. Of course, the ACA would not stand today as a pillar of health and financial security for millions of American families without the visionary leadership and unwavering commitment of President Barack Obama. And thanks to President Joe Biden, the ACA is stronger than ever. I'd also like to thank a respected White House staffer, Phil Schiliro, who advised on the ACA chapter in this book. On my staff, Wendell Primus was essential to the enactment and implementation of the ACA—and from the very beginning, Steve Morin helped shape our health care principles, especially on HIV/AIDS.

Out of one of the darkest days in American history, a beacon of patriotism emerged: our bipartisan Select Committee to Investigate the January 6th attack. Under the formidable leadership of Chair Bennie Thompson of Mississippi and Vice Chair Liz Cheney of Wyoming—and with the strong participation of our members—the work of the Select Committee lives on in the evidence they uncovered and the legal cases proceeding in the courts. Let us also salute the managers of the two impeachment trials of Donald Trump to hold him accountable for his crimes. I am forever grateful to Congressman Adam Schiff of California, who managed the first, and Congressman Jamie Raskin of Maryland, who managed the second. On the staff level, I was guided with great wisdom and patriotism by Terri McCullough, my chief of staff, and Jamie Fleet, staff director of the Committee on House Administration. The Select Committee was similarly well served by its staff.

I always say that it was my privilege in leadership to have the greatest staff ever assembled in the history of the United States Congress. Day in and day out, talented, optimistic, principled, patriotic professionals made the difficult easy and the impossible possible—paving the way for legislation that has touched the lives of millions and will stand for generations. Terri McCullough, who started working for me as an intern when I was a junior congresswoman from California and rose to become the first woman to serve as chief of staff to the Speaker of the House. Terri follows in the long-serving footsteps of my earlier chiefs, including Judy Lemons from the start, George Crawford, John Lawrence, and Nadeam Elshami. My leadership office has benefited from many brilliant and long-serving staffers with whom I worked on a daily basis, including, at the end: George Kundanis, Drew Hammill, Diane Dewhirst, Emily Berret, Dick Meltzer, Michael Tecklenburg, Michael Long, Kelsey Smith, Keith Stern, and Kate Knudson, to name just a few. Helping me keep the San Francisco home fires burning were Robert Edmonson and Dan Bernal. But there are so many more: they know who they are, and I know who they are. While I do want to name everyone, I consider those who worked in my office to be among the finest group of public servants Congress has ever known. Please know how deeply grateful I am for your commitment and contributions to our cause.

It is important to note that, when legislating in Congress, our inside maneuvering can only take us so far. Always, as my daughter Christine insists, it is the outside mobilization that makes all the difference. On every issue—from health care to climate to LGBTQ+ equality and more—the relentless, persistent advocacy of everyday Americans has made change possible.

On a personal note, I am deeply grateful to the many members of my US Capitol Police security detail over the years, including those who have been with me for so long: Shannon Croom, Dorman Simmons, Sade Bryant, Tiffany Brown, Kevin Bull, Stacy Clark, Dwight Littlejohn, Robert Delman, Gene Petty, Steve Moran, and David Lazarus.

Writing a book—let alone one that spans nearly forty years of public life—is a challenge. I am grateful for the support of Jon Karp and Priscilla Painton at Simon & Schuster for their excellent guidance, and for Richard Lovett, Mollie Glick, and David Lara-bell at CAA for introducing us and facilitating our communications. I am grateful to Lyric Winik for her patience and invaluable assistance in making my message more understandable to more people. I want to thank Aaron Bennett for always being there and for his ready acceptance of my not always understandable humor. And in spite of strange happenings on the House floor disrupting our schedule, his diligence and firm and frank suggestions helped keep me on course.

Additionally, at Simon & Schuster, I would also like to thank Hana Park, Johanna Li, Kayley Hoffman, Julia Prosser, and Elizabeth Herman, and also Janet Byrne, for their great support of this book and their willingness to accommodate the many demands of my schedule.

To the people of San Francisco: thank you for entrusting me with the high honor of being your voice in Congress. No matter what title has been bestowed upon me—Speaker, leader, whip—there is no greater honor for me than to stand on the floor of the House and speak for you. Know that I am always striving to honor the call of Saint Francis: "Lord, make me an instrument of your peace." And I will always hold Sala Burton in my heart—for believing in me, for seeing what I was capable of, and for encouraging me to reach my heights.

I will end where I began: with my family. Through their example, Mommy and Daddy taught my brothers and me that public service is a noble calling, and that we all have a responsibility to help others. The many lessons that they imparted—about faith, family, and service—have been the light leading the way in my lifelong public service.

My career in Congress would not have been possible without the loving embrace of my family. To our darling children, Nancy

Corinne, Christine, Jacqueline, Paul Jr., and Alexandra, and their spouses, and our darling grandchildren: you are the joy of our lives and an irreplaceable source of comfort to our family. Please know how proud Pop and I are of you and how grateful I am for your constant support.

And to my dear husband, Paul, my beloved partner in life: thank you. Without your love, support, encouragement, and good humor, I would never have served in Congress—let alone as Speaker of the House—as a voice that would truly be heard.

Author's Note

Throughout the writing of this book, I was fortunate to be able to speak with many colleagues, present and past, as well as House staff, congressional staff, historians, friends, and family, who augmented my own recollections about key moments, issues, and events. I thank them for their time and efforts. In addition, I relied on private notes, papers, schedules, and other documents. This is my story of what I saw and what I heard at some of the most momentous events of the last four decades, and I am glad to be able to tell it at last.

Photo Credits

Index

auto industry, after 2008 financial crisis, 178

Bachus, Spencer, 152, 159
Baker, James, 109
banks and financial institutions
  Dodd-Frank, 178–179
  financial crisis (2008), 156–157, 163, 178–179, 182–183
  Volcker Rule, 179
Banks, Jim, 283
Barr, Bill, 274
Bassnan, Osama, 100
Baucus, Max, 128, 129, 193, 211
Bayoumi, Omar al-, 100
Bear Stearns, financial crisis (2008), 156, 158
Beastie Boys, 135
Becerra, Xavier, 241
Benioff, Marc, 143
Bennett, Tony, 42
Bernanke, Ben, 152–153, 175–176
Beutler, Jaime Herrera, 280
Biden, Hunter, 274
Biden, Joe
  about, 212, 239, 279, 293
  American Rescue Plan, 294
  Biden Tax Credit, 294, 296
  Bipartisan Infrastructure Bill, 294
  Build Back Better Act, 296
  CHIPS and Science Act, 295
  election victory, 247–248
  Equality Act, 299–301, 302
  gun violence prevention legislation, 294
  health care reform, 237, 238, 239
  Honoring our PACT Act, 295
  Inflation Reduction Act, 295–296
  Respect for Marriage Act, 302
Biden Child Tax Credit, 294, 296
Biden election (2020)
  congressional certification, 248–249, 269, 271–272
  Electoral College vote, 248, 269
  Trump's challenge, 247–254
Big Pharma, 70, 211, 296
bin Laden, Osama, 93, 97, 98, 99, 102
Bipartisan Infrastructure Bill, 294
Birmingham, Cynthia, 22
Blinder, Alan, 158
Blinken, Antony, 144
Boehner, John, 152, 164, 166, 242
Boggs, Lindy, 4, 5
Bolten, Josh, 165
Bonior, David, 38
Braley, Bruce, 221
Brown, Scott, 213
Burton, Sala, 4–5, 299
Bush, Barbara, 54, 69
Bush, George H. W.
  about, 68, 69
  China policy, 120, 121, 122, 125, 127
  Pelosi and, 54–55
  President's Emergency Plan for AIDS Relief (PEPFAR), 68–69
Bush, George W.
  calls for impeachment, 109
  Dalai Lama and, 136
  financial crisis (2008), 150, 157–158, 165, 166–167, 168, 171, 181
  Iraq War, 81, 84, 88–89, 91–92, 106, 109, 110, 113

INDEX

INDEX

INDEX

INDEX